Marcelo
BIELSA

Marcelo BIELSA

13 STEPS TO THE PREMIER LEAGUE

LEE SCOTT

First published by Pitch Publishing, 2021

Pitch Publishing
A2 Yeoman Gate
Yeoman Way
Worthing
Sussex
BN13 3QZ
www.pitchpublishing.co.uk
info@pitchpublishing.co.uk

ISBN 978 1 78531 822 1

Typesetting and origination by Pitch Publishing

Printed and bound in Great Britain by TJ Books, Padstow

Contents

For Kelly, Alex, Thomas and Harry. Your love and support means everything and makes this possible.

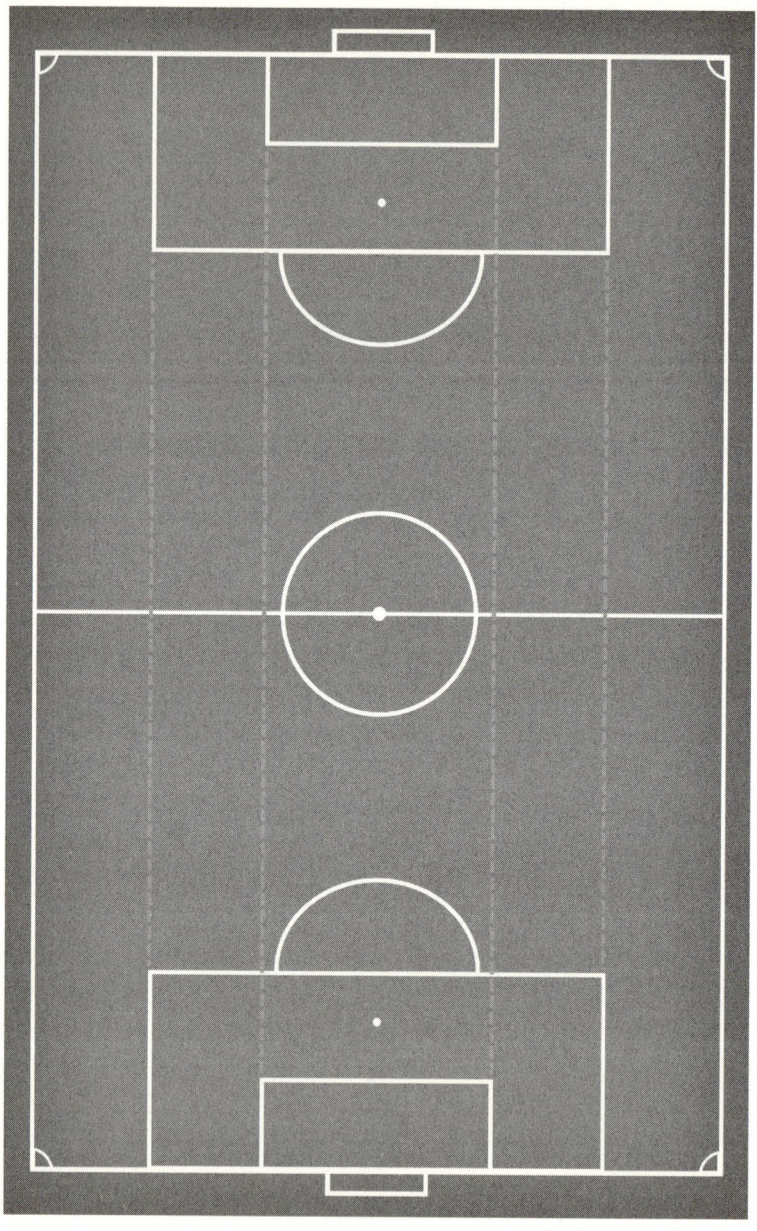

Figure 1

Chapter 1
4-1-4-1 or 3-3-1-3

When assessing the tactical model of Leeds under Marcelo Bielsa in the 2019/20 season, it makes sense that we first have to understand the structures that were used. There is an argument, of course, that formations in and of themselves do not matter. This is predicated on the belief that players' positions can be relatively fluid and based around other important reference points; the position of the ball, the position of the opposition and the position of your team-mates, for example. The truth, I believe, sits somewhere in the middle.

We cannot fully discount the importance of positional structures and team shape. Although at the same time, a coach like Bielsa has very specific tactical concepts both in and out of possession that can see players occupy different positions on the pitch depending on the factors that I have listed above. As you, the reader, progress through this book you will find that each chapter concentrates on these concepts one at a time before giving specific examples using key players from the season as case studies from a tactical perspective.

For most of his coaching career, Bielsa has been known for having a very specific tactical style of play. When he coached the Chilean national side, for example, they became known for playing an extremely aggressive 3-3-1-3 system which they rarely deviated from. While coaching in club football, however, Bielsa has shown a degree of tactical flexibility that belies his reputation as a coach who relies on one system above all. At Athletic Bilbao we began to see a willingness to morph into a more structured 4-1-4-1 system although the 3-3-1-3 was also still used. More recently, at Marseille, there were matches in which the tactical structure was primarily a 4-2-3-1 with a double pivot occupying the midfield zone.

Suddenly Bielsa was exhibiting a willingness to change structurally that was largely unexpected. What lay below these structures was incredibly interesting as whichever system was used in any given game, the underpinning tactical concepts that formed Bielsa's game model were still evident.

When Bielsa was appointed as the Leeds head coach on 15 June 2018, there was a sense of genuine excitement, and not just among Leeds fans but from those around the world who were fascinated by the tactical approach. So what would Bielsa do from a tactical point of view with players who were perhaps at a level below those with which he had worked in the past? The answer, in his first season at the club, was to play a loosely structured 4-1-4-1 system although there were some instances in which the 3-3-1-3 was used.

Going into the 2019/20 promotion season, however, there was a sense of a shift from a tactical perspective and that season saw 3-3-1-3 used more often, although the 4-1-4-1 was still the primary system of choice from Bielsa and his coaching staff. In order to fully understand why these two structures are so important to Bielsa, though, we have to first understand the difference between the two.

In order to achieve this we will break down each positional group one at a time to see how they act differently depending on the numerical structure. As a note, this will be done without reference to the goalkeeper who is a constant in the same position regardless of which structure we are discussing.

We will start then with the defensive line, which gives the greatest difference between the two structures. In terms of tactical concepts, one of the most famous that surrounds Bielsa is his preference to maintain a +1 structure on the first line (or defensive line), which means that he always wants to keep one defender more than the opposition have strikers. In other words, if the opposition are playing with one striker then Bielsa wants to have at least two central defenders. If the opposition plays with two strikers then he wants to have three central defenders and so on. This concept is built around the idea that Bielsa wants to maintain one free man on the first line. This provides cover and allows for additional flexibility in terms of his marking schemes. So, straight away we can see the value in having two defined tactical structures. In the first line the 3-3-1-3 allows for two markers and one free man while the 4-1-4-1 allows for one marker and one spare man. This is, of course, not including the full-backs in the 4-1-4-1 who have a more dynamic role which we will discuss later.

Next we will move to the following line and discuss the space between the defence and the midfield. Here, we have the '6' position that was made his own by a player developed through Leeds' own academy, Kalvin Phillips. The role of the 6 is one of the most important in the Bielsa system as that player has so many responsibilities whether in or out of possession. In 4-1-4-1 the 6 is positioned on that line on his own and he has a larger defensive responsibility as he forms a defensive triangle with the two central defenders. This allows the central defenders to split wide in possession as they allow the 6 to control the central areas. In moments of quick transition from defence to attack from the opposition it is the 6 who is most proactive in moving to cover space and denying the opposition the opportunity to attack the available space before the rest of the defensive block can reset.

In possession, it is not unusual to see the 6 take up a variety of positions in order to help with the progression of the ball. At times, he will drop back into the defensive line to form a three with the two central defenders. What is especially interesting about this movement is that this does not necessarily mean that he will drop centrally to split the central defenders wide. Instead, we will see the 6 situationally drop back to the sides of the two central defenders, into the space between the central defender and the full-back. This tends to happen when the opposition are pressing in a high and aggressive manner and the 6 dropping into that slot simply allows Leeds to change the angle of the build-up with a vertical passing option being more likely from that previously unoccupied positional slot.

In possession in the 4-1-4-1 the 6 is important for his ability to receive possession of the ball before playing vertically. We will examine the importance of 'verticality' to Bielsa in chapter three but the concept is simple. Instead of looking to maintain possession of the ball in these areas with passes back or to the side, the 6 is expected to hit a higher line wherever possible. When playing in this role, Phillips displays an excellent passing range with the ability to change the angle via long diagonal passes to the wingers or to find driven vertical passes into the central midfielders, who tend to move high, or the striker who can receive with his back to goal before linking with attacking team-mates. It is in the 4-1-4-1 that we then see the slightly different roles of the full-backs under Bielsa as it is not unusual, when Leeds are in possession, to see at least one of the two move into a more inverted position in order to support the 6 and provide a further option on that line.

In the 3-3-1-3, of course, the two full-backs, who have now become wing-backs, start, at least nominally on that second line along with the 6. The presence of a third central defender changes the role of the 6 in this shape somewhat with less of an expectation that this player holds a defensive structure with the central defenders. Instead, we tend to see the 6 roam more freely and look to take up supporting positions to allow the ball to be cleanly progressed through the thirds of the pitch. He will also move into spaces on the pitch that are vulnerable as the opposition looks to transition to the attack.

In the attacking phase the 6 is supported by the wing-backs who look to occupy the half-spaces. This allows the wide forwards in this attacking shape to isolate themselves in the wide lane against the opposition full-back and suddenly the spatial occupation from Leeds in the opposition half allows them to dominate and keep their opponents pressed in their own half. The role of the wing-backs in this system is key as their positioning is fluid and can change quickly depending on the location of the ball. They can support the wide player to form overloads against the opposition full-back or move inside to occupy the central spaces that are created when the central midfielders move on to occupy a higher line.

Next, we move on to the midfield line of the two structures – the four in 4-1-4-1 or the one in 3-3-1-3. First of all we will look at 4-1-4-1. Here, the line of four is made up of two central midfielders and two wide players. In the attacking phase the overriding characteristic of this line is that it moves high quickly. The wide players very much play as wingers and look to stay high and wide as Leeds are attacking. This movement profile is designed to achieve two clear aims from Bielsa. First of all, the wide positioning forces the opposition to commit defensive players to mark the wingers. This prevents the opposition from forming a deep and compact defensive block and creates space centrally that the central midfielders and striker can take advantage of. The second aim is to create opportunities for the wide players on the weak side (furthest away from the ball) to isolate against the opposition full-back. The ball can then be played to this side where Leeds will have a one v one opportunity. The central midfielders also look to move high. They would often completely empty the central area of the pitch and leave a gap between their line and that of Phillips as the 6. This would mean that when the ball was played vertically, again referring to the concept of verticality, the midfielders or 8s would be positioned on a line that is close to the centre-forward.

In the 3-3-1-3 we are, of course, only referring to a single player on this line and most often this would be the Polish international midfielder Mateusz Klich. In this system the central midfielder has been described by Bielsa as his *'enganche'* – this is a term used in Argentina to describe a team's 'number 10'; the player who links the midfield and attack. It is in this role that Klich in particular has excelled. He tends to play across the full width of the pitch and can be seen on a regular basis moving into the half-space or wide area in order to further overload the opposition in this area.

The role of the central midfielders, or 8s, is similar in the 4-1-4-1. Here we saw Klich partnered with several different players although the experienced Spaniard Pablo Hernandez made this position his own towards the end of the season. In this system the two 8s will push forward to link with the striker or provide rotation options in the wide areas. In doing so they naturally stretch the space between them and the 6 and this is where the full-backs are again important as they can look to occupy these central spaces situationally to allow for the ball to be circulated through the central area of the pitch.

Lastly, we have to consider the highest line. In the 3-3-1-3 there are, of course, three players on this line with two wide forwards and a single '9'. The wide forwards perform the same roles as the wide midfielders in the 4-1-4-1 and tend to stay high and wide. The 9 on the other hand tends to stay either centrally or in the half-spaces where he can receive the ball with his back to goal before linking play. When the ball is progressed to the final third, the 9 then looks to make intelligent movements to attack the spaces that the opposition leave unoccupied in the penalty area. Patrick Bamford was Bielsa's preferred option as the 9 throughout the promotion-winning season and although he gained a reputation for missing chances his technical ability allowed him to play the role that his head coach wanted perfectly. The role of the 4-1-4-1 is, of course, identical from the 9's point of view.

Now that we have discussed the theory around the two systems we will go through some practical examples to show how each line interacts and works with one another.

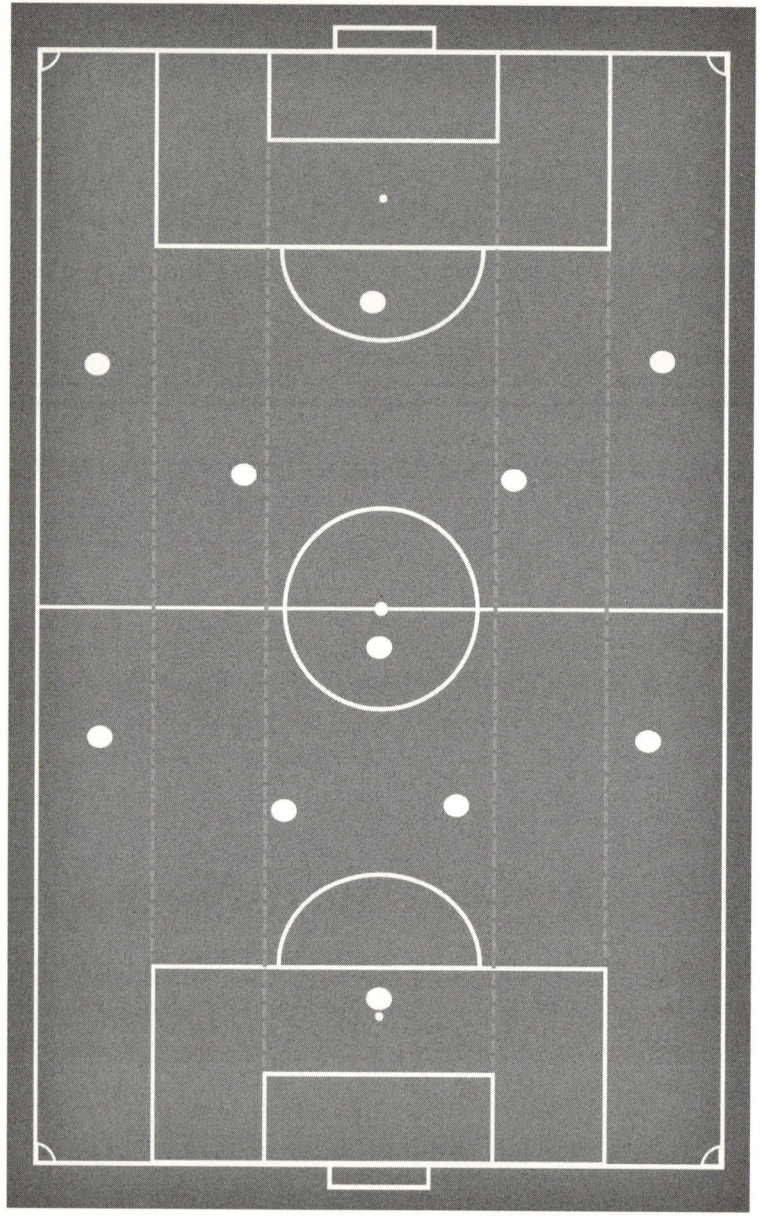

Figure 2

First of all we will break down the positional structures of the two shapes that we have been discussing in this chapter. While I appreciate that there are some among you who are more than comfortable picturing the systems and positions from what was written above, there are others who would prefer a more visual representation of what we have been talking about so far.

First of all we have the 4-1-4-1 system and it has been plotted without any opposition shape so that we have full clarity.

The first line is the defensive line with four players across the pitch. When Leeds have possession, of course, that line shifts with the full-backs moving high or into central spaces to support the attacking phase.

Next, we have a line of one with the 6 sitting in the space between the first line and the third line. This line is one of the keys to the way that Bielsa wants to play the 4-1-4-1 as he is not only expected to provide defensive strength and cover, he also becomes one of the key ball progressors for his side.

The third line has four midfielders with two central 8s and two wide players. As with the first line, however, the positioning here is largely nominal as all four players will move quickly into advanced positions when Leeds are in possession. Both 8s move high to link with the highest line and the two wide players stretch wide and move high. Even when out of possession we do not necessarily see a structured midfield block from the third line as each player will mark their individual man closely.

Finally we have the last line with, of course, only one player. The 9 here has an important role as they need to find pockets of space or create separation from the defensive players in order to provide an option to receive the ball as Leeds play to the highest line.

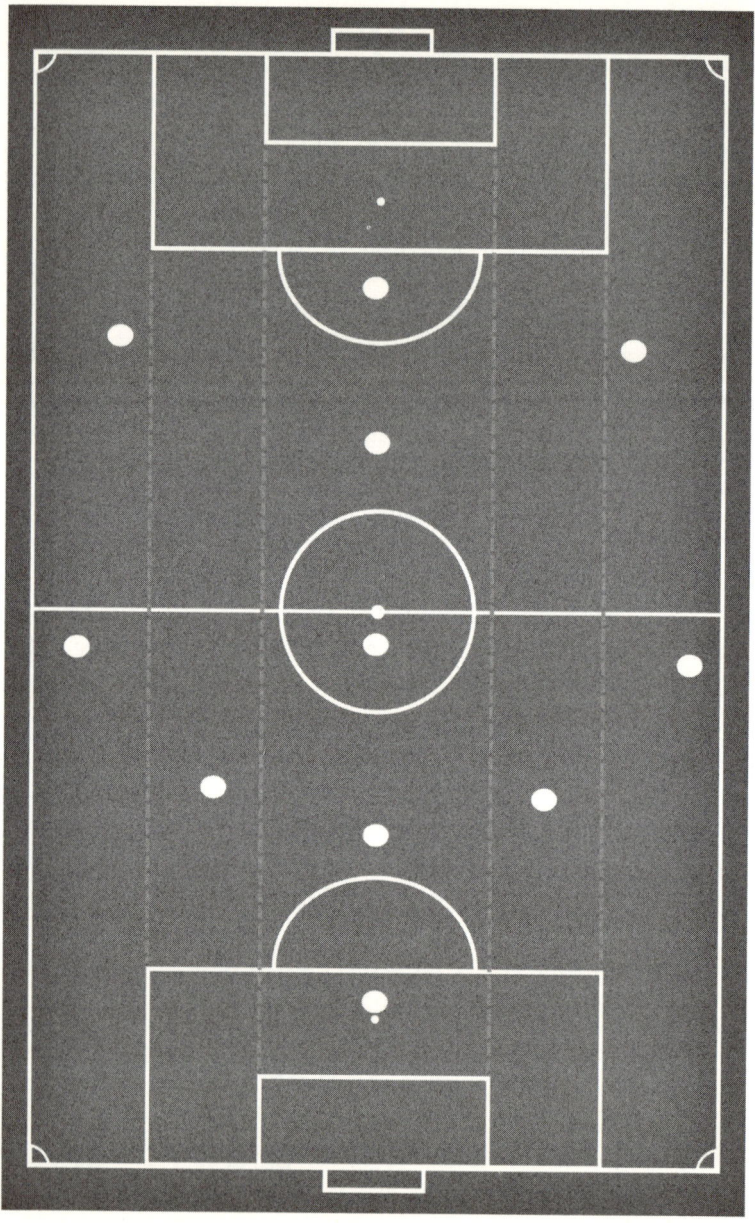

Figure 3

Next, we have plotted out the 3-3-1-3 system so that we can go through the same process.

On the first line we now have three players stretched out. This means that when the opposition field two strikers, Leeds can still maintain their +1 on the first line with a free defender.

The second line now has three players with the 6 supported by two wing-backs who do not necessarily move high immediately when Leeds are in possession. Instead, they will play in more inverted positions or even lower positions to support the progression of the ball. Such is the tactical flexibility from Leeds under Bielsa, however, these wing-backs can then move higher to overload the wide spaces as the ball progresses through the thirds and into the final third.

Now, the third line is the one with only one player and instead of the 6 it is now the 8 who is isolated on this line. This line is integral in the 3-3-1-3 system as this player provides the platform from which Leeds can build their attacking play. He will drift into the half-spaces in order to combine with either the wingers or the wing-backs and can dictate the angle and pace of the Leeds attack.

Finally we have the fourth line and now there are three players positioned high. Once again the wide forwards stretch wide and try to get isolation against the opposition full-backs. The 9 will have the same function as in the 4-1-4-1 as he moves to create angles in which he can receive vertical passes into feet.

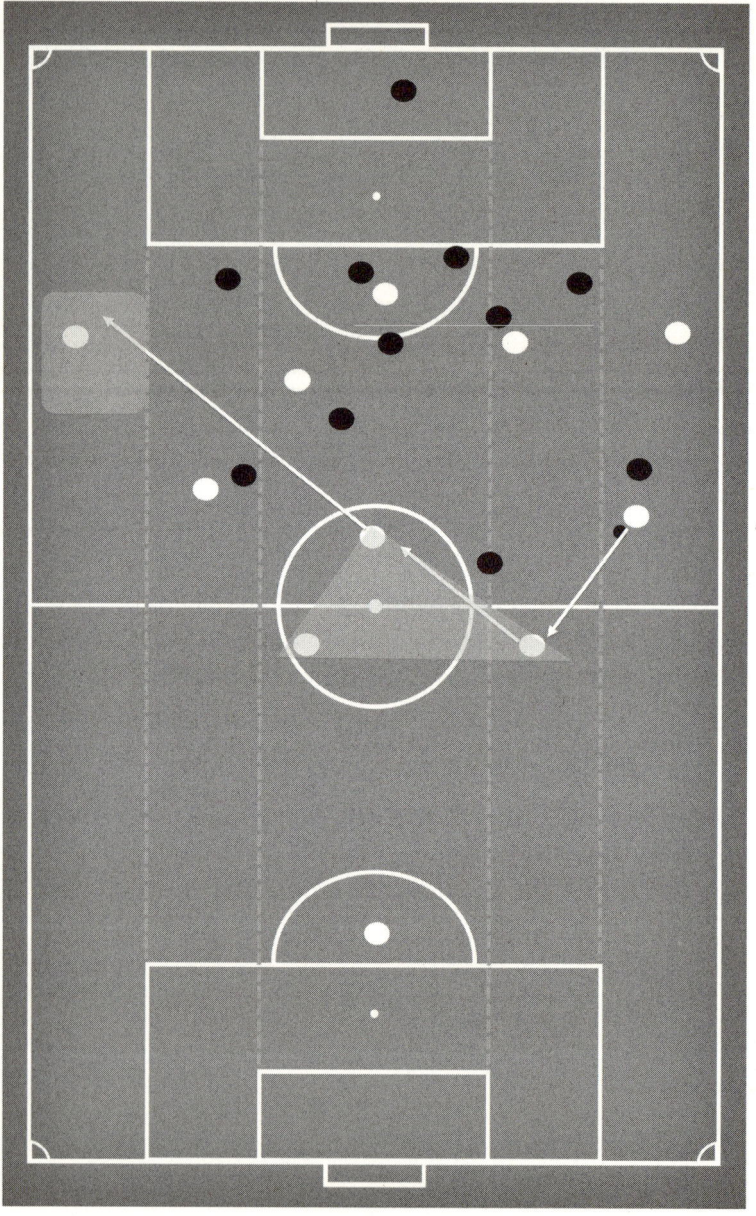

Figure 4

Next, we will start to examine some of the most important functions in these systems from individual players or roles, starting with the role of the 6 or single pivot in the 4-1-4-1 system.

First of all we have highlighted the importance of the 6 from a defensive perspective. This player tends to stay in central areas or at most drift into the half-spaces and he creates a defensive triangle with the two central defenders. This defensive positioning means that even if they win the ball and look to play quickly in transition the opposition still cannot easily occupy and overload the key space in front of the Leeds defensive line. The positioning and intelligence of the 6, especially when the role is occupied by Kalvin Phillips, means that vertical passes from the opposition into the feet of the strikers are very hard to achieve.

This deeper positioning from the 6 is also important for Leeds when they are in possession and looking to progress the ball. The 6 is often the player that Leeds use in order to change the angle of the attack quickly. We have an example of this in *figure 4* as the ball is sent back to the central defender before being moved quickly to the 6. From this position the diagonal pass can then be played to access the wide forward on the left who is in space and then isolated against the opposition full-back.

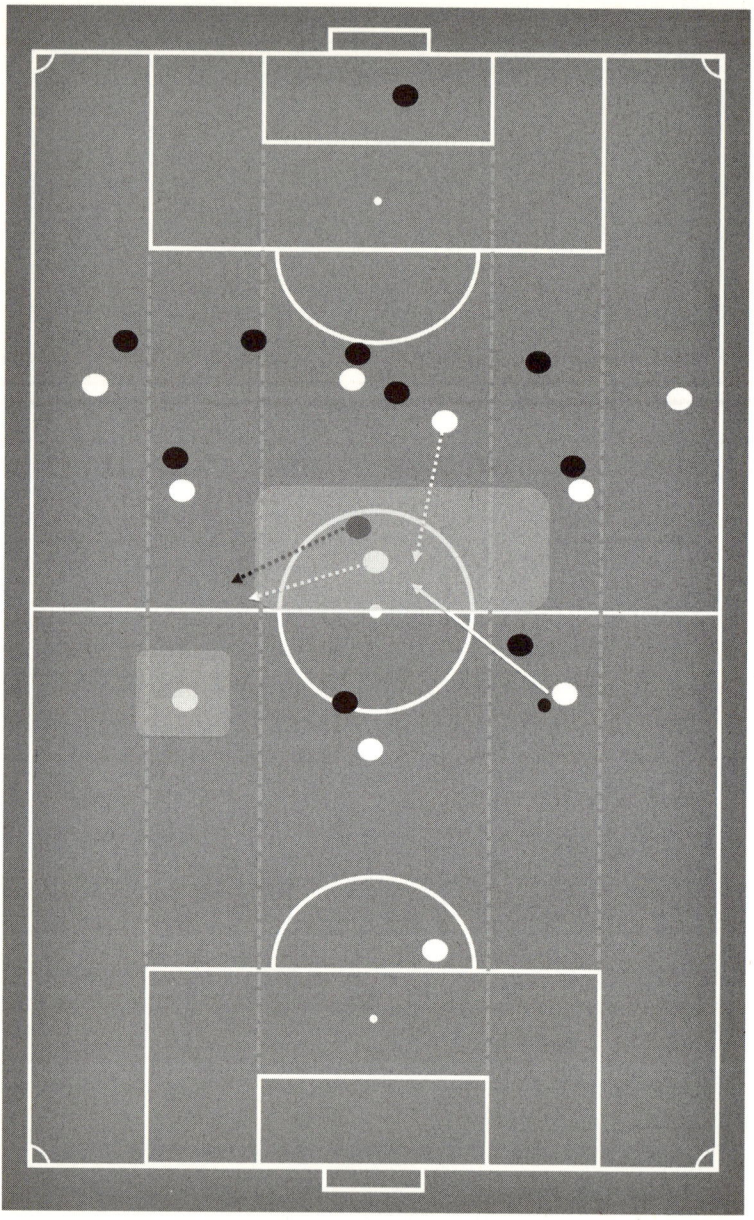

Figure 5

In *figure 5* we see an example of the behaviour of the 6 in the 3-3-1-3 system as Leeds are trying to progress the ball from their own first line. The first thing to note is that despite the opposition pressing the first line with two players, Leeds still maintain a +1 with one free player on the first line.

In the previous example, as part of the 4-1-4-1 system, we saw how important the 6 was in progressing the ball. Now, his role is slightly different and it is not unusual to see the 6 making movements to the left or the right in order to try to remove himself from the attention of his direct opponent or to draw the opposition player out of the central zone.

We see this kind of movement in *figure 5* as Phillips, as the 6, makes a movement away from the ball and pulls the defensive player out of position as he moves to cover. This empties space in the central zone and the 8 rotates back from a higher line in order to occupy this space and receive the pass from the central defender.

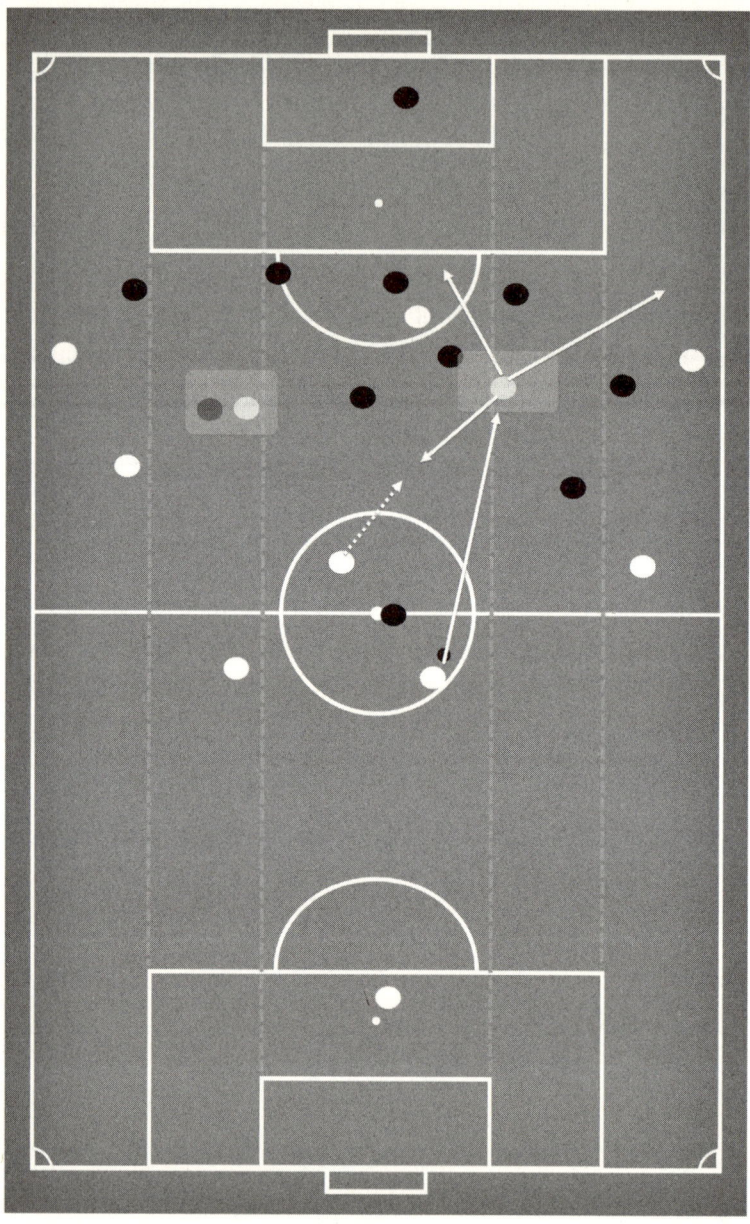

Figure 6

In *figure 6* we have gone back to the 4-1-4-1 structure but this time we are concentrating on the role and positions of the two 8s who move high in order to create chaos in the opposition defensive structure. With the vertical movement from these two players, they essentially form a block of five with the two wide attackers and the 9. With the 6 retaining a deep line with the central defenders we then start to see a separation between two clear units when Leeds are in possession. This separation is mitigated and linked by the behaviour and movements of the full-backs who have different instructions depending on the position of the ball. As the play is being built up they will be narrow or deep but as it moves high the ball-side full-back will move to overload in the wide space.

Here though we are concentrating on the 8s and their positioning is highlighted. The 8 nearest the ball is able to find a pocket of space to receive the vertical pass and as he does so he is threatening the penalty area. From this position he immediately has options. He can play to the wide player, play through to the 9 or set the ball back to the 6 if they are looking for an up, back and through movement. More on that later.

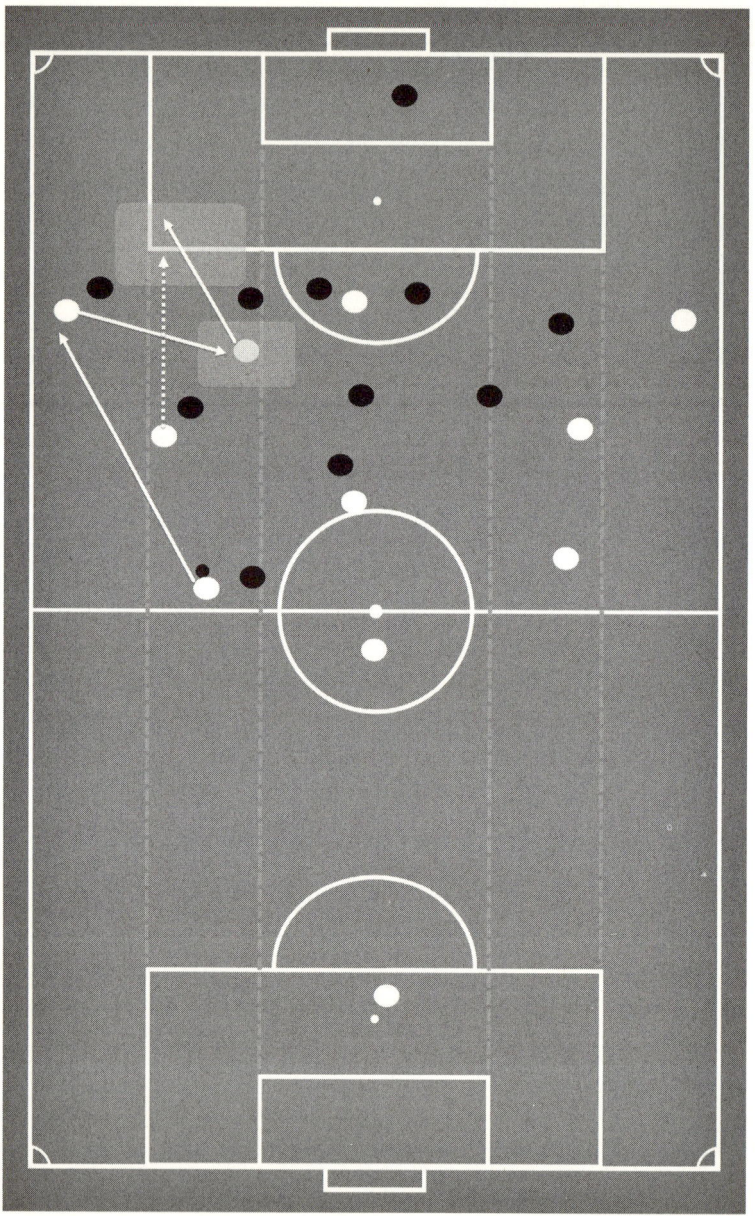

Figure 7

Finally, in *figure 7,* we see the importance of the player on the third line in the 3-3-1-3, the 8 or *enganche.*

As the central defender on the left-hand side has possession of the ball he is able to play a vertical pass that accesses the feet of the left-sided wide forward. In these situations we will often see the wide man look to engage the defender quickly one v one but there is a potential overload on that side of the field thanks to the positioning of the 8 and the supporting position of the wing-back.

As the wide player receives the ball he immediately moves it inside to the 8. Here we see the importance of the wide positioning of the wide attackers as he has stretched the defensive line. You can see the gap between the opposition full-back and central defender.

As the 8 receives the ball the wing-back makes a run off of his defender's blind side and looks to use this gap in the line. The 8 has the vision and timing to play the ball into the space perfectly for the wing-back to collect and break beyond the defensive line.

Chapter 2

Man-Orientated Marking

In football there are two distinct styles in which a team can mark the opposition when they are in the defensive phase. These are man marking and zonal marking. Both terms are widely known and understood and used almost on a weekly basis by the pundits who appear on our television. The merits of each are often discussed and debated but the truth is that it is rare in football for a team to adopt one over the other. Instead, most teams, especially at the professional level, adopt a hybrid approach. This means that teams will mark differently during the game depending on the position of the ball. This is also known as using the ball as a reference point. In other words, if the opposition have the ball in their own half then the first two lines, defence and midfield, will often be marking zonally with each player being responsible for marking his own space and picking up any player who drifts into it. As the ball progresses towards the final third, however, then the first line, the defence, will often shift to a man-marking system in order to deny the opposition players space in and around the penalty area.

Very few coaches use marking systems in their defensive game model that are purely man- or zonal-based. Marcelo Bielsa is, of course, one of the exceptions to this rule as he prefers a fully man-orientated system. At the time of writing this book, the 2020/21 season has started and Leeds have got their Premier League campaign under way. While the focus of this book is on the promotion-winning campaign of 2019/20, there is an interesting example that we can call upon to illustrate this point perfectly. This came from the opening match of the Premier League season as Leeds travelled to play against champions Liverpool at Anfield. Leeds came up against Roberto Firmino, a Brazilian '9' who is almost unique in his tactical profile and movement patterns. One of the key tactical characteristics of Liverpool in their attack is the way that Firmino drops off of the front line in order to link with the midfield. In doing so he poses a difficult choice for any opposition defender. Do they follow the Brazilian into midfield and leave space in the defensive line? Or do they allow Firmino free movement despite this allowing him to receive the ball unopposed?

At one point in this match Firmino dropped so deep that he was on the second line (as a 6) looking to receive the ball. As he checked his shoulder, however, he was shocked to find that the Leeds central defender Robin Koch had followed him all of the way into the Liverpool half. This perfectly displays how intense the man-marking system preferred by Bielsa is and shows the lengths that Leeds players will go to in order to shadow their designated man.

In order to fully understand why Leeds defend in this highly unusual manner we have to first understand exactly how it all works.

The defensive structure of the Bielsa model of play can be broadly broken down in a concept that is similar to his belief in maintaining a +1 advantage in terms of players in his first line (defenders) to opposition attackers. In the initial press, Leeds like to press -1 or with one player fewer than the opposition have on their first line. If a team is building up with two central defenders then just one Leeds player will enact the initial press. If there are three central defenders then two Leeds players will press and so on. This allows for the rest of the defensive block to adopt a man-to-man system behind the initial pressure. There are times in which this will switch with other players being triggered to join the press but pressing will be the topic of chapter three and as such we will leave that there.

So Leeds press with -1 but they still defend in their first line with +1. This means that in their first line they like to maintain a balance of at least one free defender who offers cover. In most instances across the 2019/20 season this free player would be Ben White, the young English defender who was on loan from Premier League side Brighton. White has excellent defensive instincts and is mobile enough to provide cover across the defensive line.

This free man concept gave an extra layer of security to a defensive system that is quite intense in the risk vs reward stakes. It is, after all, incredibly unlikely that no opposition player would be able to create separation from the Leeds player marking them, so how does the defensive system react to an opposition player moving forward into their half in space? The answer to this question is relatively simple; they react intuitively. This means that the Leeds squad is drilled and coached to understand threats such as these and to adjust their marking assignments accordingly.

To do so effectively they once again use the position of the ball as the key reference point. In other words the players who are closest to the ball will adjust their position and change who they are marking. This means that if a Leeds player is beaten in a one v one duel in the centre of the pitch and the opposition are moving towards the goal in possession of the ball then every player under Bielsa understands that they need to adjust their marking to cover the threat. The only rule in this adjustment of marking profiles is that the cover has to come from behind the ball. Leeds will still maintain their +1 concept in the first line and will avoid compromising that at all costs. As such the wide players in either the 4-1-4-1 or the 3-3-1-3 systems will often be the ones to sprint back into the defensive block in order to maintain balance.

There is a second answer to how Leeds react when an opposition player is moving into space within their defensive structure. If a player is left without the capacity to mark a specific opponent then they will move to close off potential passing lanes that would allow the opposition to move into even more advanced positions.

In an interview in *The Athletic* in July 2020, we saw Kalvin Phillips give an insight into this while in conversation with Phil Hay. On his actions on the first moment of defensive transition Phillips said, 'The first thing I think is, "Where's my man?" I'll take a quick look to try and spot him and I'll get as tight to him as I can as quickly as I can. If I'm close to him already, then I'm in a good position and the shape's fine. If I'm not, then I'll look to cut off the passing line from whoever's got the ball, because if my man gets the ball and I'm not with him, it's a problem. If I'm nowhere near him, then I'm in completely the wrong position but we've always played man-to-man and that makes it easier. "Keep track of your own player and you'll be in a good way." I keep that thought in my head.'

This interview and this quote in particular gives valuable insight into the decisions that a Leeds player has to cycle through in the first moment of defensive transition. It also tells us that cutting passing lanes and preventing the progression of the ball is a close second for Bielsa to ensuring that you are close enough to your man to cover them. Once again this provides the flexibility that the defensive system needs to prevent it from breaking altogether.

A pure man-marking system like this is extremely taxing on players, both from a physical and mental point of view. The level of concentration that the Leeds players have to maintain in order to track their man and understand the importance of the ball as a reference point can be extremely difficult to maintain. The fact that this defensive system is not only possible but effective demonstrates the level and quality of training sessions that Bielsa and his coaching staff provide for the players at the club.

Much has been made of the intense midweek sessions, which have been assigned the code name 'Murderball' because of the physical and mental intensity that they demand. In these sessions the Leeds squad play in a normal 11 v 11 match but if the ball goes out of play then a member of the coaching staff immediately feeds another one in. This ensures that the players on the pitch are constantly moving and having to concentrate on the various reference points in the match. By training in this manner, Bielsa is preparing his side to be able to concentrate on their defensive responsibilities when in the defensive phase of play during matches.

The physical aspect of this training, combined with other days in which Leeds still train in double sessions, is one of the key reasons that they were one of the fittest sides in the Championship during 2019/20. Indeed, it became something of a trend during the course of the season that Leeds' attacking output was hugely improved in the second half of games.

While the man-marking system that Leeds use is intriguing and even effective given that it is so hard to break, there are also times in which players can be moved out of their positional slots. This occurs when an opposition player drifts to the wing from the central area or from the centre out to the wide space. When this happens and the Leeds player in question follows them there can be a structural issue when they win the ball back and look to transition into the attacking phase. This is solved somewhat by the fact that Leeds are so fluid in possession of the ball with players able to rotate and interchange positions.

Now, we will move on to consider some practical examples with visual aides.

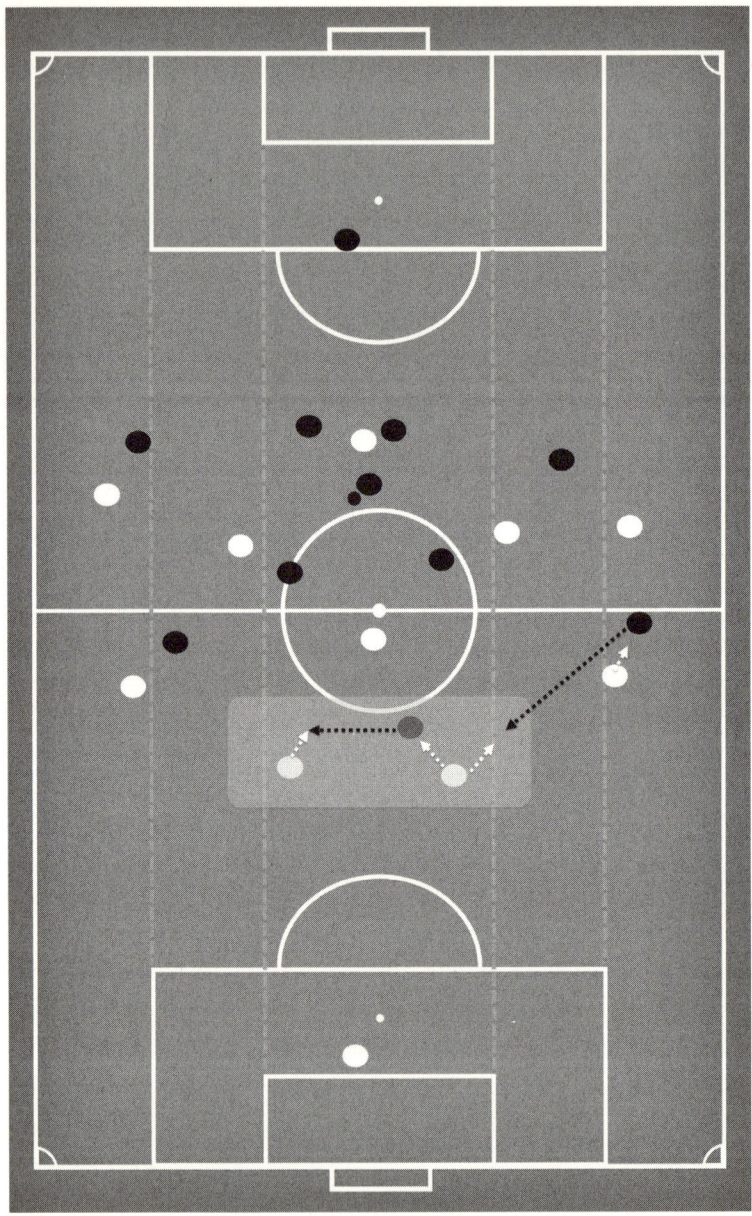

Figure 8

First of all we will provide an example of a typical zonal marking system with the kinds of movement profiles that we can see from defensive players as attackers move around the pitch.

This is displayed in *figure 8* and we have set Leeds out in a 4-1-4-1 system as they would be were they using a zonal marking system in the defensive phase. Initially the opposition have the ball centrally and in a relatively deep position. The section that matters the most to us has been highlighted where the two central defenders are positioned against one opposition forward player.

In the first instance the forward is being marked by the right-sided central defender but there is no open passing lane for the man in possession to access the striker from this position. So the forward moves to the left of the highlighted area and now the left-sided central defender has the responsibility to mark the forward.

There does not seem to be any structure issues with the two central defenders passing the marking duty back and forth. Bielsa, however, likes to have one player act as the free defender at all times. This player, during the 2019/20 season was almost exclusively Ben White as his profile fitted the role perfectly. If he was having to concentrate on his zonal duties then this would be more difficult.

There is also a second example included as the right-back for Leeds is initially positioned against the opposition's left-winger. The winger moves centrally and the zonal responsibility passes on to the right-sided central defender. Once again this kind of structure would not work for Bielsa and his man-marking system.

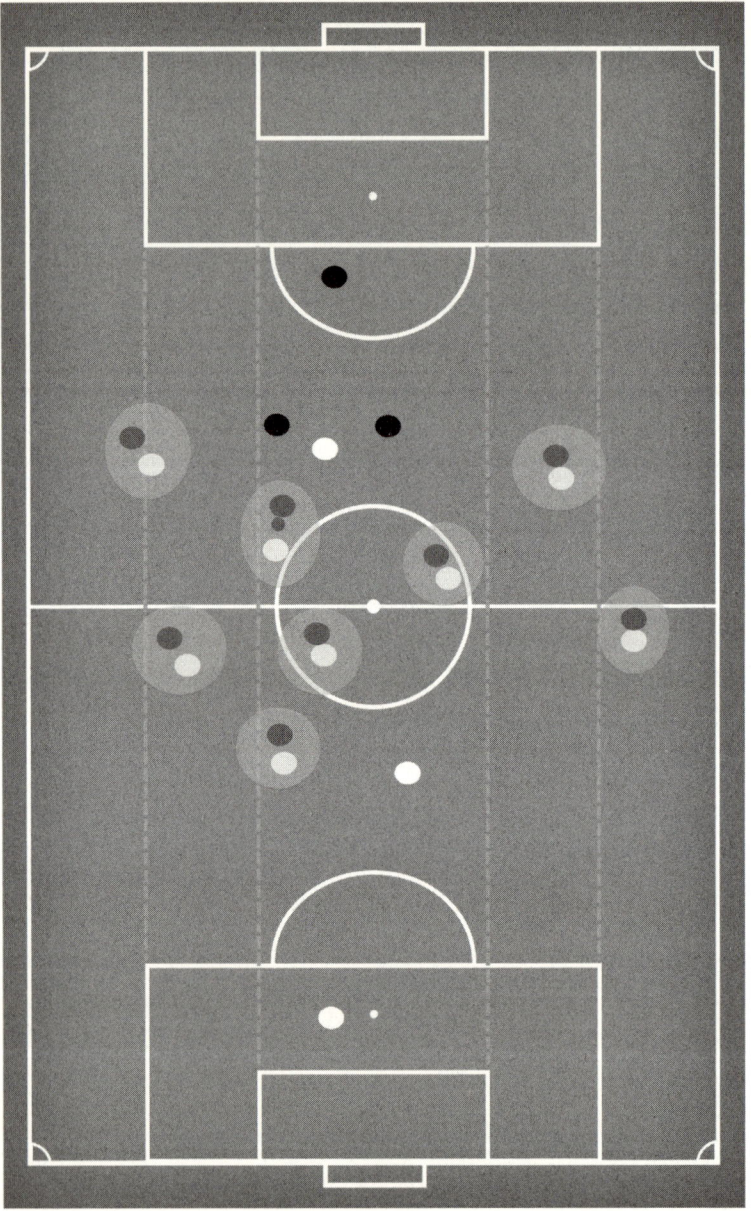

Figure 9

Next, in *figure 9*, we will examine the way that a man-orientated marking system works, again in a 4-1-4-1 shape.

As you can see we have highlighted each player to show the way that they are closely positioned with their direct opponent in a man-marking style. It is important to note that there are three players to whom this does not directly apply. The first is, perhaps obviously, the goalkeeper who does not join the marking system. The second is the spare central defender, normally White, who is free to provide cover across the width of the defensive line and the third is the 9 who does not specifically man-mark unless Leeds are pulled very deep. Instead he will move to block passing lanes back to the opposition central defenders or apply pressure deep.

You can see with the help of this visual just how difficult it is for sides to maintain a pure man-marking system for a long time over the course of a match. There is no balance or cover, apart from the spare central defender, and it takes a lot of concentration for players to maintain their defensive shape.

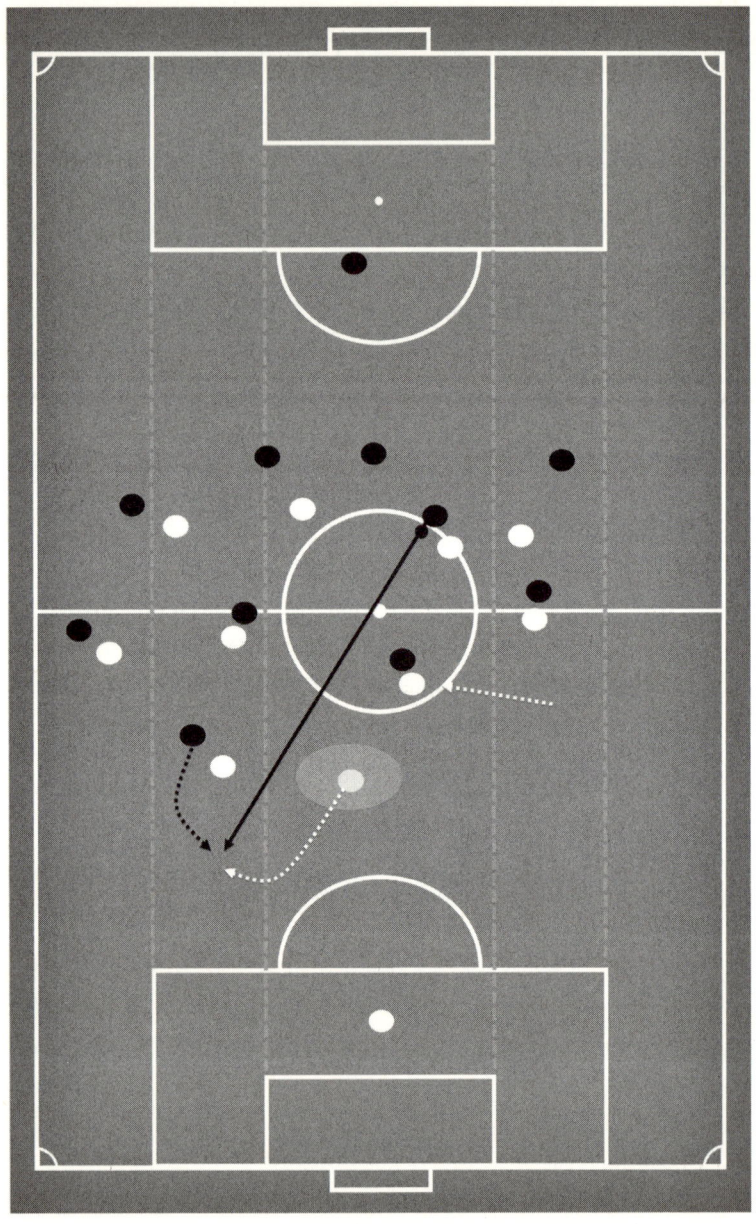

Figure 10

Now we will move on to look at why it is important for Leeds to maintain a +1 in the first line when they are in the defensive phase. One of the drawbacks of man-marking across the entire pitch in the way that Bielsa does is that you are leaving your side exposed to specific mismatches, especially on the physical side of the game. If, for example, the opposition has a wide player or a striker who is exceptionally quick then the full-backs/wing-backs or central defenders can be exposed.

This is why cover is especially important on the first line where a Leeds player being outplayed, whether physically or technically, could leave the opposition with a chance on goal. This is not as big an issue for Leeds in more advanced areas of the pitch thanks to the mechanisms put in place by Bielsa to ensure that there is cover in place should this be an issue.

In *figure 10* we see a situation where the marking central defender is exposed by a relatively simple direct pass behind the defensive line. The pass is angled beyond the defender and the striker has managed to create separation to get himself into a favourable attacking position with a chance to move in on goal. This is where the covering defender comes into his own as he reads the danger and moves around to provide cover and prevent the situation from developing into something more dangerous than it already was.

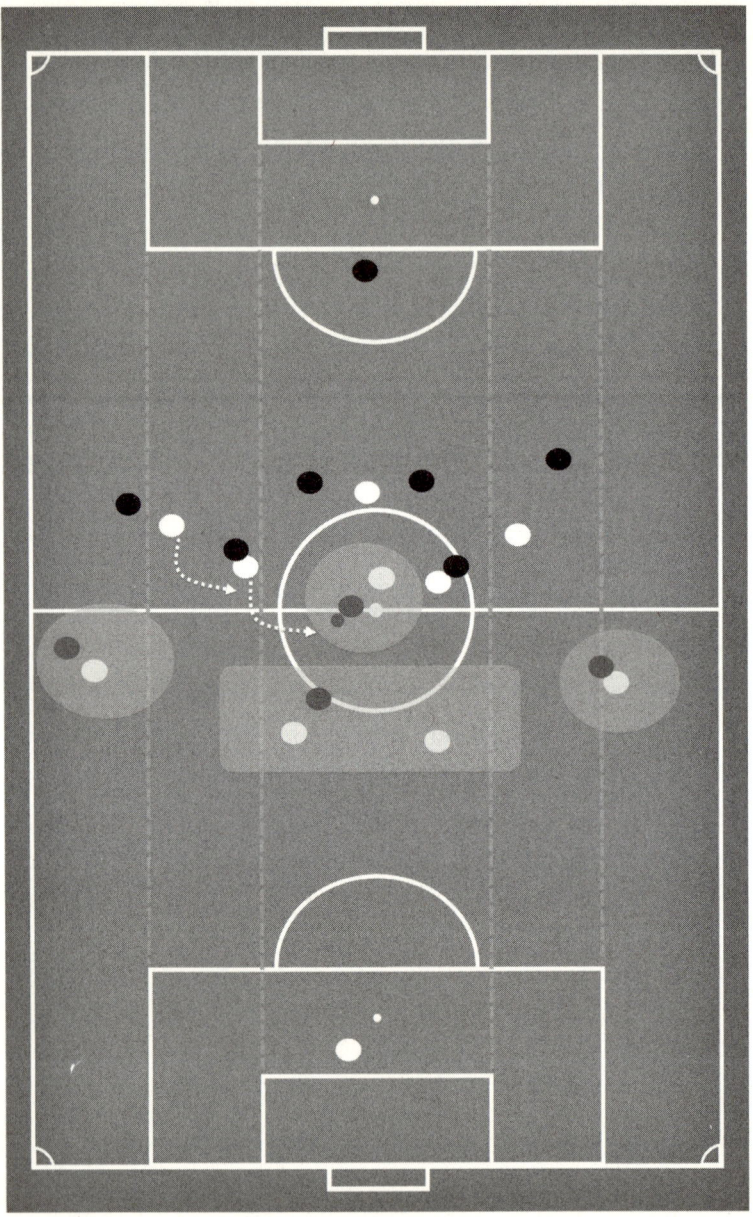

Figure 11

In *figure 11* we look more closely at the adjustments that Leeds make when an opposition player outplays their press in the centre of the park. It is after all completely unrealistic to think that a player can win all of their defensive duels across the course of a game, never mind a season, and as such Bielsa coaches his players to understand their role in balancing out the defensive structure when a player is beaten or caught out of position.

Here we see an example when Kalvin Phillips, playing as the 6, has allowed himself to be pulled up the field into a flat line with the two 8s. This lapse of concentration from a positioning point of view has allowed the opposition to create space between the first line and the third line with no cover in between.

As the opposition player looks to take advantage of this space we see an adjustment in positioning from the Leeds players that takes away the threat almost immediately. First of all the left-sided 8, Mateusz Klich in this example, bursts back to get in front of the ball carrier. This, of course, unbalances Leeds elsewhere as the man initially marked by Klich is not free and this represents an easy passing option for the player in possession. In order to retain the necessary defensive balance we then see Jack Harrison, the left-sided attacker, moving quickly to replace Klich and man-mark the free opposition player.

This is why it is important that the defensive adjustments come from behind the ball. Had one of the full-backs or the spare central defender had to step out to engage the ball then the lack of balance would have occurred on the first line, in a position that is far more dangerous for the opposition attack.

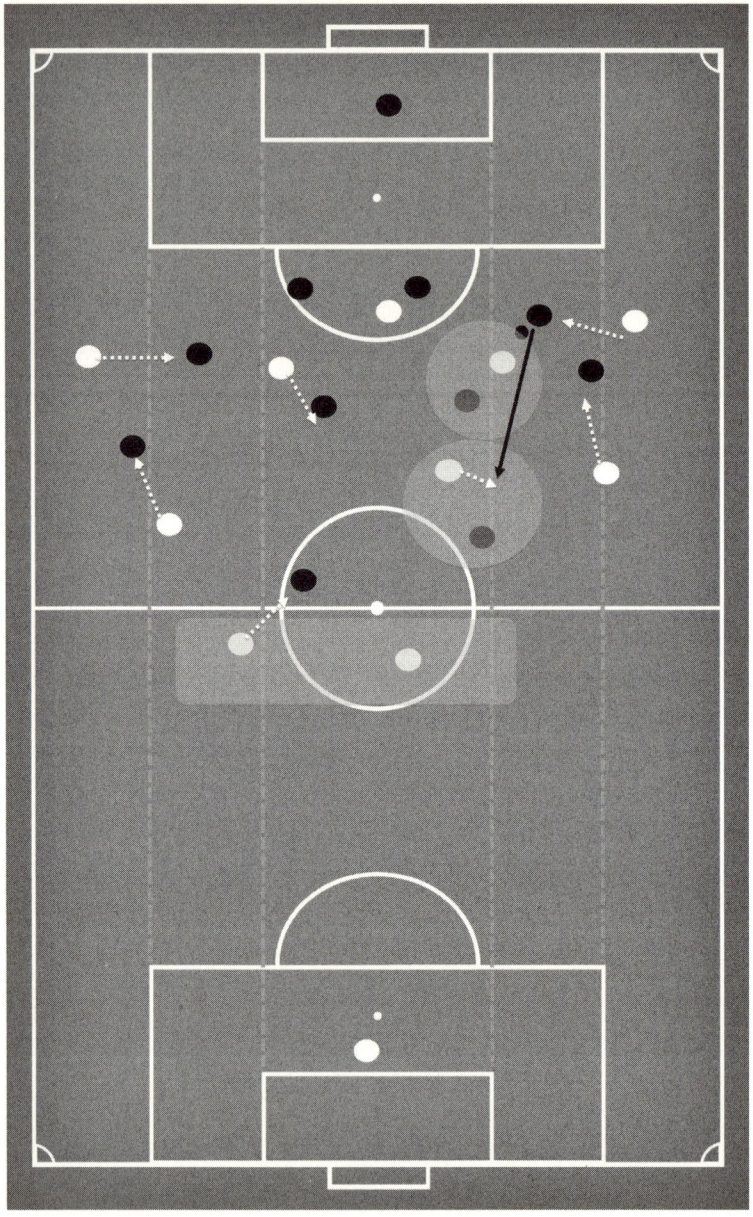

Figure 12

The moments of immediate defensive transition from Leeds are often a sight to behold as players move seamlessly into their defensive position and into a man-to-man structure. The quote that we have on page 31 from Kalvin Phillips, however, needs more exploration. How do Leeds players, and Phillips in particular, behave when they are caught significantly out of possession?

In *figure 12* we have an example of this and you can see the movements from Leeds players to get tight to their man. Phillips, however, finds himself caught between the ball and the man who would be his. One again Bielsa does not want the free central defender to have to step out to cover this threat as this would expose the first line.

Instead, we see Phillips move quickly in a lateral motion to position himself between the ball and the free attacker. This cuts the passing lane and ensures that when the ball is attempted to find the free man the young midfielder is in position to win back the ball and restart the attack for his team.

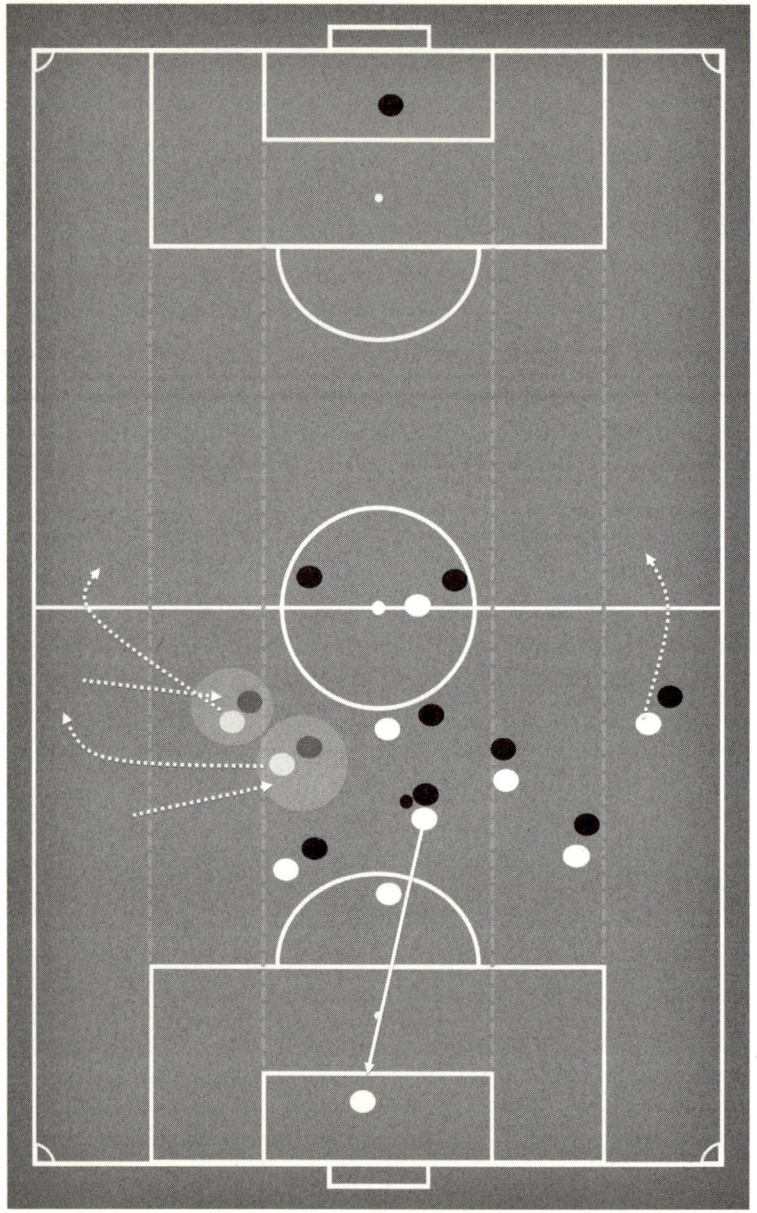

Figure 13

44

If the speed in which Leeds adjust in the immediate defensive transition is impressive, it is worth noting that this speed is matched in the way that they adjust their shape in the moments of immediate transition to the attacking phase.

It is not unusual for us to see players significantly pulled out of their positional slots when they are acting in the defensive phase. This is especially true of the wide forwards and wing-backs who will happily follow their man into central spaces in order to stop them from receiving the ball comfortably.

In *figure 13* we have examined the typical movements that we saw from Leeds in the attacking transition across the 2019/20 season.

The wide forward and full-back have both been pulled centrally as the opposition try to attack through a very compact shape. As Leeds regain possession and the ball is played back to the goalkeeper we immediately see those wide players make sprinting movements back out to occupy the wide spaces.

This is a pure example at the professional level of why we hear youth coaches telling their charges to 'make the pitch big' when in possession of the ball.

Chapter 3

Pressing

In the modern game, one of the most discussed aspects of any team's defensive organisation is the way that they press when out of possession. A lot of analysis, both at the amateur and the professional level, is designed to understand how the top teams do this and whether any trends can be identified and duplicated. The truth, however, is that there is no right or wrong way to press the ball, just the way that fits into your overall defensive structure.

There is no point, after all, in committing to a high and aggressive press if you do not maintain a layer of support behind it. Without this support the press can be broken comfortably and played around. Equally, there is no point in pressing from a low block with little aggression without knowing how you will transition into the attack should you win the ball back. In this situation it is easy for your side to become trapped in their own half with no easy way to play through and beyond the opposition block.

There are some coaches who have very defined pressing schemes that have to an extent defined their coaching style. Take Liverpool's Jurgen Klopp, for example, and we see a coach who was linked constantly to the concept of *gegenpressing* or counter-pressing. This was a style that Klopp used to great effect when he was the coach of Borussia Dortmund in Germany, his last role prior to taking over at Liverpool. The central principle of this style was that the team would commit to pressing aggressively in order to win the ball back as close to the opposition goal as possible. This then results in goalscoring opportunities for your team.

The key behind counter-pressing was that when used properly it became the overriding defensive principle that defined a team's play when out of possession. This means that not only did the attacking line press, the midfield line would also press to cut off any potential passing options and gradually teams were pushed back and forced to play long, hopeful passes that could be comfortably intercepted by the defending team.

Another example of this comes from another coach who now works in the Premier League in the shape of Pep Guardiola. While at Barcelona, the Spaniard also favoured a high and aggressive press although not to the extent that it could be compared to counter-pressing. Instead Guardiola coached his side to use what became known as the 'five-second rule'. The simple principle was that when his side lost the ball and entered a defensive transition he wanted them to press aggressively for five seconds. If after that period the ball was not regained then the side was expected to drop into a more compact block and, at times, look to commit a foul to slow down the opposition and prevent them from countering effectively.

What is especially interesting when analysing Leeds under Bielsa is that he is generally known as a pressing coach, but in truth his system of applying pressure to the ball is more nuanced than just all-out pressing and pure aggression. Instead, once again, there is a specific tactical concept or principle that dictates the way that Leeds will press the opposition.

We have already discussed the +1 principle in relation to the way that Leeds like to maintain a one-man advantage on the first line. Now, with pressing, we need to discuss the -1 principle. This idea works in much the same way as the +1 does in that Leeds will press the opposition defensive line with one fewer player than they are trying to build up with. This means that if the opposition has two central defenders building play then one Leeds player will engage to press. If there are three central defenders then the 9 and the ball-side wide forward will look to engage and press the ball. This principle is relatively simple in action and is designed to prevent the opposition from having comfortable possession in order to progress through the thirds.

The way that the players in question press is again dependent on the positioning of the ball as a reference point. If a player in a central space has possession of the ball then the run of the player engaging in the press will be angled to cut off the closest passing lane. If the player in possession has the ball in a wider space then the run of the player initiating or supporting the press will be angled to force the man in possession wider as the touchline can be used effectively as a second defender.

These simple pressing principles are designed to stop clean ball progression but also to delay the opposition's attacking movement and allow the rest of the Leeds defensive structure to drop back into their man-marking system. There are rarely more than two players involved in the initial pressing movement and if someone is not one of those two then their first responsibility is to pick up the closest opposition and mark them tightly. This goes for the entire team with the only exception being the free man at the back who maintains the defensive balance. This defensive structure, with pressing players and a man-orientated marking system combined, works together extremely well. If teams look to drop players back to help receive the ball past the line of pressure then those players will be closely covered by a Leeds man. The more players the opposition choose to drop back towards the ball the better for Leeds as they end up pinning their opponents deep in their own half and the ability to escape the press is then made much harder.

The most important aspect of the pressing style that we saw from Leeds as they gained promotion was that the players were willing to fully commit to it. In pressing and maintaining man-to-man structures such as this there will always be opportunities for the opposition to play through and break your press. Once again the conditioning of the Leeds players is key as even if the opposition do manage to break through the initial pressing structure we then see Bielsa's side able to drop their structure to maintain their man-to-man marking as they get back behind the ball.

The -1 concept is one part of the pressing system utilised by Bielsa, but as with all coaches at the top level there are several pressing triggers he uses in order to dictate when Leeds move into a more aggressive pressing style. Two of the most common pressing triggers we saw during 2019/20 were to press when the ball is played into a wide position or to press when the ball is played to a player in a central area who is facing his own goal. Once again, these specific principles deserve a little more exploration.

The first of these triggers, with the ball played to the wide area, is relatively simple and is often forced when the player in possession in the central space of the opposition half is pressed from the inside out. This essentially means that the first pressing player is moving at an angle to prevent the central defender in possession from playing a lateral pass to the second central defender. The angle of the press is then combined with the positioning and marking of the next line as they pick up opposition players in a man-to-man structure.

That leaves the pass out to the near-side full-back as the safest option. As soon as that pass is played we see the initial presser move beyond the central defender to block the passing lane back to him or the goalkeeper. The man in possession is now pressed intensely and as his team-mates look to drop to support we then see the Leeds players continue to squeeze up. This effectively pins the opposition into the corner of the field and a turnover can then be forced.

The second trigger of note is when an opposition player receives the ball while facing his own goal. Once again the pressing from the first player is designed to deny the opposition easy circulation of the ball and to force an opportunity to win it back close to the opposition goal. Often, the way an opposition team will look to escape the first press will be with a pass to a deeper central midfielder. This is a trap that Bielsa's team will press quickly and from more than one angle. As the opposition player receiving the ball and facing his goal takes possession the initial presser will immediately approach from the goal side. This prevents a comfortable pass back into the central defenders and applies pressure to win the ball back. There is secondary pressure, usually from one of the 8s or from a wide forward who is closest to the man in possession. Once again the result of this period of play is that the opposition looks to move players back and into supporting positions. Leeds then squeeze up and look to force a turnover or a mistake.

In order to fully understand the way that Leeds play though it tends to help to look at some practical examples.

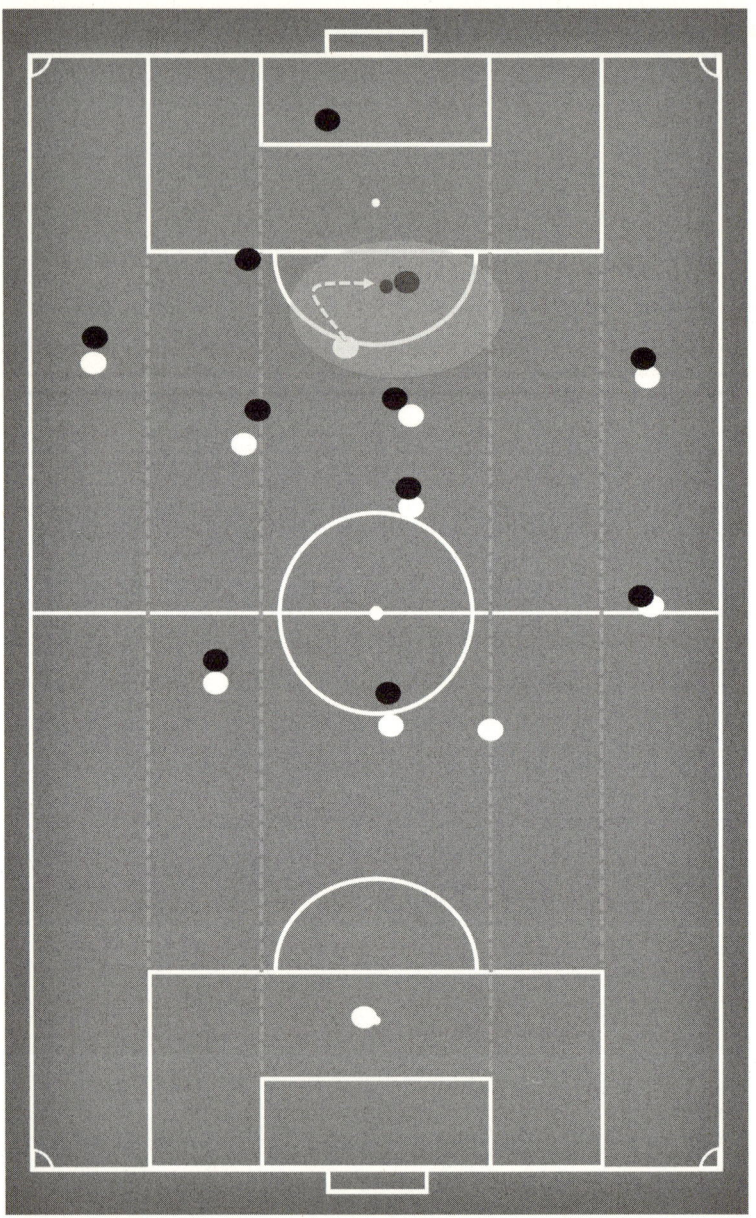

Figure 14

First of all, in *figure 14* we need to look at the kind of runs that the 9 will tend to make against a two-man build-up. In the build-up phase we tend to ignore the full-backs and consider the number of central defenders that a team is using, unless of course the full-back drops back into the defensive line and changes the dynamic and the shape.

As discussed earlier in the chapter, the structure of the Leeds press is versatile and depends on how many players the opposition have on their first line when building the play and trying to progress the ball.

In this example it is a two-man partnership looking to move the ball and as such Patrick Bamford, playing as the 9, is the only man who is actively involved in the pressing action. He deliberately angles his run to approach the ball carrier in a way that shuts down the passing angle to play the ball across to the second central defender. This pressing movement and the angle of the run from Bamford is designed to take away a safe passing option for the man in possession. This is then combined with the man-to-man marking structure behind the line of pressure. We can see that in this example every opposition player ahead of the ball is being closely marked by a Leeds player. This forces the man in possession to play a pass into an area where they have no immediate advantage over the Leeds defensive structure.

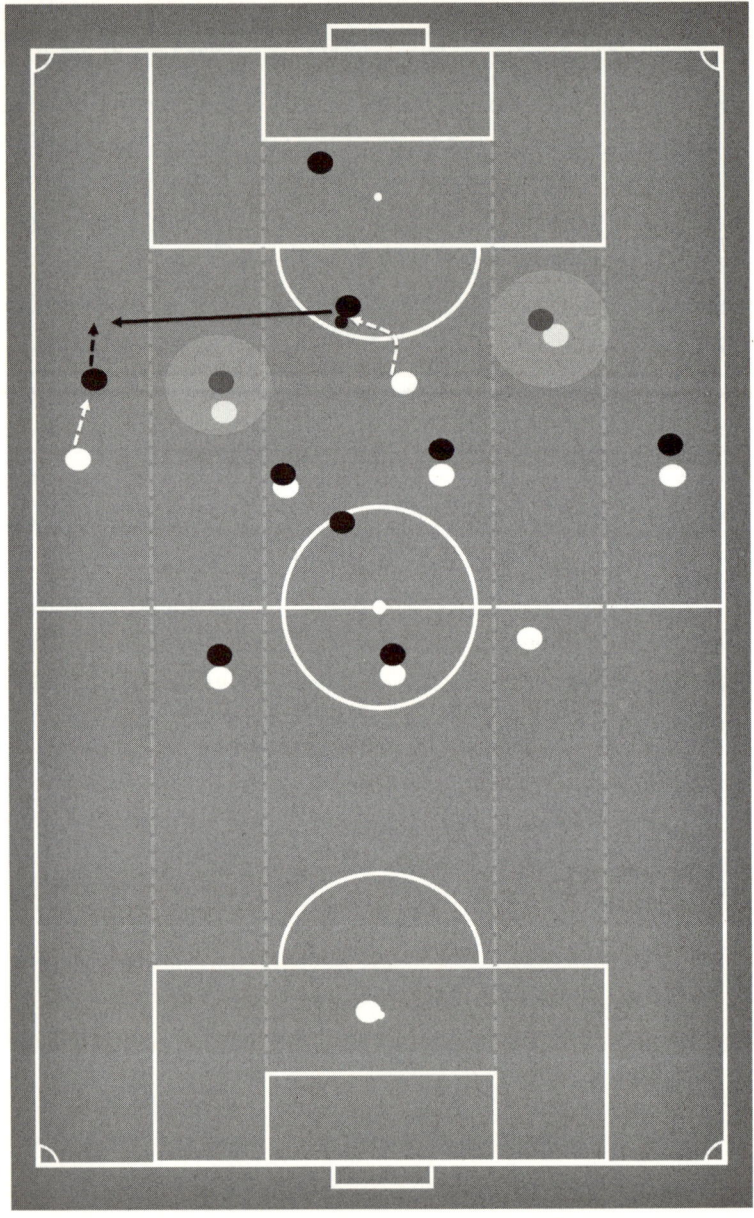

Figure 15

This time, in *figure 15,* the opposition are trying to build the attack from a three-man base on the first line. This structure means that the wide forwards now become involved in the pressing action for Leeds.

Once again the key from the structure wanted by Bielsa is that there has to be balance between those who are pressing the ball and those who are closely marking the opposition players behind the press.

Which wide forward is pressing depends on the position of the ball and which way it is likely to be played. In this example the player at the centre of the back three is the one who has possession of the ball. Once again we see Bamford as the 9 as the first player to apply pressure to the ball. He, again, angles his run in such a way to shut off one of the easy passing options for the man in possession of the ball. The angle of this run then dictates which wide forward joins to press. As Bamford engages, the left-sided attacker is the one whose man has a clear passing option and as such he moves to engage on the ball. On the other side the wide player simply squeezes in to man-mark his player on that side.

The receiving player is then under extreme pressure with Bamford poised to cut the passing lane to the central defender in the middle or back to the goalkeeper.

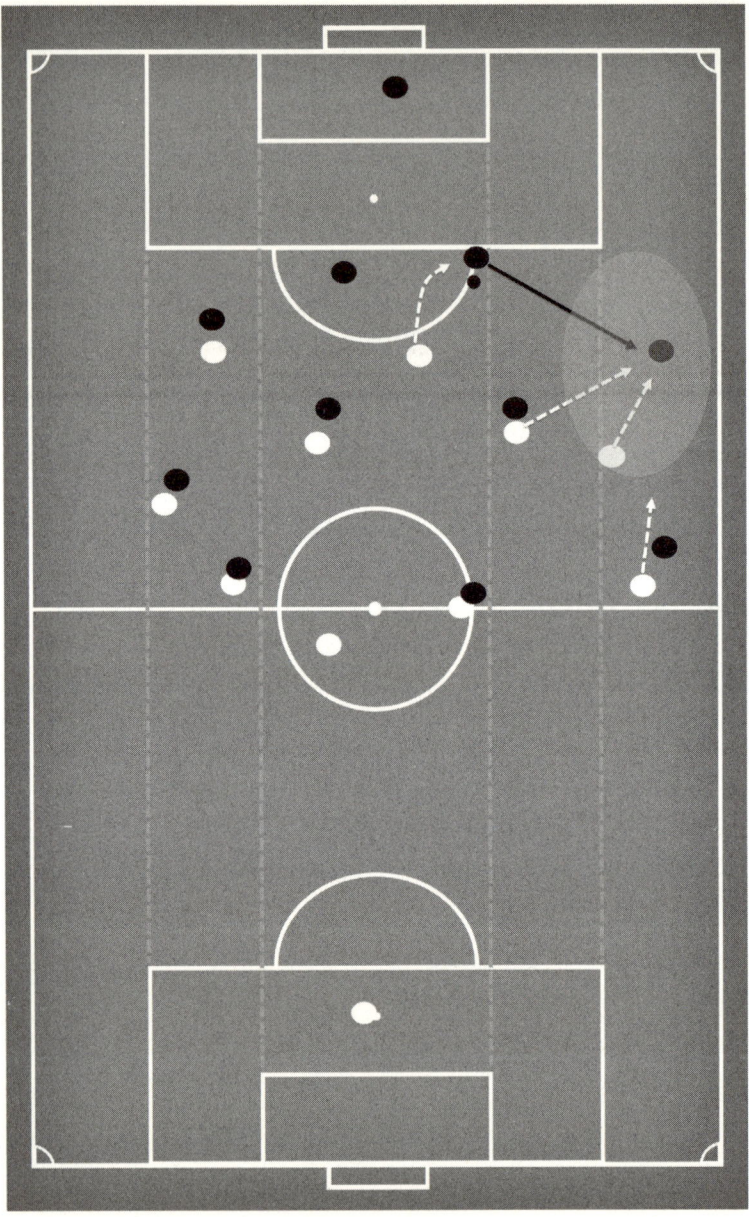

Figure 16

Now let's take a closer look at one of the clear pressing triggers that Bielsa likes to use with his team. In *figure 16* we see a situation when the opposition were looking to build up from the back and one of the Leeds players was caught out of position, thus leaving the opposition relatively free to receive the ball.

Once again we see the 9, Eddie Nketiah this time, moving to engage the ball carrier and cut off the option of passing back across to the second central defender. On this occasion, however, there is what seems to be an easy escape with a pass to the left-back. It is at this point though, as the ball reaches a player on the touchline, that a pressing trigger is activated.

The fact that the receiving player is so close to the line is helpful from a defensive perspective because it limits the options for the man receiving the ball in terms of where he can move or pass the ball.

As soon as the trigger occurs we see Leeds players on that side of the field leave their immediate marking assignments and move to engage the ball. What is crucial though is that they angle the runs that they are making in order to keep the opposition player they were marking in their cover shadow. This prevents the player with the ball from easily escaping the press.

As two players move to press the ball a third steps in front of the vertical passing option to cut that passing lane. With this press the opposition are forced to play passes without control that can be easily won back by Leeds.

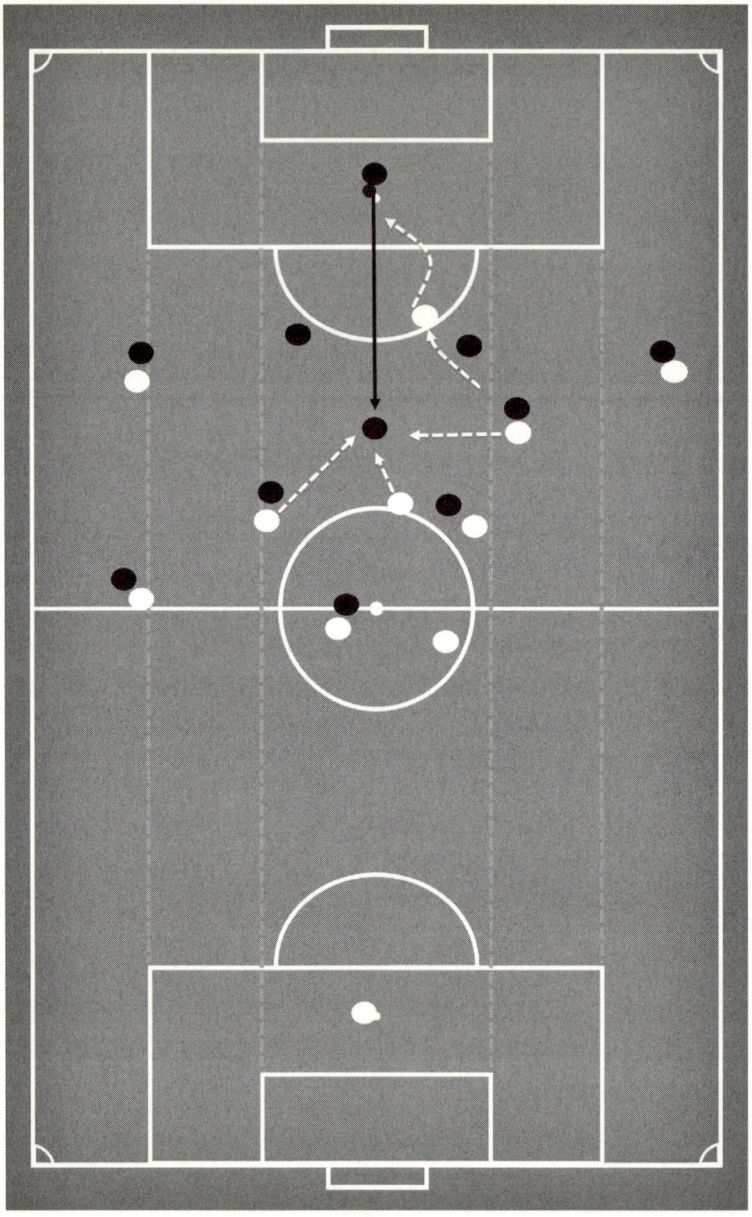

Figure 17

The second regular pressing trigger that Leeds used over the course of 2019/20 saw them move to engage and press the ball when the receiving player was positioned centrally but was facing his own goal.

The idea behind this trap is that the receiving player is poorly positioned to be able to receive the pass and then look forward in order to play through the oncoming press. We have an example of this trigger in action in *figure 17.*

This time the goalkeeper is in possession with the ball at his feet. In order to prevent comfortable and clean ball progression we see Bamford looking to move to apply pressure; once more though he angles this press to cut off one of the passing options that the goalkeeper has available to him. The goalkeeper then takes the option to play the vertical pass into the feet of his 6, who receives facing his own goal. As soon as this pass is played the press is triggered.

As with the previous example we then see the three Leeds players who are positioned closest to the ball moving to engage and press the player who has now received the pass. What is crucial though is that the 9 also moves back towards the ball and balances his movement to make any pass back to one of the central defenders dangerous. When Leeds were able to win the ball back in these areas they were very quick to flood into the area and attack the opposition goal.

Figure 184

There is no such thing as a perfect system in football, whether in the attacking or the defensive phase, and any pressing structure can, at times, be played through. The key thing for any team to understand though is how to recover their position when this happens without losing balance through the rest of their defensive structure.

In *figure 18* we see an example of this in action.

Bamford, again as the 9, was looking to move across to place pressure on the goalkeeper who had possession. As he did so the ball was played out to the central defender and Bamford had to adjust his run towards the player who now received the pass.

Mateusz Klich, playing as the left-sided 8, was caught out of position as he was attracted forward towards the ball. This allowed the pass to be played vertically to a free man and immediately the Leeds man-marking structure was threatened. In order to recover their position in this area the left-sided attacker leaves his man and looks to burst back to engage the new ball carrier. Klich also adjusts his position and looks to press the man who now has the ball.

It is key for Leeds to recover their position when the press is played through from behind. This retains defensive balance between the ball carrier and the ball. It is also notable that when the press is bypassed in this manner the recovery and pressing from Leeds is extremely aggressive as they look to immediately take away the threat from the opposition player on the ball.

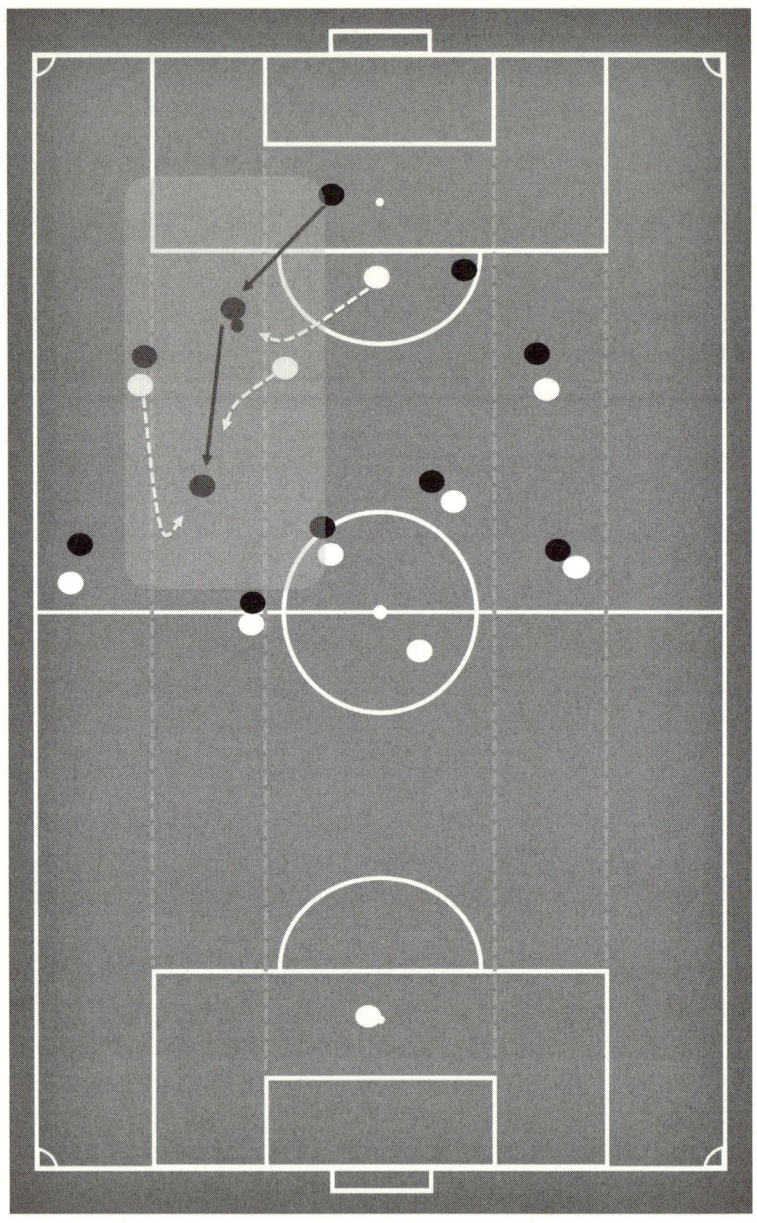

Figure 19

In *figure 19* we see another example of the initial press being opened in the same position. This is something that we tended to see when Klich, in particular, was being overly aggressive out of possession instead of having the patience to remain with his man defensively.

He was once again caught out of position in a high line as he tried to support Bamford. The pass was played through into the same defensive zone and the reaction from the Leeds players was the same as the left-sided attacker moved to engage and recover in the first instance.

That each player knows his role and understands the need to be fluid in moving and recovering should a team-mate be outplayed shows a very well-coached team.

Chapter 4

Verticality

If there was one term to describe the attacking aspect of the game model used by Marcelo Bielsa at Leeds in the 2019/20 season then it would be verticality. This simply refers to a tendency to look for forward passes that break the lines of the opposition as opposed to using safer backwards or lateral passes to simply maintain possession.

These safer options were largely prevalent during a period of football in which *tiki-taka* reigned supreme as the most *en vogue* of concepts. This term was coined by a Spanish football journalist when referring to the style played under Pep Guardiola. It was also, however, an intrinsic misunderstanding of what made that side and the football that they played so effective.

Tiki-taka became synonymous with possession-orientated football where teams would go to great lengths in order to keep the ball, although they would rarely be effective with it. In fact, one of the greatest strengths of the Barcelona side in question was that although their possession statistics were very impressive there was still an expectation that the play would be concentrated in the opposition half and that the vertical pass that broke the defensive line of the opposition would be sought in order to create goalscoring opportunities. The idea of *tiki-taka* was perhaps best displayed in a major league by Swansea City under Brendan Rodgers. His team were widely lauded for playing in what became known as the 'Swansea way' although in truth most of their possession and play with the ball took place in their own half with little in the way of passes that threatened to break the structure of the opposition.

This form of what became known as possession for possession's sake or as possession without purpose led to some insipid displays as teams prioritised security of the ball over moving into areas in which they could hurt their opponents.

Indeed, that is perhaps the best way to think about the concept of verticality within football. It's a style of play that is predicated on a desire to break through the opposition defence and to threaten the first line of their structure, in order to directly hurt your opponent. This encapsulates the attacking model of Marcelo Bielsa rather nicely. The first priority is to access the final third and the second is to create a high-quality shooting opportunity. The idea behind verticality is that when a player receives possession of the ball, whether in transition or in the attacking phase, the first priority that they have is to play a vertical pass to a player who is positioned on a higher line. It really is that simple, or is it?

The process in itself for a player in a side that was as well coached as this Leeds team was is actually reasonably similar to that of an NFL quarterback before they look to pass the ball. There is an expectation that you work your way through a series of progressions that are dictated by the priorities that they have in possession of the ball. The first priority for every Leeds player would be to play a vertical pass that breaks the first line of the opposition defensive block and would access the central space between the opposition goalkeeper and defensive line. The second priority is to play a similar vertical pass but one that accesses the wide space between the opposition goalkeeper and defensive line. The third priority sees a pass that accesses the central space in front of the defensive line and the fourth a pass that accesses the space in the wide areas in front of the defensive line. The fifth and sixth priorities are passes that find the space between the first line of pressure from the opposition and the midfield line, in the central space and then the wide space respectively.

So the first priority is always to play a pass that can create a direct goalscoring opportunity but this is only possible if all other variables on the pitch fall into space. If a Leeds player had possession of the ball in a deeper area, for example, they first need to recognise the reference point that is the positioning of their team-mates. Do they have a central player on the furthest line who can take advantage of a pass that is played behind the defensive line? If not, is there a central player in a pocket of space who can receive in the space in front of the opposition defensive line? Beyond that, the player in possession has to recognise and understand the reference point that is the positioning of the opposition players. Are they being pressed? If so, can they make a pass to the furthest line? Is there a player positioned on the furthest line that is double covered? If so, that pass may not be the safest. All of this information has to be processed and understood by a Leeds player almost immediately on taking possession of the ball before the correct decision can be made.

The pass to the furthest line, and beyond, is the best pass but not always the safest. It is at this point that we have to understand that while the player in possession has a set of progressions to work through, they are also coached to understand that while ball progression is key the safe progression of the ball is equally important. In other words, the movement of the ball through the thirds has to be as clean as possible to ensure that Leeds have control as they progress into the final third. This sense of control is key for Bielsa as he understands the importance of creating strong openings and good shooting opportunities for his side. In order to achieve this, Leeds have to shift the ball quickly, through verticality, but safely, through understanding the various reference points that exist on the field.

So now that we understand the priorities that a Leeds player has in possession of the ball, we then have to figure out how exactly they will look to access these spaces and passes. There were two key concepts within verticality that are used specifically by Leeds in order to maintain control of the ball as they are attacking.

The first is widely known as the 'up, back and through' and with this system there are two vertical passes played in quick succession with one backwards lay-off to link the two. So if the 6 has possession of the ball they may, for example, look for a pass to the feet of the 9 on the furthest line. This pass will be received but set straight back to one of the 8s who then play a second vertical pass that can break the defensive line of the opposition and find the run of a winger who is attacking from outside to inside on a diagonal line.

The second concept is similar but accesses different spaces and can be known as the 'out, in and out'. The principle is similar to the more vertical up, back and through with the key difference being that the final ball accesses wide spaces. Here the first pass moved from the central areas out to a player in the half-space. The ball can then be set back again before being played through and into the wide space for a full-back or wide forward to step into space. These movements are particularly important under Bielsa given the desire of the coach to create opportunities in wide spaces for overloads that can break through the defensive block of the opposition.

In order to fully understand the way that Leeds used verticality in their attacking play throughout the 2019/20 season, it is worth considering the specific role that Kalvin Phillips played in possession. Playing as the 6 in the 4-1-4-1 shape it was Phillips who shouldered the bulk of the responsibility for the progression of the ball through the thirds. This is further enhanced when we consider that the other central midfielders, the two 8s, would move immediately when Leeds transitioned into their attacking phase into more advanced positions where they could receive the ball in front of the opposition defensive line. Phillips, in particular, has the kind of passing range that Bielsa values at this position. He has the capacity and the passing range to access all zones of the pitch from a deep, central location. This means that play can be quickly switched from one side of the pitch to the other in order to take advantage of situations in which there is a chance of isolating a wide forward against an opposition full-back.

While verticality is always the first choice for this Leeds side under Bielsa we have to, of course, understand that there are still times in which the ball has to be played laterally in order to change the angle of the attack. This is particularly true when Leeds are building out from the back in the initial stages of the attacking phase. If there is no vertical passing channel available to the man in possession then the ball can be quickly switched across the line to find a man who does have the option to play the vertical pass. This tends to occur between one central defender to the other or if the 6 drops back into the defensive line it can come to the 6 as he forms a back three with the central defender.

Now, we will move on to some practical examples of the theories and concepts that have been discussed above.

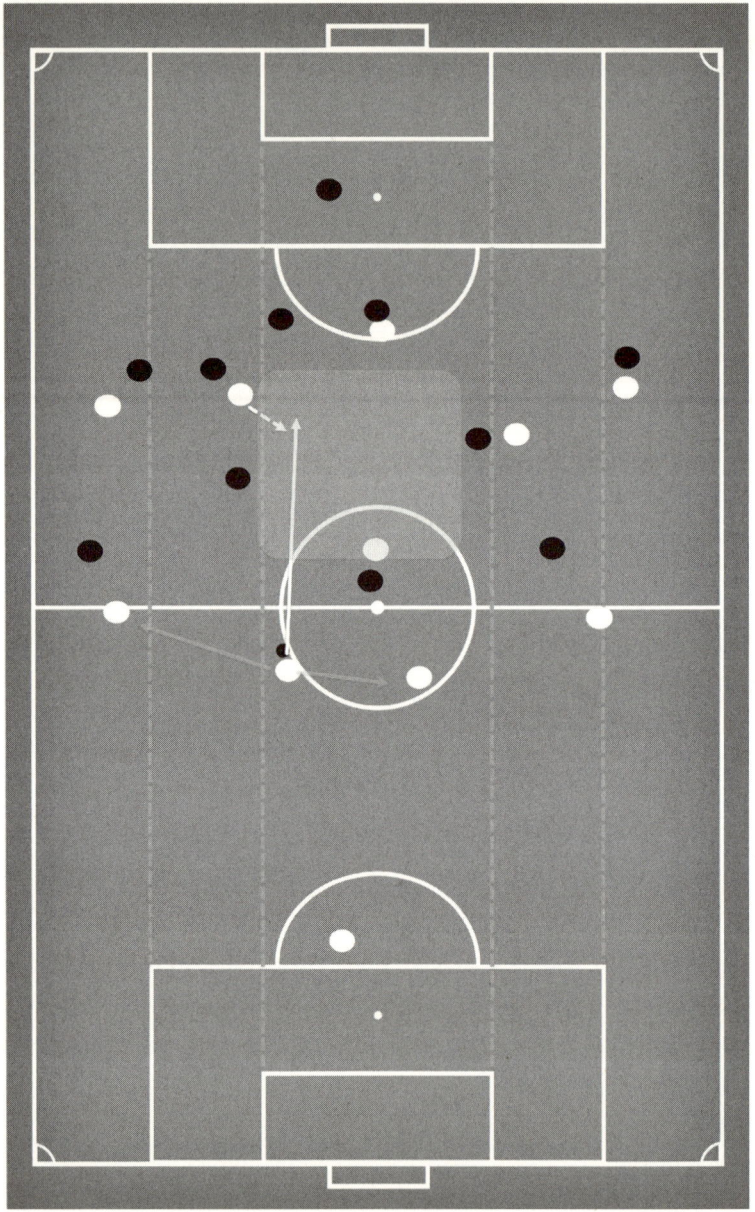

Figure 20

The first priority for a Leeds player in possession is to look for the vertical passing option to progress the ball cleanly through the thirds of the field. This generally means that the player in possession will ignore other passing options that may be safer but that would slow down the progression.

We see an example of this in *figure 20* with Liam Cooper in possession on the first line. The opposition are defending in a 4-5-1 shape and there is no immediate pressure on the ball. There are safer passing options out to Stuart Dallas, playing at left-back, or back across to Ben White, the second central defender.

Instead of accessing these options and playing in a safe manner, Cooper instead looks for the vertical pass through the lines of the opposition. The pass is played to Mateusz Klich, who had initially moved higher to link in with the attack. As Cooper has possession of the ball, Klich drops back into a deeper position and is able to receive it cleanly through the vertical pass. What is especially important in these situations and especially here is that the one vertical pass outplays five opposition players and allows Leeds to create an overload on the defensive line.

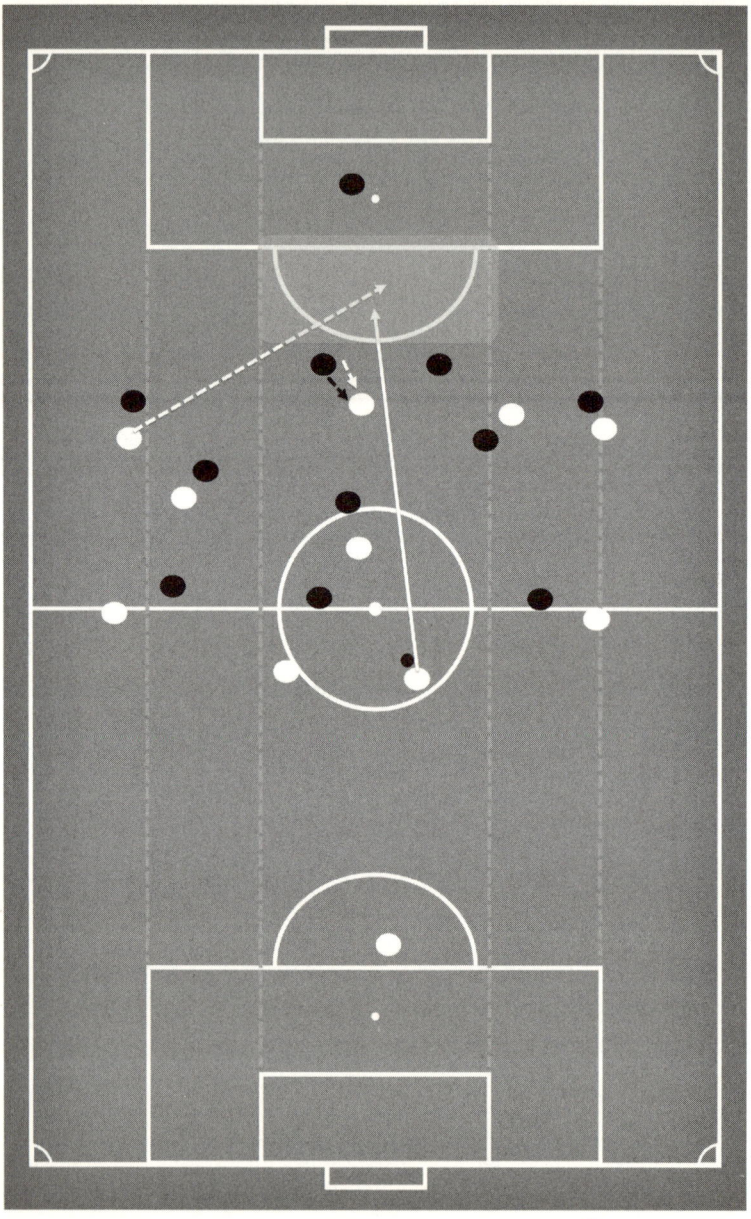

Figure 21

As discussed earlier in the chapter, the first priority of the man in possession for this Leeds team was to play a vertical pass but wherever possible the pass should be played in such a way to break the defensive line and find the space in behind.

We see an example of this kind of passing style in *figure 21*. The ball is initially on the first line with White in possession. There are easier passing options that could be accessed in order to move the ball forward. The pass to Kalvin Phillips as the 6 or out to the right-hand side of the pitch was open but neither pass would create that many problems for the opposition.

What we tended to see in these circumstances was the 9 dropping back towards the ball to offer a vertical passing option. This is part of the reason that Bielsa showed a clear preference for Patrick Bamford over Eddie Nketiah as Bamford was stronger in linking in with his midfield to aid the ball progression. Nketiah, on the other hand, was more of a penalty box finisher.

In this example, as Bamford moves back towards the ball he pulls a defender with him. This empties a space centrally that Jack Harrison can attack as he moves diagonally from the left. Now, as White plays the ball forward into this zone he accesses the run of Harrison. This pass is given the highest priority because it immediately takes all ten opposition outfield players out of the game.

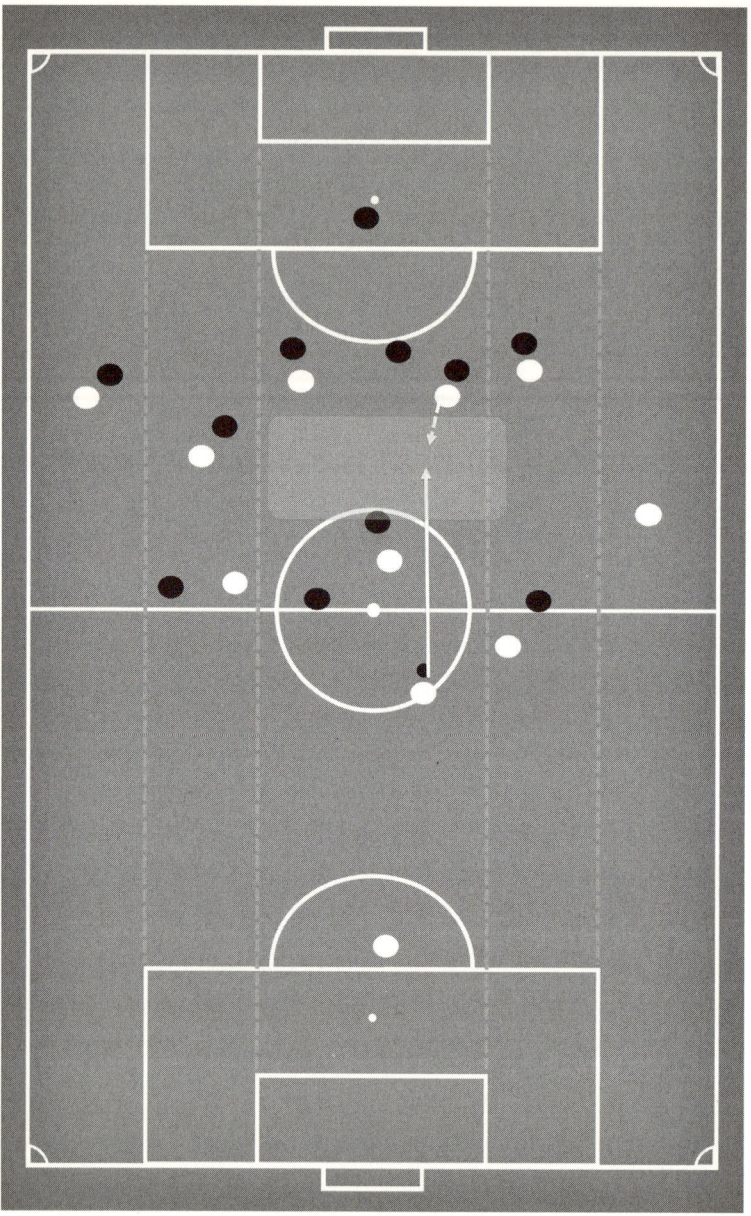

Figure 22

Another key space in the field that we tend to see Leeds try to access as quickly as possible is the space between the opposition defensive line and midfield.

We see this in action in *figure 22*. Once again the ball is on the first line for Leeds as the central defenders are trying to progress it. The vertical pass is always looked for but it is really important that this vertical pass is clean to allow for the ball to move into key areas where Leeds will be able to receive it and then build.

The space in question tended not to be occupied in the first instance as the 8s moved high to join a higher line. This meant that in order to access this pocket of space, players would tend to rotate in from other positional slots into this area.

We see this in action here as Pablo Hernandez, playing as one of the 8s, moves back towards the ball in order to create separation from his immediate marker and receive the vertical pass. This pass immediately outplays four opposition players.

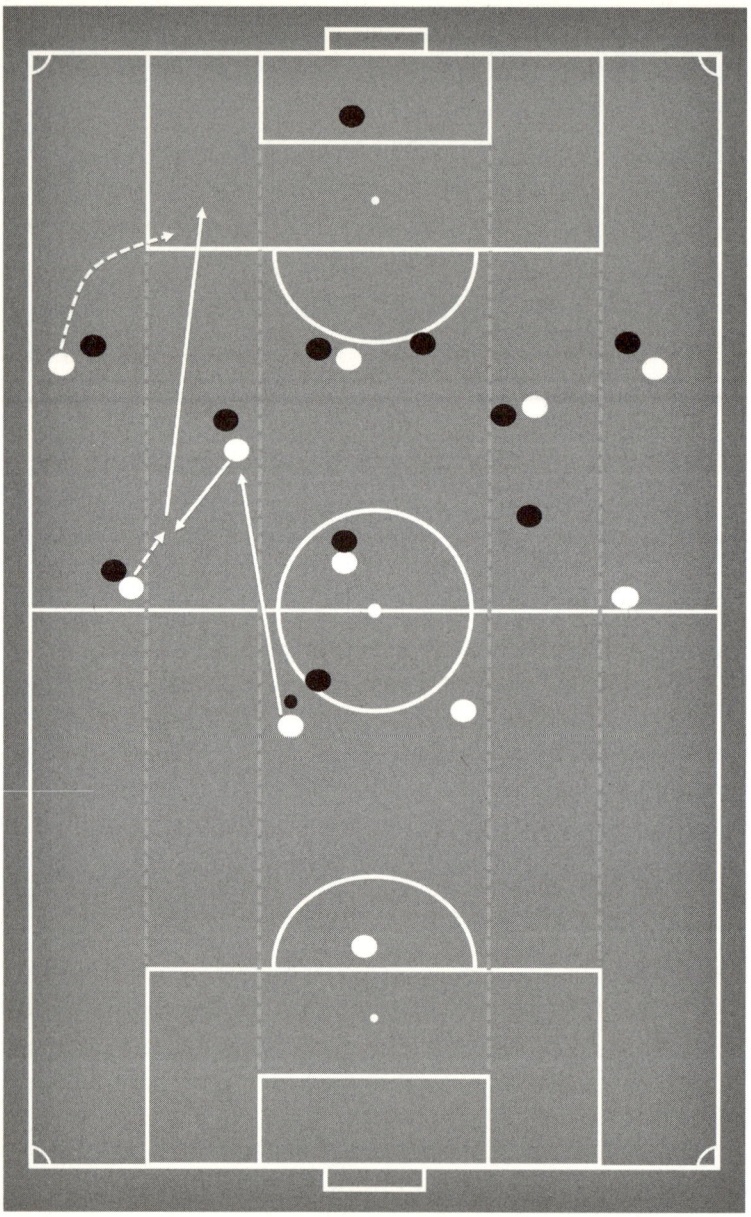

Figure 23

One of the key concepts within the idea of a vertical passing style of football is the idea of playing the up, back and through, which describes a series of passes that tend to be played very quickly. When these passing movements are played successfully they are exceptionally difficult to defend effectively.

We have given an example of this kind of passing in *figure 23*.

The ball is initially in the possession of Liam Cooper and he is being pressed by the opposition striker. In order to escape the press, Cooper is able to play an immediate vertical pass forward. Now the tempo of the pass really picks up. The player receiving the ball, Mateusz Klich, plays first time and sets the ball back to Stuart Dallas, who is moving inside from the left-back slot.

The attacking movement is then completed as Dallas plays another first-time pass, this time vertically through the gap between the opposition central defender and full-back to an area where Jack Harrison can attack diagonally.

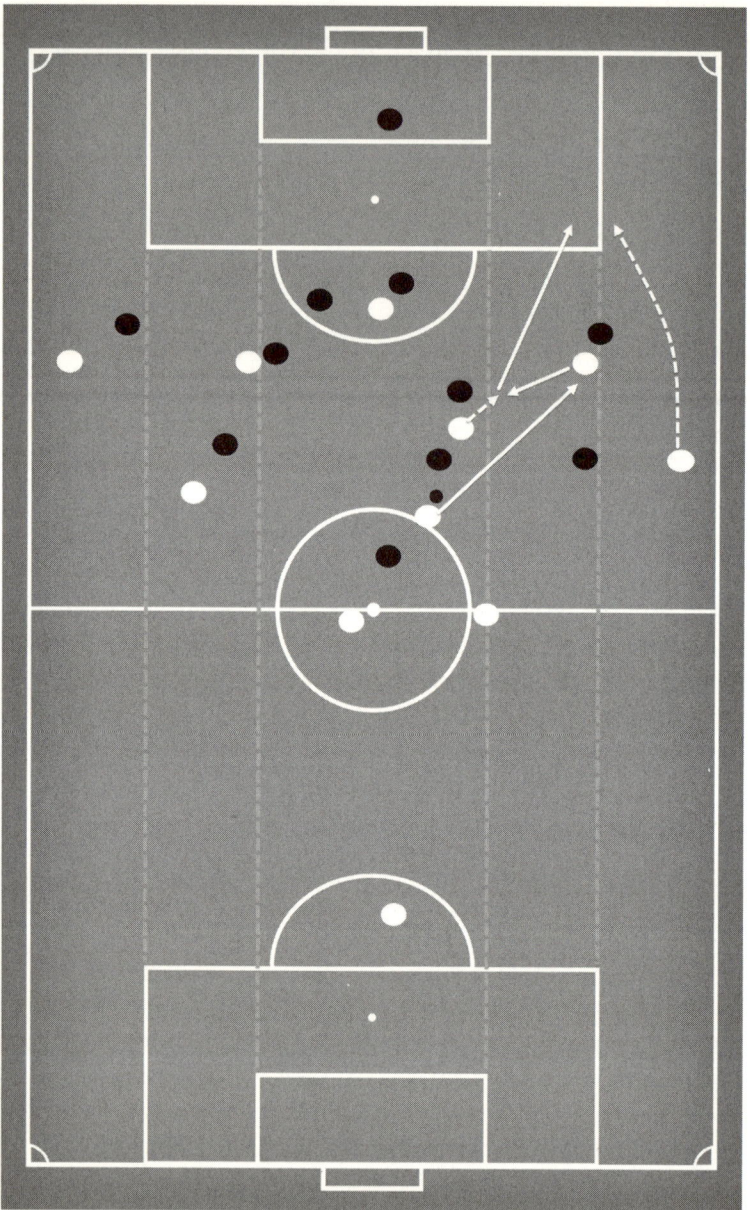

Figure 24

There is a second variant to the up, back and through that was used regularly by Leeds under Bielsa in their promotion campaign. This variant is called outside, inside and outside. This is a similar idea but instead of the ball being moved vertically it is moved diagonally or even laterally into space for a player to be able to attack from.

This is shown in *figure 24*.

The ball is initially with Kalvin Phillips as the 6. But as he receives it there are no clear vertical passing options. Instead, the initial pass moves outside to the half-space as the right-winger, Helder Costa, moves inside to receive. Once again the key here is that the passes are played quickly and therefore it is difficult for the opposition to react properly. As Costa receives the ball he sets the ball back to the near-side 8, Pablo Hernandez, who then in turn plays a first-time pass diagonally out to the right. This accesses the run made from right-back by Luke Ayling.

The final pass being played wide and behind the defensive line creates an immediate opportunity for Ayling to access the penalty area and create a goalscoring opportunity.

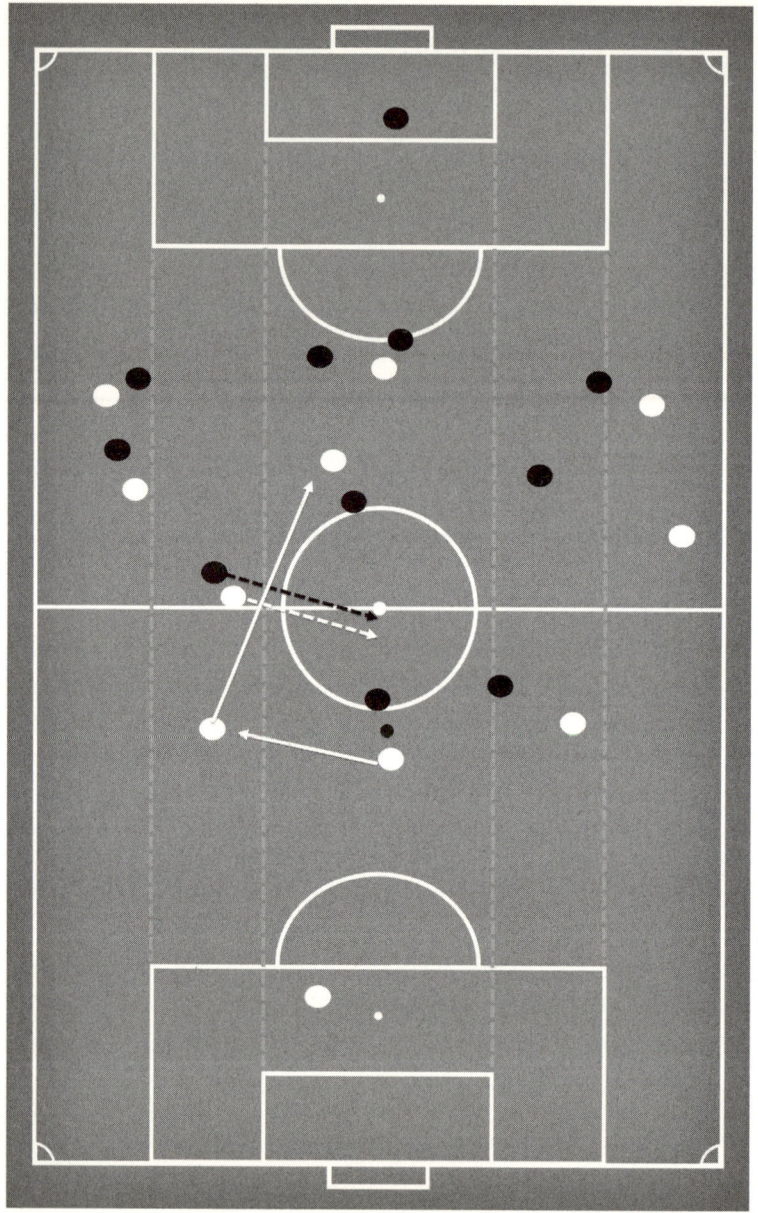

Figure 25

With football being as fluid a game as it is there were, of course, times when Leeds were in possession of the ball when they could not immediately play vertically. It is at this point that we start to see the difference from a flexible tactical system with priorities and progressions and a structured system with little scope for players to think for themselves.

The system that Bielsa created is very much the former with players being coached and taught to run through their progressions and choose the best option for the situation.

Here we see Leeds, playing in their 3-3-1-3 system and the player at the centre of the first line in possession of the ball. The first pass is played sideways to access the player on the first line who is free and not under pressure. From this point on the man in possession will start the progressions again and look in the first instance for the vertical passing option.

This pass was not immediately evident but Phillips read the situation and, in the 6 slot, made a later movement that dragged a defensive player out of his position. This then gave the man in possession the freedom to play the vertical line to access the central attacking midfielder, who could receive and then turn to attack the defensive line.

Chapter 5

Rotations

In the last chapter we were clear that the first priority for a Leeds United player in possession during the 2019/20 season was to play with verticality. If you cannot shoot from a good position then you should look to create a good shooting opportunity for a team-mate. This is, for Marcelo Bielsa, the ideal for his side in possession. You only win games if you are able to score more goals than the opposition and to score more goals you need to create chances to shoot.

The issue with this concept, however, is that you cannot always attack with perfect structures and the ability to progress the ball cleanly. There is, after all, one very important variable that will, to an extent, dictate the efficiency of your attacking game model, even for a coach as well prepared as Bielsa: the opposition.

There is a huge variety of ways in which an opposition coach could set out their defensive structure. Some teams, like Leeds, are aggressive and mark tightly with pressure applied to the ball high. Others are equally aggressive with their press but maintain a zonal structure behind the first line of pressure. Then you have the teams who are more cautious in their defensive approach and will drop to a medium or deep defensive block in order to prevent their opponents from having a clean progression of the ball into the final third. These deep structures would include pressing triggers that would see the ball carrier engaged in certain key areas.

There were some teams in the Championship during 2019/20 who were willing to press and engage Leeds aggressively, such as Barnsley under Gerhard Struber, but in most cases teams would drop back to try to defend in a medium or low block in order to slow the extremely effective Leeds attack.

So if the vertical option is not there due to the defensive positioning of the opposition then how did Leeds create opportunities to progress the ball cleanly? In chapter four we touched upon one of these with the idea that the ball could be circulated horizontally to find an open passing lane that would allow for the ball to be progressed vertically. This option in itself, however, is still relatively passive and Bielsa prefers to use a more aggressive option in order to create opportunities for the ball to be played vertically. This option comes in the form of rotations ahead of the ball.

Rotations within the attacking phase are not a new concept. They have been used as a key principle of the attacking style in positional play by a wide array for coaches ranging from Pep Guardiola to Bielsa's Argentinean compatriot Ricardo La Volpe, but often they are used to achieve very specific results. Guardiola, for example, uses rotations to dominate the central area of the pitch while La Volpe uses them in order to create clean build-up of the ball from the first line. Bielsa, however, employs them in all areas of the pitch in order to manipulate and break the defensive structure of the opposition.

The idea of rotations is relatively simple and they act as a means to move the opposition out of their defensive slot in order to create space further up the pitch. These rotations are designed to allow for the ball to be progressed but also, when used in higher positions, to create openings that can lead to goalscoring chances. In order to achieve this, attacking rotations, when used well, allow a side to create positional superiorities over their opponents in key areas of the pitch. This was especially true of this Leeds side who combined attacking rotations, both in ball progressions and in terms of chance creation, with quick interchanges of possession in order to pull their opposition out of position and then find passing lanes that allow the ball to be moved safely into advanced areas.

In order to fully understand the way that Bielsa coached this side to move and rotate positions, we first of all have to acknowledge that there is one specific way that Bielsa differs from almost all other coaches in his approach to the attacking phase. In football, as in chess, one of the most common concepts when in possession is for teams to try to occupy and dominate the centre. This can be achieved through positional superiority or having players positioned in front of and behind the opposition defensive line or through numerical superiority in terms of having clear overloads centrally. These tend to be when a 4-3-3 faces a 4-4-2 and there is a three v two superiority in the centre for one side or the other.

Typically, coaches believe that superiority in these areas is key to allow for an effective attacking structure. Bielsa, however, sees things differently. When Leeds were progressing the ball it was not unusual to see their midfielders completely empty the centre of the pitch. The 6 in the 4-1-4-1 would drop deeper to receive the ball while the two 8s would move to a higher line to support the striker. This meant that the game was effectively stretched with the opposition's midfield line now being left in central areas almost on their own.

This is not to say, however, that Bielsa does not recognise the importance of the central spaces being used to enable ball progression into the final third. Instead, Leeds would only rotate into the central spaces in order to receive the ball and never from fixed positions. These very specific movements and rotations were designed to create opportunities for vertical rotations to enable vertical passing, which we already know is the first priority for Leeds in possession.

When Leeds played with Pablo Hernandez and Mateusz Klich as their 8s these rotations from high positions back into the centre of the pitch were especially useful. Both Hernandez and Klich have excellent instincts and timed their movements back into the centre perfectly in order to create separation from their marker and then to receive the ball perfectly in the central space. The key thing is that when these players moved backwards to receive possession in central spaces they still tended to be receiving the ball behind the line of opposition midfielders. These movements back towards the ball make it very difficult for the opposition to close these spaces. If the midfield line drops back then the man in possession looking to progress the ball can carry it forward. If players move from the defensive line to close down the space then space is created which can be accessed and exploited by the 9 or by the wide forwards.

These spaces then allow the first priority for Leeds to be accessed: the vertical pass that finds the space in the middle or wide areas of the pitch behind the defensive line of the opposition. These are in essence the kind of questions that Bielsa's Leeds asked of sides in the Championship and time and time again the opposition coaches were unable to find answers.

There are two very specific forms of rotations that can be used to create space in the attacking phase. The type described above, with players moving back to receive the ball from advanced areas, is known as vertical rotations. These can be utilised simply by one player moving high or low to enable ball progression but they can also be used by two players when one moves low to empty the space and another moves high to occupy that same space. Again, these rotational movements are designed to force opposition defenders to move out of their positional slot.

The second distinct type are horizontal rotations. These see a player move to the left or the right of their initial position. This movement can either allow the player to lose their marker and get into space or, if the opponent follows the movement, it can create a vertical passing option to a man who was initially blocked by the players who have moved and rotated.

What is especially impressive about this Leeds side under Bielsa is that they utilised both forms consistently on their way to winning the title and gaining promotion to the Premier League. Players would move in and out of their positional slot consistently with midfielders moving into wide spaces or moving from one side of the field to the other in order to gain some separation and to take advantage of gaps and spaces in the opposition defensive block. Indeed, it was not unusual to see one of the two 8s from Leeds move over to the same space as the other 8 with the opposition often finding themselves overloaded in this section of the pitch. This movement from one side of the pitch to the other was also part of a rotation with one 8 dropping back to receive the ball in front of the midfield line while the other moved across from right to left into the half-space. This rotational movement was enough for Leeds to be able to play vertically through the lines of the opposition defensive block and to create an attacking platform from which they could attack the penalty area.

These rotations were also prevalent when Leeds were looking to build their attack in the wide spaces with the structures that they created in these areas designed to allow them to manipulate the opposition defensive structure. Here we saw the interaction between the 8s and the wide players in particular as key factors in Leeds managing to progress the ball cleanly into advanced areas of the pitch. The shape would usually form something like a loose diamond with the player at the bottom of the structure being a central defender, a full-back or even the 6. The wide forward would either be the tip of the diamond or, if the full-back was in possession at the base, the wide player in the shape.

From these positions the player at the tip of the diamond would often act as the ball progression option as they dropped towards the ball. The 8, on the inside of the diamond, would then move to the space at the tip of the diamond. These movements along created opportunities for Leeds to play to either level. The ball could be progressed through the player dropping towards the ball or beyond that player to the 8 who should now be moving in space.

Once again we will move on now to consider these tactical tendencies through the use of practical and visual examples.

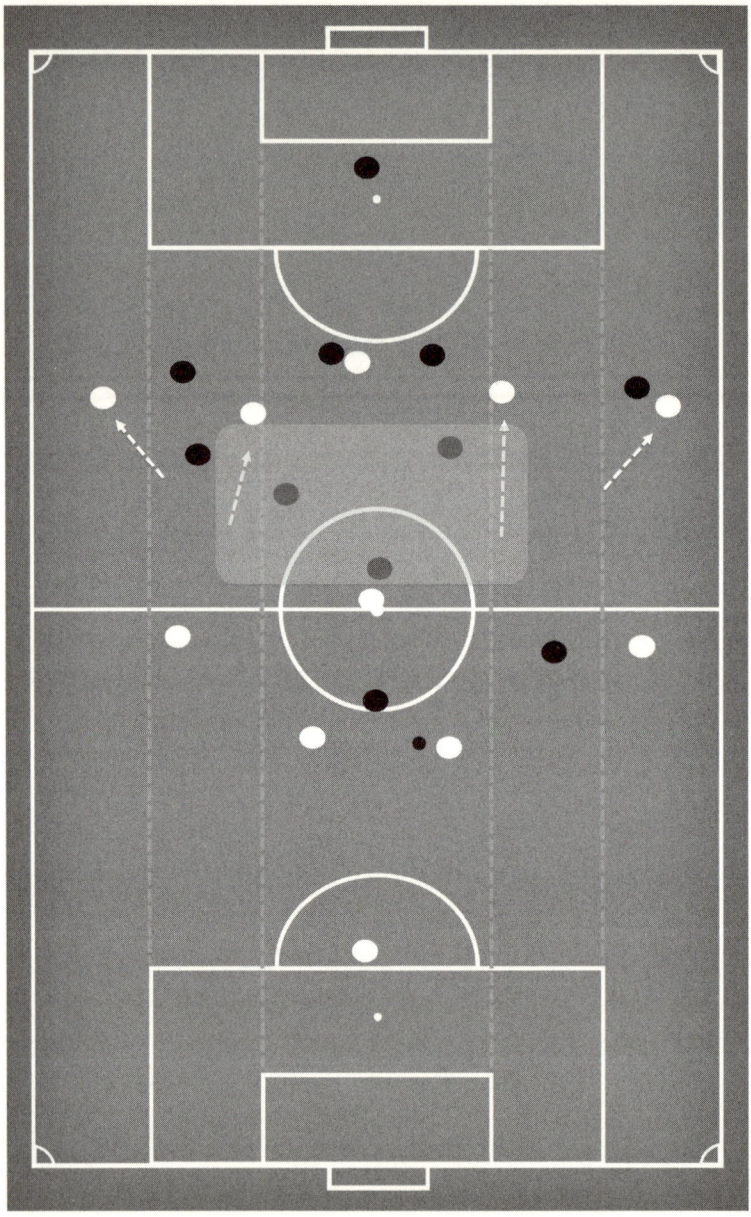

Figure 26

First of all we will consider more closely the way that the 8s in this system moved in the attacking phase in order to empty the central space and create opportunities for Leeds to progress through the thirds.

This example is shown in *figure 26.*

The ball is positioned initially on the first line with Ben White, and the opposition are not pressing overly aggressively. Almost immediately we see vertical movements from the two 8s who move towards the 9 and effectively empty the central space. This is coupled by diagonal movements from the wide attackers who move quickly to occupy wide spaces. These movements then almost create a split structure for Leeds with five players in the first block and five players in the second block.

The key is that the full-backs for Leeds are comfortable when asked to step inside to occupy this empty space when the situation demands it. This, when combined with the movements back towards the ball from the 8s as they drop into the highlighted space, allows Leeds to still effectively control the central areas when they are in possession. They just do so without actually occupying it.

Having players like Kalvin Phillips and Ben White, who were so comfortable in possession of the ball and who had the range of passing to access these spaces, helped facilitate these movements.

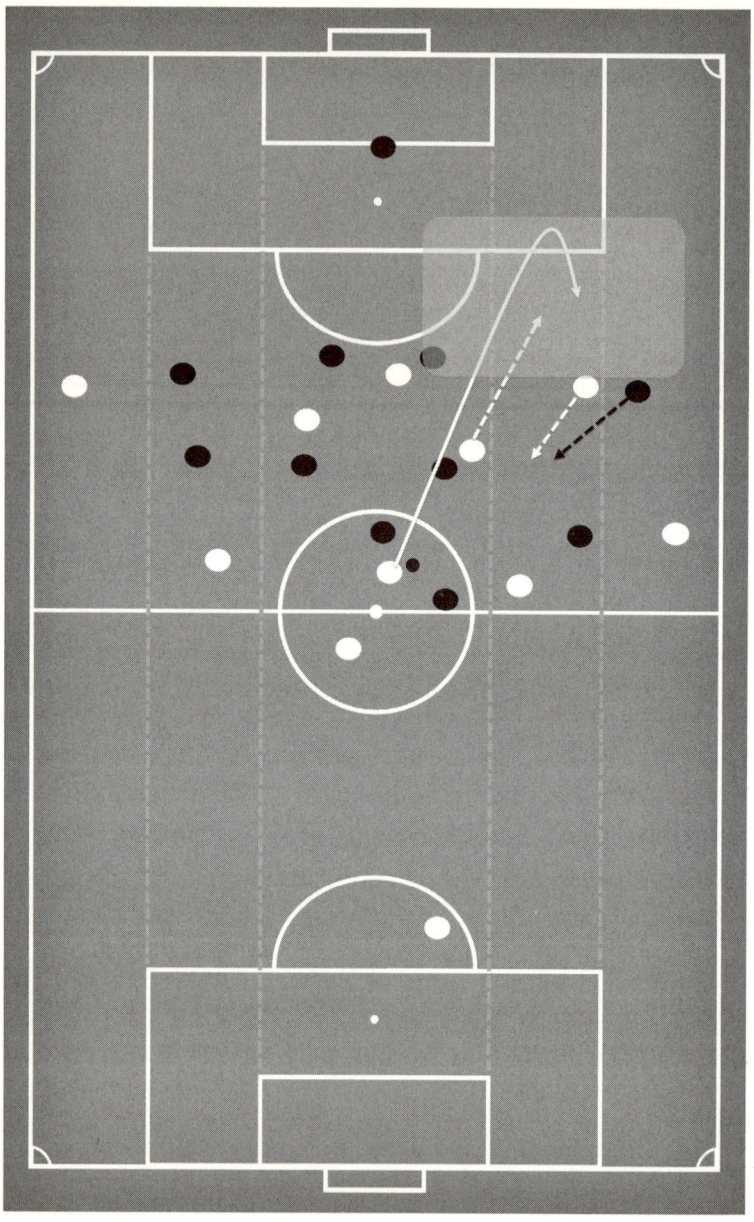

Figure 27

During the 2019/20 promotion season Leeds made great use of the versatility and intelligence of their attacking players when they were looking to access spaces in the final third. This was especially true when they had players creating space for themselves using vertical rotations.

We see an example of this in *figure 27.*

Once again the example that we have taken from a match starts with Kalvin Phillips in possession of the ball as the 6. On the right-hand side of the pitch, Helder Costa makes a movement back towards the ball looking for a vertical passing option. This movement pulls an opposition defender along and out of his positional slot.

In most instances these rotations, from different positions, allow them to manipulate the positioning of the opposition defensive structure. This time, as Costa drops towards the ball, we see vertical rotation as Pablo Hernandez makes a vertical movement to attack the space that has been left behind. This rotation makes the vertical pass from Phillips possible.

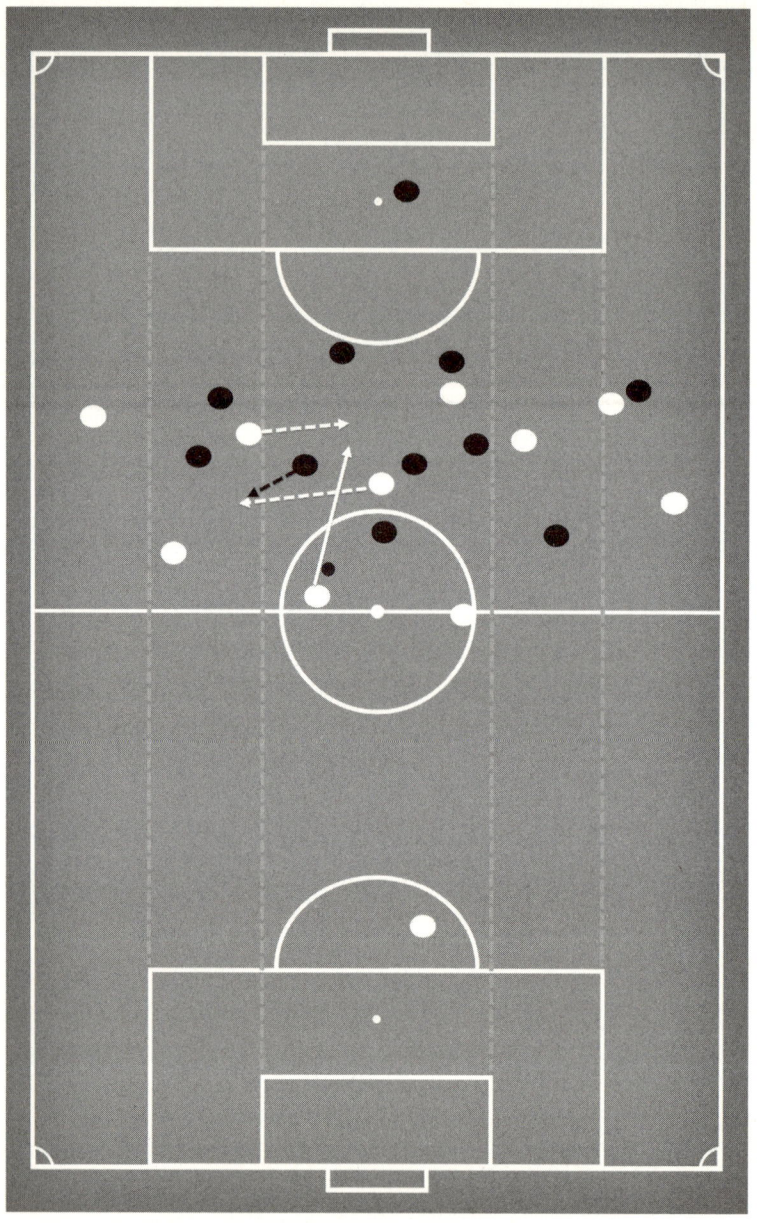

Figure 28

While vertical rotations create depth to the attacking structure that Leeds used, they also employed horizontal rotations to create superiority and passing lanes that allowed them to play through the structure of the opposition.

In *figure 28* we see an example of how this was done in order to progress the ball in a more measured way as opposed to looking for a vertical passing option behind the defensive line.

As the central defender has possession of the ball, he is looking to access the space between the opposition defensive line and midfield line. There is no clean option but the pass could be forced through. Instead, however, a clever piece of movement by Kalvin Phillips and Mateusz Klich opens the space and allows the pass to be played through cleanly.

The first movement comes from Phillips, who moves from the central area across into the left-sided half-space. This movement effectively takes the attention of a key defensive player for the opposition. As he moves to cover the movement of Phillips we then see the second part to the rotation as Klich, positioned behind this defensive player, can move on the defender's blind side in order to give the man in possession a vertical passing option to occupy a key position and create a platform from which Leeds can attack.

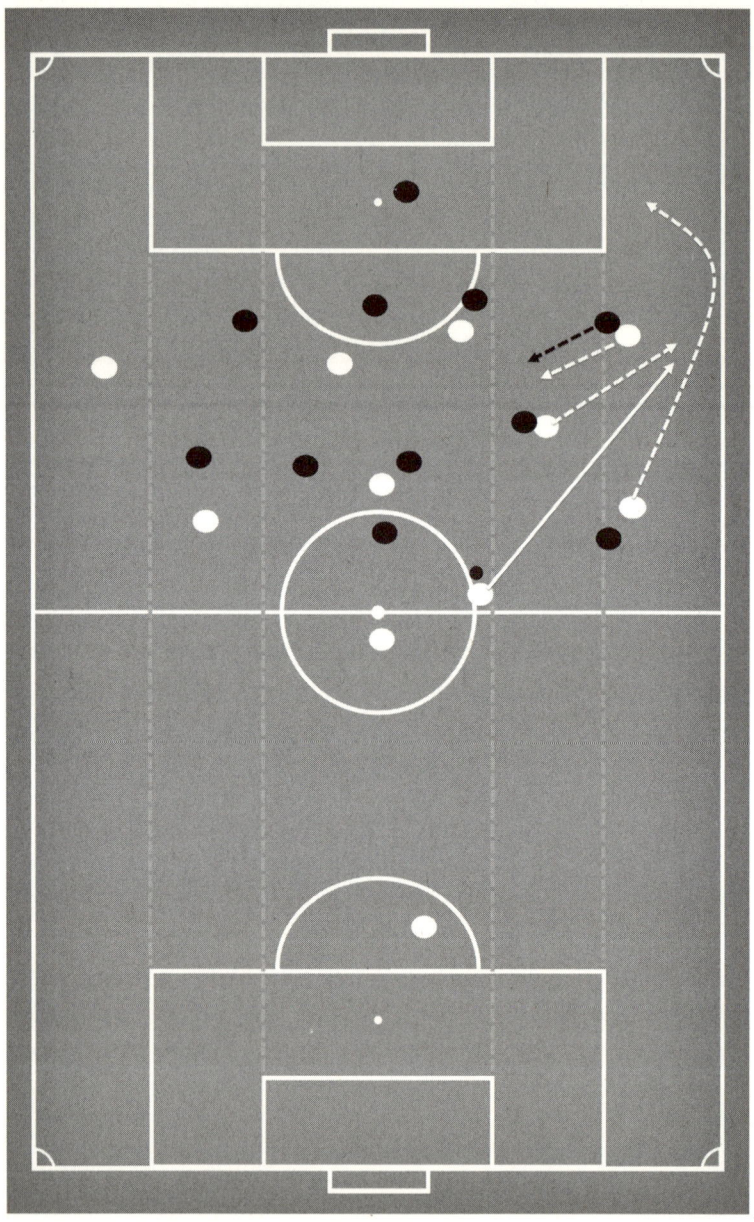

Figure 29

Because the more advanced midfielders were not having to position themselves and occupy the central space, they were then able to rotate into the wide spaces more cleanly. This movement of the 8s from the half-space or the central zone into the wide areas was key for Leeds when they were looking to overload the wide spaces.

Figure 29 shows an example of these rotations in action.

With White on the ball in space and with time there was a chance for them to create an opportunity to play through. The first rotational movement comes from the right-sided attacker, Helder Costa, as he drops diagonally back towards the ball. Once again the key with these movements is that they manipulate the defensive structure of the opposition and pull people out of position.

This idea is central to the way that Bielsa wants his side to play but at the same time it is incredibly simple. As a defensive player is pulled from their slot an opportunity is created for a Leeds man to make a run to occupy that space. We see this in this example with Hernandez moving from the 8 position to occupy the space that Costa has created with his movement. As the Spaniard then collects the ball there is a further movement from Luke Ayling at right-back who advances beyond the ball and stretches the opposition defensive line vertically.

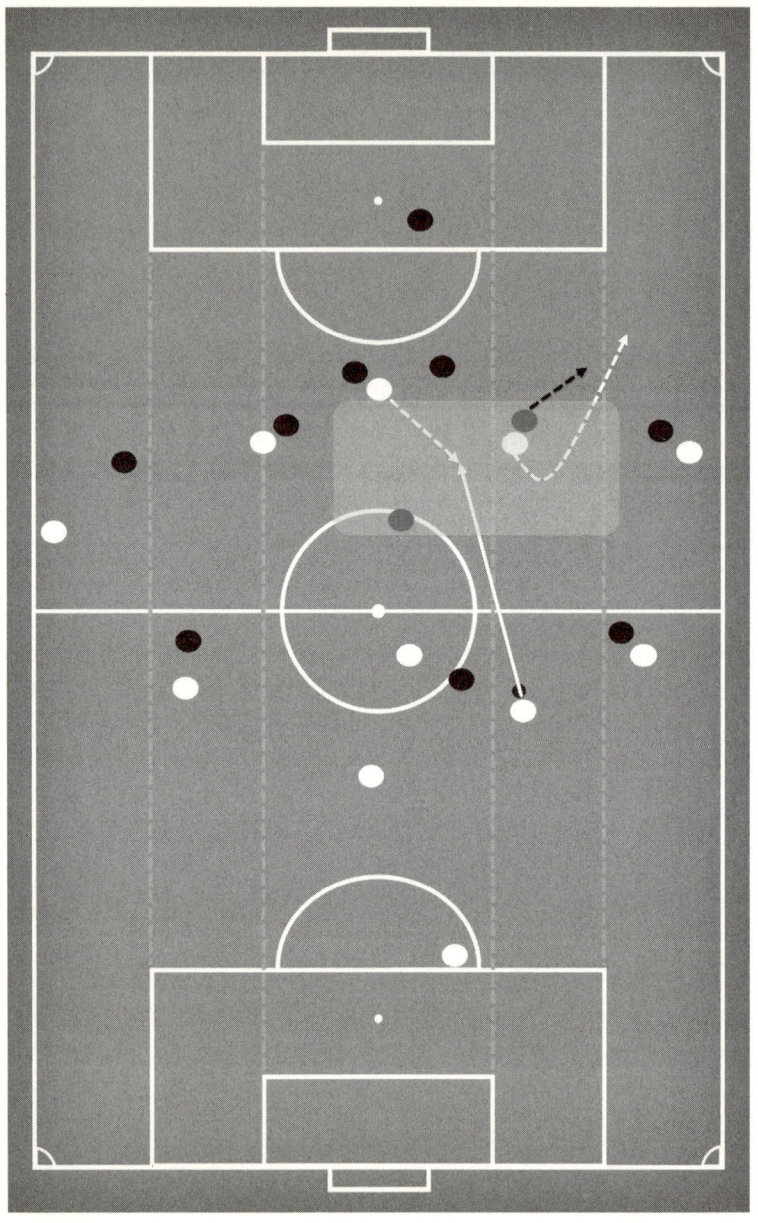

Figure 30

These rotations and the way that they affect the opposition can take place anywhere across the final third of the pitch and can involve any player as the player that moves out of slot or the one who receives the ball.

We see an example of this *figure 30*.

White is, once again, the player in possession. Indeed, with the exception of Kalvin Phillips, there are no players who were more impressive and important in the progression of the ball than White. This time White is once again looking for an opportunity to play a pass into an area of the pitch from where Leeds could hurt the opposition.

This time the rotational movement comes from Hernandez, in the half-space, who rotates out and towards the wide space. Once again the key in these rotational movements is that they have to pull the opposition player with them. As the defender follows Hernandez wide the space is created for Patrick Bamford to drop in and receive an easy vertical pass from White.

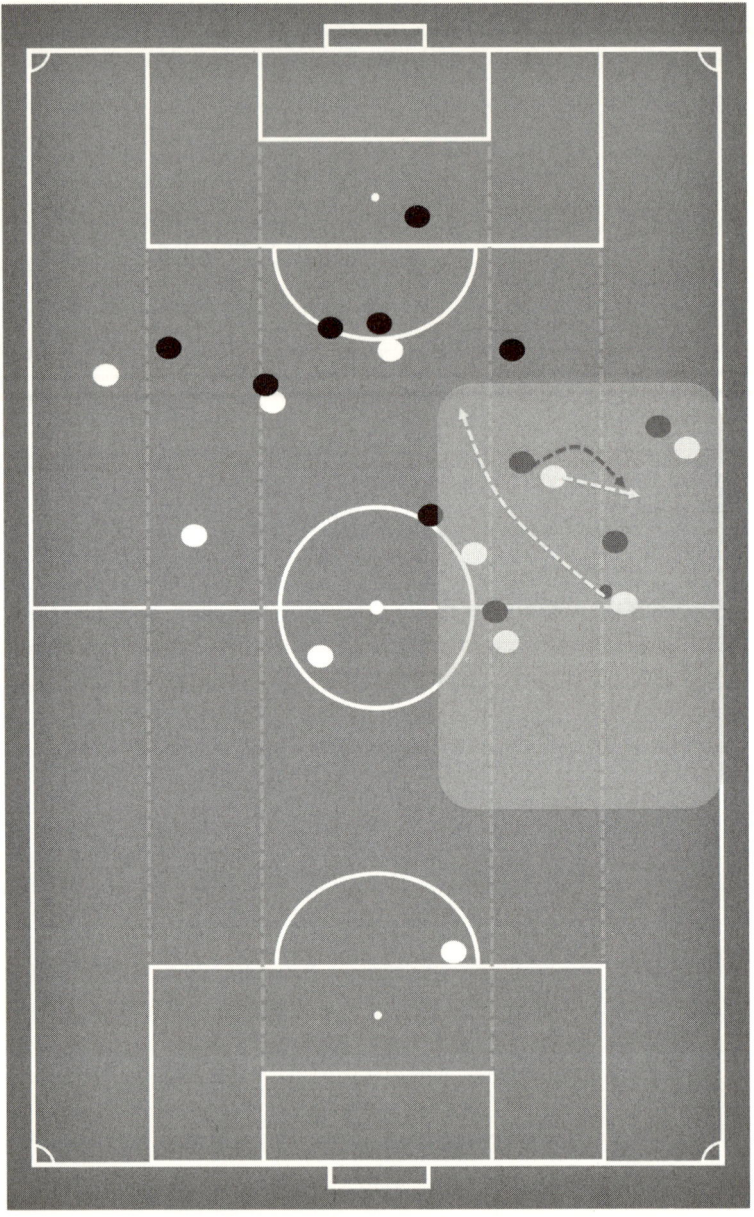

Figure 31

To this point we have talked a lot about how rotations allow the Leeds players to interact with one another and facilitate the vertical passing concept. These rotations, which create space in the opposition defensive structure, can also be accessed by allowing the man in rotation to drive forward in possession of the ball.

We can see an example of this in *figure 31*.

Ayling, positioned in the traditional right-back position, has possession of the ball. There are passing options open to him, one wide to Costa and one inside to Phillips, but ahead of the ball Klich makes a movement from the half-space to the wide area. Once again this pulls a defender out of position and Ayling is able to take advantage of that by driving through the half-space and into an advanced area with the ball at his feet.

This added versatility in terms of attacking movement was a significant factor in allowing Leeds to break down sides who looked to defend consistently from a low defensive block. By driving inside in possession in this manner, Ayling automatically affects the defensive structure of the opposition as a defensive player has to move from their positional slot in order to engage the ball carrier. This, in turn, will create space that another Leeds player can look to occupy in order to offer a passing option into a pocket of space.

Chapter 6

Role of the Wide Players

On paper it can look as though Leeds were tactically dynamic during the 2019/20 season with their tendency to switch between their 4-1-4-1 and 3-3-1-3 systems. In truth, however, while there were some variances in the systems as set out in chapter one, the key in allowing the side to switch systems comfortably was that the concepts and principles that underpinned those systems remained constant. In no positional slot was this more important than with the wide attackers.

As with many of the concepts we are discussing within this book, we have to take the time to understand the expectations that Bielsa has of his wide players. With the vertical movements of the 8s and the expectation that they occupy the spaces between the lines of the opposition midfield and defence, there is a need for space to be created in those areas. In order to achieve this space Bielsa used his wide players to effectively stretch the opposition defensive line. In the build-up phase the wide players on both sides were instructed to take up wide positions, generally tight to the touchline, which meant that the opposition defensive line could not be as compact as they wanted.

If the opposition full-back tucked in, for example, and tried to position themselves close to their central defender then there would be space for the wide player to receive the ball comfortably. If, on the other hand, the full-back moved out to close the space on the Leeds wide player, then there was space within the defensive structure that the 8s could move into in order to receive the ball.

It is this choice that perhaps best defines the key attacking concepts used by Bielsa. It was exceptionally difficult for the opposition to find the correct balance between defending the wide and central areas. The wide positioning of the wide forward from Bielsa, however, also had another key function within the attacking game plan that Leeds utilised across the course of their Championship-winning season, seeing them create opportunities to overload and isolate the opposition.

We have, in the previous chapter, touched on the concept of overloads in the wide areas as Leeds looked to create numerical superiority over the opposition in order to cleanly progress the ball. This is achieved by the 8s moving towards the wide areas to combine with the full-back and the wide forward in order to create favourable match-ups against the opposition defender. It is at this point that we begin to see how the concepts that we have been breaking down interact with one another.

The central areas of the pitch are left empty, as the 8s move high, and these players can then move into wide areas in order to create overloads. This is made possible because of the vertical passing style that Leeds used over the course of the season and because they were not fixated on the need to constantly have control of the centre of the pitch. These factors combined meant that they were comfortable committing players into wide areas to force breakthroughs against the opposition block there. These overloads would always take place on the ball side of the pitch with the right-hand side especially prevalent.

The right was used more often by Leeds as they were building up towards the final third because they tended to use the Spaniard Pablo Hernandez as the right-sided 8. His ability to find pockets of space in dangerous areas and to receive the ball cleanly meant that Leeds were often able to build up on that side of the pitch. The Portuguese winger Helder Costa, purchased from Wolverhampton Wanderers, tended to play on that side and he possessed the technical skills to combine intelligently with Hernandez. In overloading one side of the pitch you naturally pull the opposition defensive block over to the ball-side of the field. With the ball positioned towards the right then, and with the left-sided wide player maintaining their wide positioning, there came an opportunity for Leeds to switch the play quickly from one side of the pitch to the other. The left-sided player tended to be Jack Harrison, on loan from Manchester City, and when receiving the ball in these areas Harrison would quickly move to engage the defender in a one v one situation. Although there was a clear preference for building up on the right side the same situation could be mirrored when the ball was on the left.

This preference for creating isolations for the wide players against the opposition full-back highlights the type of wide players that Bielsa likes his side to recruit. For the most part during the 2019/20 season we saw Costa play on the right and Harrison on the left. Costa is mainly left-footed and would therefore naturally look to play inside when in possession of the ball. Harrison is also left-footed and can therefore play more as a conventional winger. Harrison, however, is also comfortable coming inside to play on his right foot. The wide players were expected to be comfortable carrying the ball but also when looking to combine and interchange possession with supporting team-mates.

Interestingly, when we use data to compare performance from the two players we begin to see the similarities between the two. In 3,178 minutes of league football we saw Costa average 6.17 dribbles per 90 minutes and 1.78 shots per 90 minutes. Costa scored on average 0.11 goals from an expected goals (xG) of 0.18. Now, let's consider the same metrics for Harrison. He played an impressive 4,050 minutes across the league campaign and averaged 6.04 dribbles per 90 with 1.64 shots per 90. He averaged 0.13 goals from an xG of 0.21. These metrics are incredibly similar, especially when you consider the significant sample size from both players. Using data in this manner allows us to further emphasise the similarities in the roles that Bielsa expects from his wide players in the attacking phase.

That has covered the role of the wide players in the attacking phase but they also had an important job to perform when Leeds were out of possession.

The positional slots are slightly different as in the 3-3-1-3 they are positioned on the highest line. In the 4-1-4-1 they are in the third line and not the fourth. These differences can be subtle but important as they dictate the immediate role of the player when Leeds are transitioning from the attacking to the defensive phases of the game. This is a more notable variance when in the defensive phase rather than the attacking when the role and responsibility of the wide players tends to be constant regardless of the overall structure of the team.

We have already looked at the role that the wide players have in pressing the opposition in chapter three but it deserves a more nuanced discussion now that we are considering position-specific roles.

Whether a wide player joins the initial press, when the ball is on the first line of the opposition structure, depends on how many players the opposition are building up. Remember the -1 rule discussed previously in terms of pressing. If the opposition are building up with three central defenders or with two central defenders and a 6 who is dropping back then the ball-sided wide player will engage and press to support the striker in stopping clean ball progression from the opposition. Again, this simple expectation requires significant practice and concentration as these players need to understand the position of the ball and the structure of the opposition team at all times. If one of the wide players moves to press then the other one drops to man-mark their most direct opponent. It is in these moments that the Leeds players have to display flexibility though as there was an expectation that the covering wide player would join the press as soon as a pressing trigger was activated.

We have discussed the technical requirements of the wide players in the system used by Bielsa in the Championship but there were also significant physical requirements. The wide players had to have speed but this was not only to be active in the attacking phase and to create separation from their direct opponent but also to ensure that they were able to recover their defensive position when the opposition were able to play out of the line of pressure. In the established defensive phase of the game the wide players were expected to perform recovery runs to either track their direct opponent and mark them closely, as part of the overall defensive structure, or be ready to rotate their marking duties should a team-mate be outplayed elsewhere in the defensive block.

It was not unusual for us to see either of the wide players in this side tracking their opponent deep into their own half or even into central areas of the pitch. While this can look unusual to the casual eye it was essential that these players understood that there was an expectation that they fulfilled these roles in the defensive phase.

Once again we can use data to show just how effective the wide forwards were off the ball, primarily in the way that they were able to win possession back close to the opposition goal. With the same sample size of minutes played (3,178 for Helder Costa and 4,050 for Jack Harrison) we saw Costa average 3.94 recoveries in the opposition half per 90 minutes and Harrison average 3.67.

Now we will move on to consider some visual examples of the concepts discussed. These visuals are designed to show these tactical ideas on a way that will enable more visual learners to follow what we are talking about.

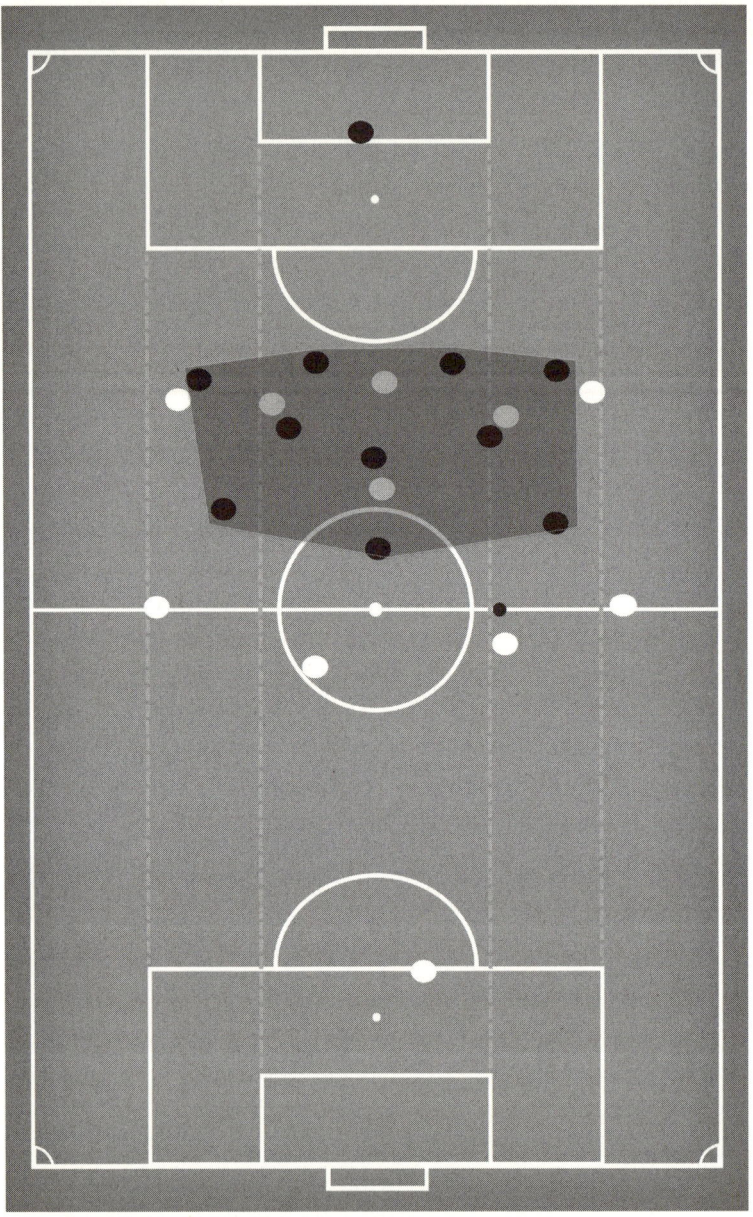

Figure 32

First of all we can look at how the spaces on the pitch appear when the opposition are able to maintain a deep and compact defensive block. This is shown in *figure 32*.

You can clearly see that the issue for the attacking side in these situations is that there is no space in the central areas to find pockets of space in which to receive the ball. Indeed, in order to break down a side that defends in this manner, and most importantly does so well, teams have to play around the outsides and create width to try to affect the defensive block.

A team that is well coached in defending in this manner will simply slide their block across in a pendulum style depending on the location of the ball at the time. If the attacking side attacks down the left then every defender shades over to that side while maintaining their defensive spacing. This is an ideal situation in terms of defensive positioning but it is, of course, extremely difficult to maintain.

The way to break down this kind of defensive structure most efficiently is to continually force the opposition to make hard choices. This is something that Leeds managed very effectively during their promotion-winning campaign, as we will see in the next example.

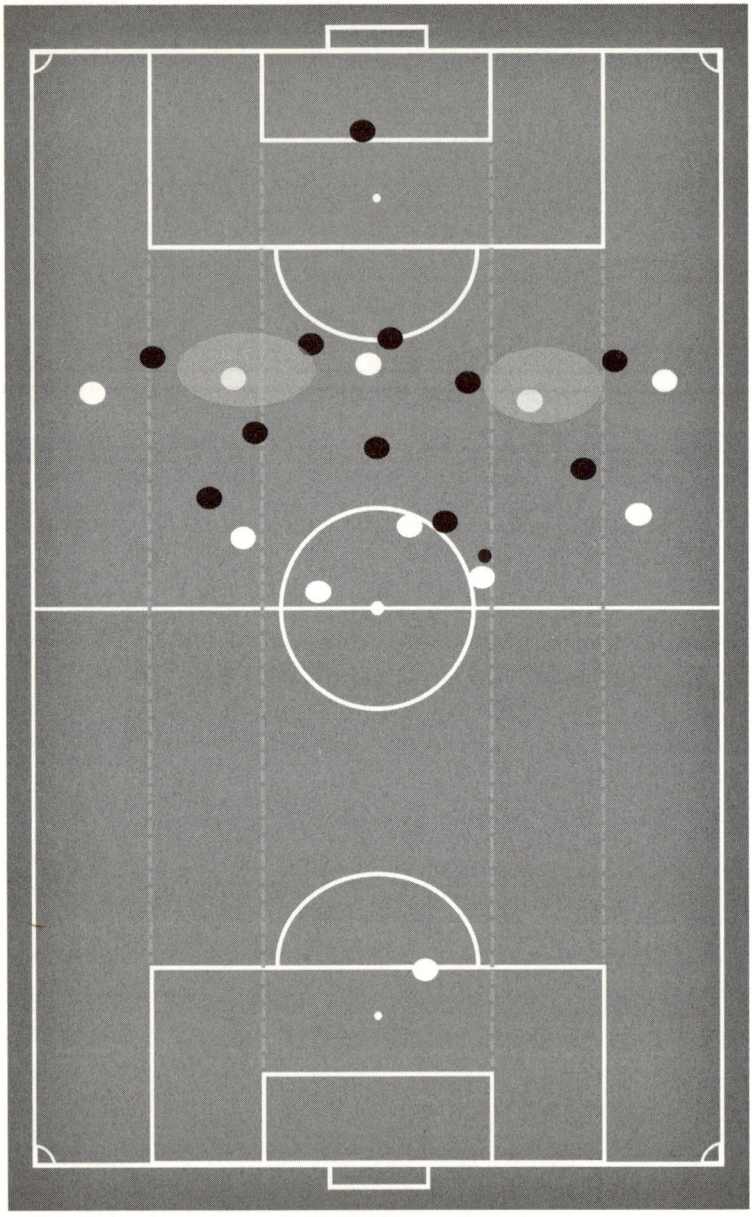

Figure 33

The key to breaking down teams who defend in such a narrow and compact defensive block is to use your wide forwards effectively in order to space the pitch horizontally. We can see an example of this kind of spacing in *figure 33*.

Here, the attacking side maintain width through positioning of their two wingers. By staying wide and close to the touchline the wide players are immediately forcing the opposition full-backs to make a difficult decision. Do they stay in their compact position in order to negate opportunities for the attacking team to play through the block? Or do they move out to cover the threat in the wide spaces and create pockets of space that the attacking team can look to exploit centrally?

This is what Leeds did so effectively. The fact that their wide players stayed out towards the touchline and the two 8s moved into high positions gave opposition teams a dilemma as Leeds were progressing the ball. They were often unable to shift their defensive block effectively to negate these dual threats and this allowed Leeds to attack the weak points in the defensive structure. The key to this was that Leeds were so fluid and flexible in the way that they were able to play.

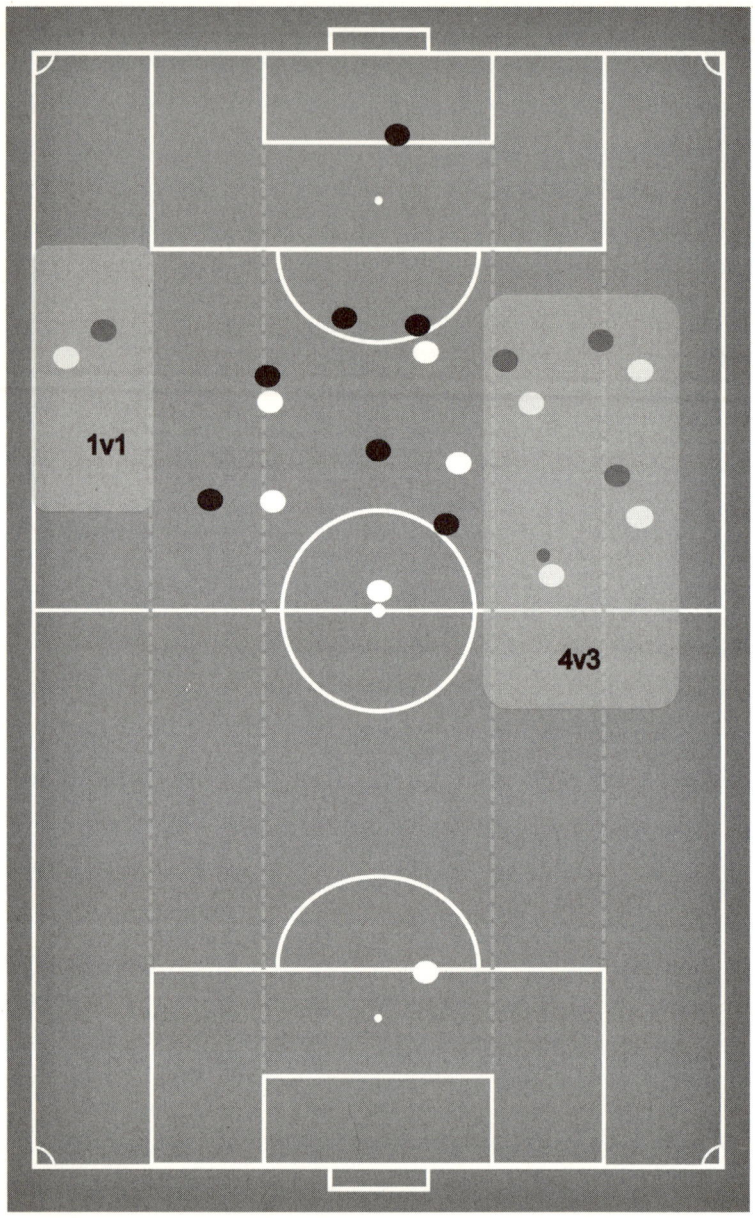

Figure 34

Within Bielsa's game model, as with some other top-level coaches, the concept of overloading and isolating is integral. This is the idea that you attack on one side of the pitch and commit players to that side in order to force your opponent to make a choice defensively. In this sense it is similar to the last example in that you are looking to manipulate the defensive structure and force a decision before quickly taking advantage of any spaces and gaps that appear in their block. In this concept the role of the winger is key as the ball far player has to have the confidence and understanding that they must maintain a wide position and not allow themselves to be pulled inside and attracted towards the position of the ball.

In *figure 34* we have an example of this in action.

Leeds are attacking down their right, again as they tended to do most often across the course of the season, and Ben White is again in possession of the ball at the base of their attacking structure. In the right-side half-space and wide areas Leeds have created a four v three overload over the opposition thanks to the positioning of Luke Ayling, Pablo Hernandez and Helder Costa. This provides an immediate opportunity for the ball to be progressed through the overload and for opportunities to be created in order to outplay and play through the defensive line.

We have already discussed the way that players would rotate in these circumstances to further manipulate the defensive line of the opposition.

The key here, though, is the positioning of Jack Harrison on the far side of the field. Here he has retained his wide position and is isolated one v one against the opposing full-back. Now, as the opposition are pulled further over towards the ball we see that Leeds have a clear opportunity to switch the play quickly and take advantage of the opportunity on the left.

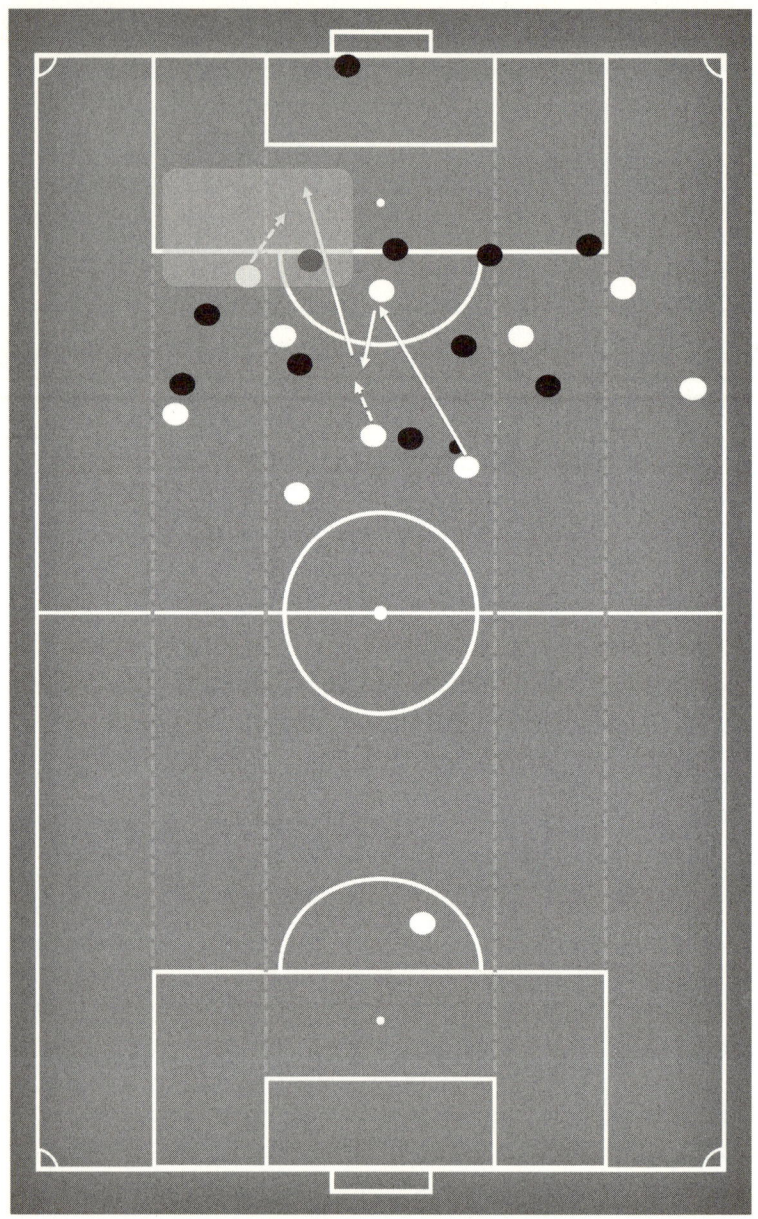

Figure 35

In the more established attacking phase, the wide players would become more active in terms of looking to access and occupy spaces in the opposition area in order to receive the ball and create shooting opportunities either for themselves or for team-mates.

In *figure 35* we have an example of how this tended to work with Harrison as the receiving player.

With Leeds attacking on the edge of the penalty area the opposition had dropped back into a flat and compact defensive structure. Their spacing, however, is still too wide and it allows Leeds to access the central areas of the pitch and to use the up, back and through passing movement to access the run of Harrison behind the defensive line. The initial pass is in to the feet of Patrick Bamford, who drops back towards the ball in order to receive with his back to goal. This angle allows Bamford to play the ball off to Mateusz Klich and then, with the defensive line distracted by the movement of Bamford and the quick passing combination, we see Harrison make a diagonal movement on the blind side of the defensive player.

This run allowed Klich to play the ball past the defensive line and created a goalscoring opportunity for Leeds.

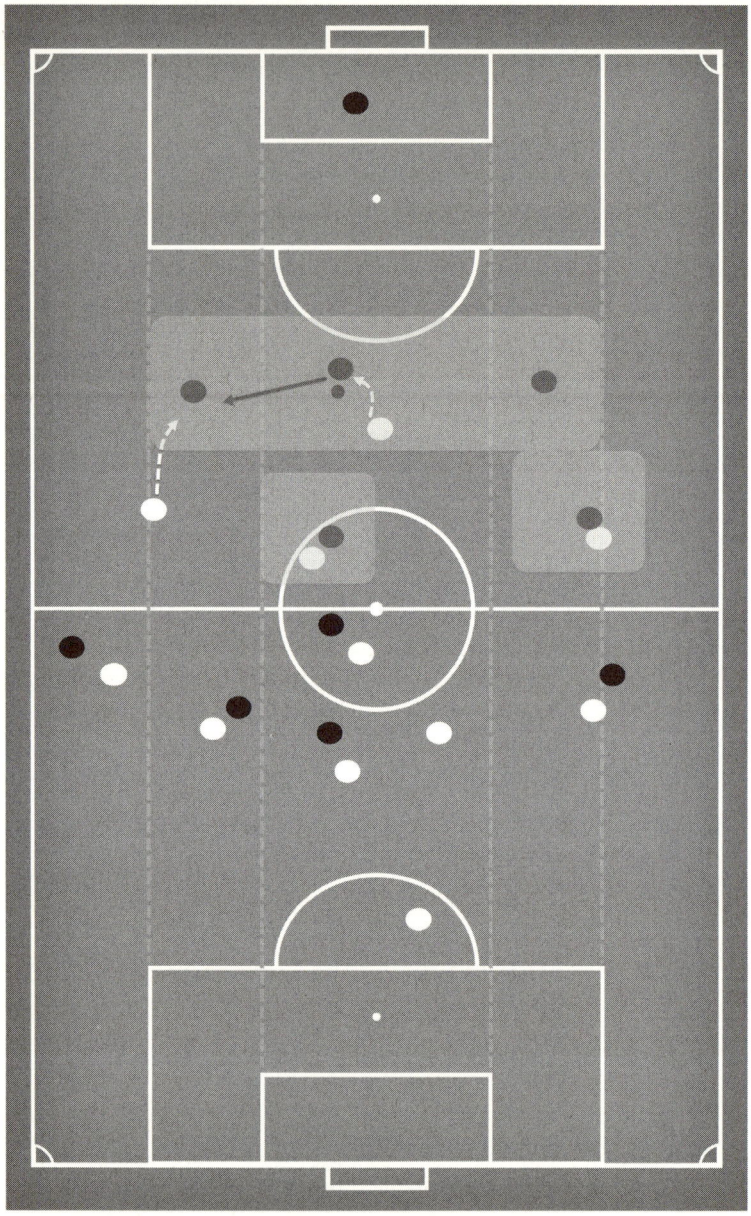

Figure 36

We have already talked about the role that the wide players perform in the defensive phase in terms of pressing in a previous chapter but it is important and therefore bears revisiting.

Once again, the important factor that Bielsa coaches into this team is the positioning on the pitch of the ball, and players are taught to use this as a key reference point in their decision-making. This is especially true in the defensive phase when deciding when to press and when to mark your man closely.

In *figure 36* we see an example of this in action.

The opposition are building out from the back with a structure that has three central defenders. As we already know the -1 rule means that Leeds then have to commit two players to press and engage the ball in order to prevent the opposition from playing through comfortably.

As the 9 presses centrally and angles his press to cut off the potential passing option to the other central defender we see that the left-winger recognises the structure and moves to engage the ball. Out of all of the players in this Leeds side it was the wide forward who had the most responsibility in terms of understanding what their defensive requirements would be. They had to be constantly alert to the shifting structures of the opposition and ready to press and engage when the situation called for it.

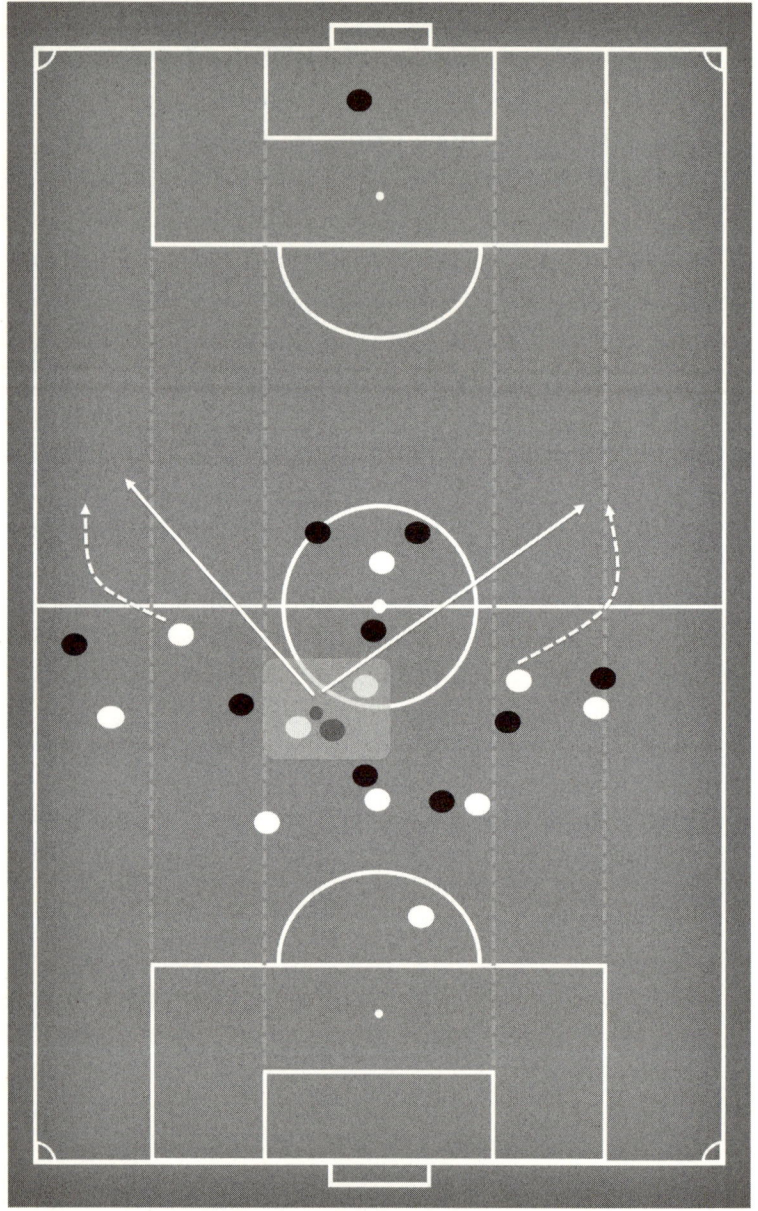

Figure 37

While Leeds were impressive in the defensive phase with their pressing structures and man-marking style, they were equally impressive when the ball was regained and they were able to transition into the attack.

Once again the key men in allowing Leeds to quickly move the ball vertically in the initial moments of transition were the wide players as they moved swiftly to provide width and stretch the defence of the opposition. We see an example of this in *figure 36*.

The opposition are attacking in the central areas and the ball is won back in the midfield. As soon as Leeds regain possession in these areas the wide forward makes movements to attack in the half-space or wide areas. They are able to do so because they trust the technical abilities of their team-mates to not only retain possession in transition but to be able to play vertically.

These movements stretch the defensive structure of the opposition and create spaces and gaps through which Leeds would attack comfortably.

Chapter 7

Free 8s

One of the most important aspects of the attacking game model that Marcelo Bielsa used during the course of the 2019/20 season was the role of the number 8s. There were, of course, differences between the way that the role was interpreted depending on whether the structure of the side was 4-1-4-1 or 3-3-1-3 but their key functions remained constant.

In order to fully understand how the 8s work, we need to consider how coaches with similar attacking principles like their midfield to function. First of all we can consider Pep Guardiola at Manchester City who utilised a similar structure to Leeds in 2019/20. It can be characterised as a 1-2 with a single pivot sitting at the base of the midfield and two 8s on a higher line.

The key differences between the midfield roles under Guardiola compared to Bielsa are relatively simple. Guardiola expects his two 8s to act as link players or ball progressors and as such they will occupy central areas in order to provide passing options. As the ball is moved in towards the final third they then have a freer role with a tendency to occupy the half-spaces in order to find space to create as the ball moves forward.

Now consider the same structure (1-2) that is utilised for the most part by Jurgen Klopp at Liverpool. The roles of the 8s in this system are again different to those that were used by Leeds as there is a tendency for the midfielders in the Liverpool system to be relatively functional as they control the central areas of the field without even moving into high areas of the pitch.

Then think of the role of the 8s under Bielsa where we saw an entirely different picture, which in turn requires a very specific profile of player to work effectively. This was particularly true when Leeds were playing in their 4-1-4-1 shape. We have already discussed in this book that the 8s are expected to move high as soon as Leeds begin the build-up phase of the attacking movement. This is a deliberate ploy to stretch and manipulate the defensive block of the opposition and to empty the central areas of the field. The purpose of this is relatively simple as the wide players maintain a wide position when Leeds are in possession of the ball. This creates pockets of space in the half-space or central areas that can be used and occupied. If the 8s are able to get into this position then they immediately create an advanced platform from which Leeds can build their attacking movement in the final third.

Advanced platforms are a concept that I first came across via the excellent Joey Lombardi, a coach who is currently involved with Brampton Soccer Club in Canada as their director of player and coach development. The idea is a simple one where players are coached to occupy pockets of space in between the lines of the opposition midfield and defence. When in these positions the player in question can then receive the ball in a relatively safe manner. The central idea behind the concept of advanced platforms is that when the ball is played into these spaces the attacking team can then take the position of the ball as their primary reference and move into and occupy advanced areas of the pitch. When the 8s were able to occupy these platforms and receive the ball they were immediately in a favourable position between the lines of the opposition defensive structure, between the midfield and the defence. By being able to occupy these spaces and create these platforms the Leeds 8s were also enabling the vertical passing style that Bielsa wants from his side in the attacking phase.

In order to play in this manner, there is a need for the 8s that Bielsa has at his disposal to be extremely well conditioned from a physical point of view. Indeed, there is a sense that if the 6 in this system acts as the brains, as the main ball progressor, then the 8s act as the heart and lungs of the side with their ability to contribute all phases of the game effectively.

This physical capacity is well documented when considering the roles of the 8s but at times their technical ability can be overlooked. While these players can move quickly in the attacking phase, emptying and occupying space as they rotate in and out of key areas of the field, they also have to be able to receive the ball cleanly and then have the technical ability and understanding of the system to be able to link play effectively. Often, in either 4-1-4-1 or 3-3-1-3, the 8s become the link players who act essentially as pivots in receiving the ball and then finding the next free player.

This mix of the physical and technical is something that the Polish international Mateusz Klich has in abundance and over the course of the season he ended up playing 4,035 minutes. Klich ended up with various partners across the whole of 2019/20 with the likes of Tyler Roberts and Stuart Dallas in particular spending time as one of the 8s. It was Pablo Hernandez, however, who made the difference when partnering Klich in the central areas. Hernandez was already in the twilight of his career when he moved to Elland Road in 2017 and although his creativity from the wide areas was never in doubt it was when he moved into the central spaces and was able to link play that Leeds took a huge step forward in the attacking phase.

If Klich had the physical capacity and technique to hurt the opposition then Hernandez had the vision and ability to find the correct pass time and time again. He is a typical Spanish midfielder in that he never looks hurried or under pressure. His ability to manipulate the ball away from pressing defenders and unerringly find the correct pass at the correct time was incredibly important for Leeds as they moved towards the Championship title. Once again the quality of these two players shows up clearly in the data that we have available.

In his 4,035 minutes Klich averaged 0.13 goals per 90 from an xG per 90 of 0.17. Although Klich was an attacking threat he was more of a creator than a shooter in the final third. He only averaged 1.65 shots per 90 but had 2.7 crosses per 90 and 4.53 passes into the penalty area per 90 minutes. The Polish midfielder was also a surprisingly important part of the ball progression for Leeds as he moved the ball up the field and did not only look to receive in high positions. He averaged an impressive 7.52 progressive passes per 90 and 5.91 passes to the final third per 90.

Hernandez, on the other hand, spent less time on the pitch with 2,685 minutes across the course of the league campaign. He averaged 0.30 goals per 90 minutes from an xG of 0.19 per 90. He took the third most shots on average in the Leeds squad with 2.45 shots per 90, behind just Patrick Bamford and Tyler Roberts. The goal contribution that Hernandez had was further enhanced by an impressive 0.37 assists per 90 from an expected assists (xA) figure of 0.31. The Spaniard was a creative force throughout his time on the field and averaged 3.52 dribbles and 2.75 crosses per 90 alongside 1.11 key passes per 90.

Now, we can move on to providing practical examples of these things in action.

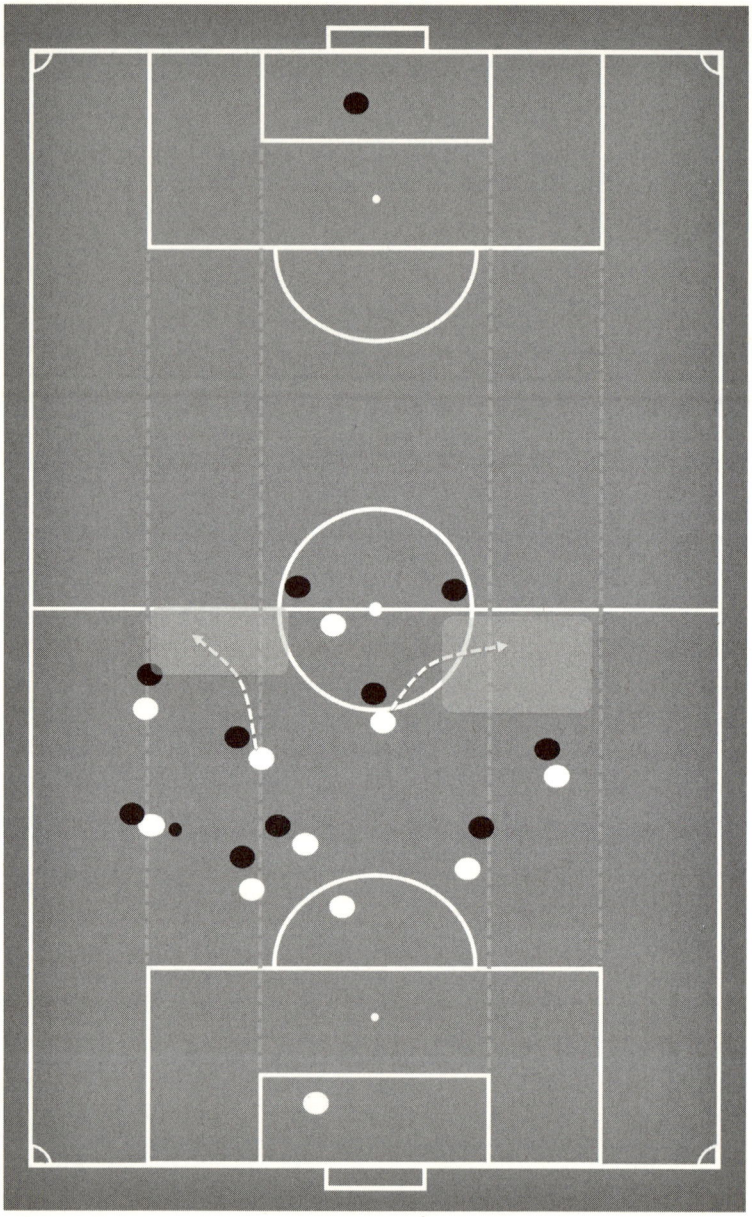

Figure 38

We have already discussed that the 8s under Bielsa would look to move to a high line immediately on Leeds gaining possession of the ball. They would empty the central space and look to link with the highest line. Again, this is key in allowing Leeds to use their vertical passing concept in order to move the ball quickly into areas that will hurt the opposition most effectively.

We see an example of these movements in *figure 38*.

Here the opposition had been attacking and were in a relatively advanced position on the pitch but Leeds regained possession as Stuart Dallas, at left-back, won a defensive duel. This meant that Leeds were immediately transitioning into the attacking phase and the 8s looked to move into positions accordingly.

The key, though, is that they did not move too high and instead held a position in space, one on the left and one on the right. This positioning allowed Leeds to access an advanced platform from which they could play and build an effective attacking movement.

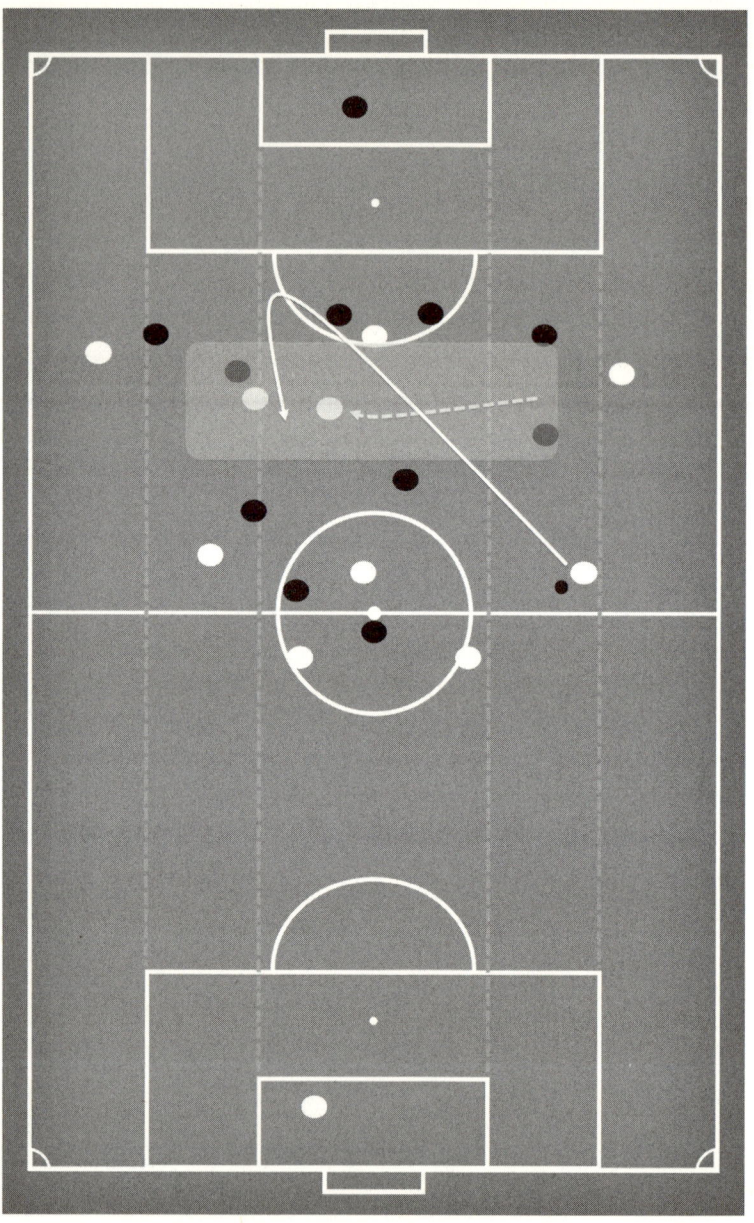

Figure 39

The positioning and movement of the 8s under Bielsa was, throughout the 2019/20 promotion season, exceptionally interesting.

Yes, they would move high to occupy higher lines and provide vertical passing options, but they would also move across the width of the pitch in order to take advantage of weak points in the opposition defensive structure. While this is a relatively normal concept for midfielders when they move wide to combine and create overloads it is less normal to see an 8 move across to occupy the same space as his opposite side 8.

This is part of the genius of Bielsa as players have the flexibility to be able to move into areas of the pitch that will affect the opposition defence. This saw the 8s occasionally taking the opportunity to move from their side of the pitch to the other into areas where they could overload and break through the opposition.

We see an example of this in *figure 39.*

Hernandez, playing as the right-sided 8, makes the movement across from that positional slot into the same areas as Klich who is playing on the opposite side of the structure. Crucially, this movement takes place on the blind side of the opposition midfielder and in the space between the midfield line and the line of the defence. As Hernandez makes this movement we see Luke Ayling look to play the ball into this overloaded area of the pitch as Leeds attack the opposition.

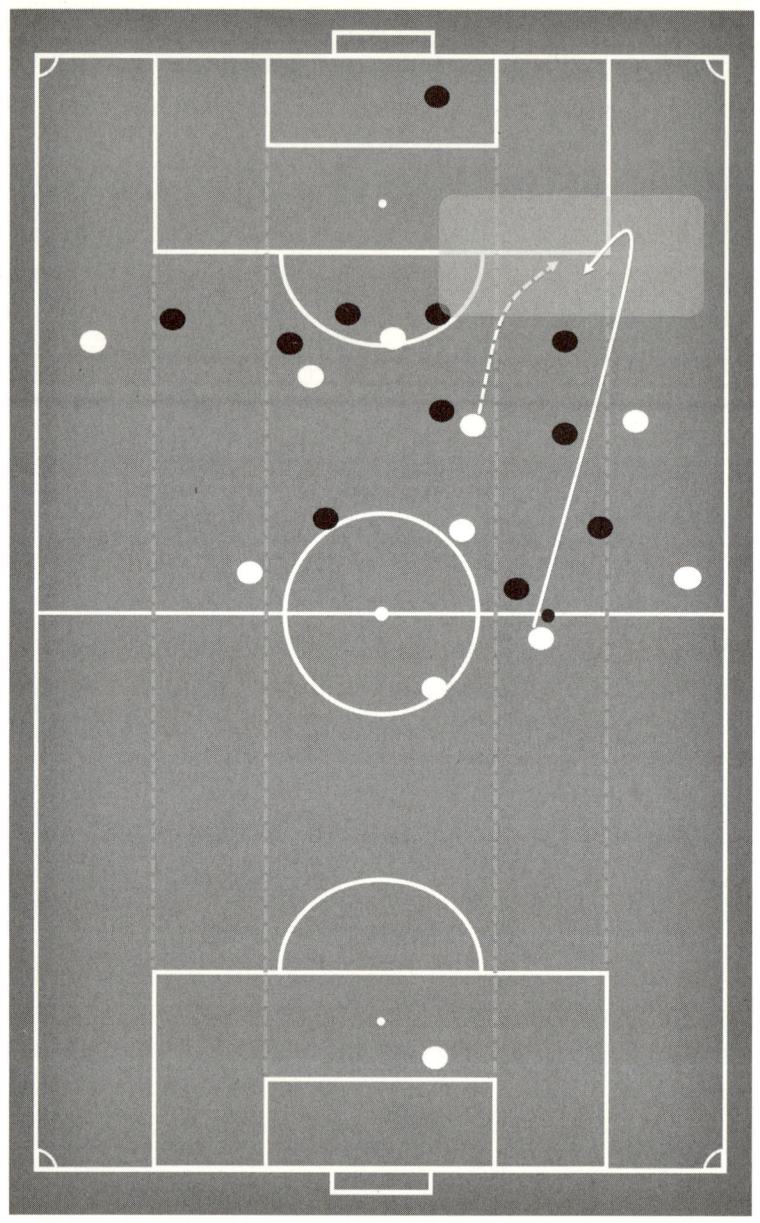

Figure 40

The 8s were so important for Leeds because of their intelligent movements across the final third of the pitch. The way that they occupied pockets of space and were constantly available to receive the ball in key areas allowed Leeds to attack constantly and look to overload and outplay the opposition structure.

The movement of the players in these positions stretched the pitch and the opposition defensive structure horizontally and also vertically.

We see an example of this vertical movement in *figure 40*.

Once again the key player in this scenario was Hernendez, who used his experience and intelligence to find the space to attack the opposition. There is a misconception that surrounded this Leeds side; that they always used short passing and passing combinations in order to play through and break through the opposition. This is absolutely not the case and as with many other top teams they would use longer and more direct passing when that was the right thing to do.

Here, we see Ben White in possession of the ball and although there are shorting passing options open to him it is the movement by Hernandez, who moves from the 8 slot and attacks the half-space behind the opposition left-back, which makes the move possible. White is able to make that pass over the defensive line and immediately Leeds are in a position to threaten the opposition goal.

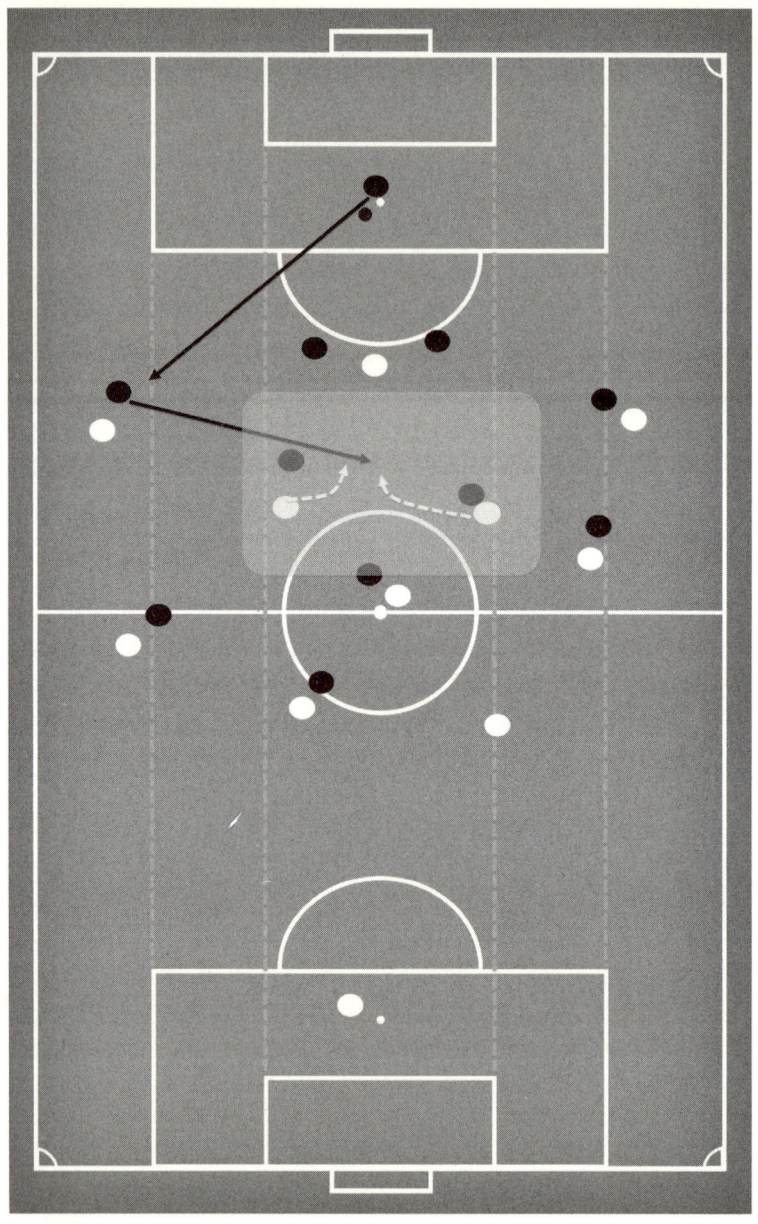

Figure 41

One of the common things that we saw from the Leeds 8s in this season was their ability to recover possession in the opposition half. This, of course, was extremely important for Bielsa as he wanted his team to win the ball back early in order to be able to attack the opposition goal in the moment of immediate transition.

The 8s tended to use their intelligence and ability to read the game to time their jump on the ball and create turnover opportunities early in the opposition attacking movement. This ties in with the idea that they would trigger to press in central areas when the receiving player for the opposition was facing his own goal.

In *figure 41* we have annotated an example of how this worked in practice.

The opposition goalkeeper is initially in possession of the ball and this time has space with no immediate pressure. He looks to play a pass out to the right-back who then comes under pressure and tries to connect a pass into the central areas. This is slightly loose and immediately the two 8s for Leeds move to press and engage the ball. They work together and are aggressive in pursuing the ball before eventually winning the duel and then being able to attack the edge of the penalty area.

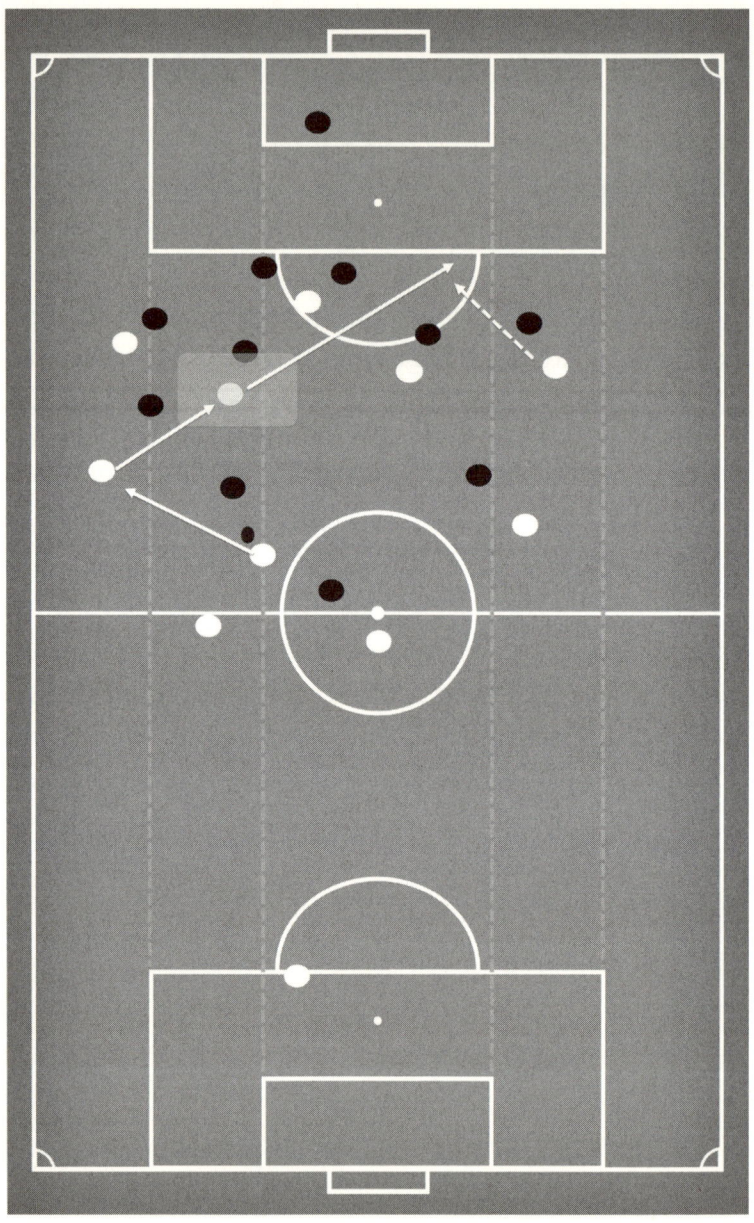

Figure 42

In the attacking phase the two 8s in the 4-1-4-1 for Leeds were incredibly important in terms of providing links in the final third to allow the ball to move into these areas safely. Often we would see the central midfielders moving towards the ball to receive the pass and then quickly link with team-mates in dangerous areas. This included close combinations and intelligent switches of play.

In *figure 42* we see this in action.

The ball is initially with Phillips at the base of the attacking structure just inside the opposition half of the pitch. He makes a quick diagonal pass to find Ezgjan Alioski who is playing at left-back in the wide space. As soon as this pass is made we see Klich as the 8 moving slightly out towards the ball but still positioned in the half-space. Klich is then able to receive the ball comfortably as Leeds start to progress the ball in this manner.

On receiving the ball here, Klich would perhaps be expected to link again out to the winger on the ball side of the field. Instead, he has the intelligence to turn out towards the other side before playing a diagonal pass that outplays the defensive line and finds the run of the opposite-side winger who is moving behind the defensive line.

The 8s consistently take up positions in these situations which provide the ability to link the play and allow Leeds to have meaningful possession.

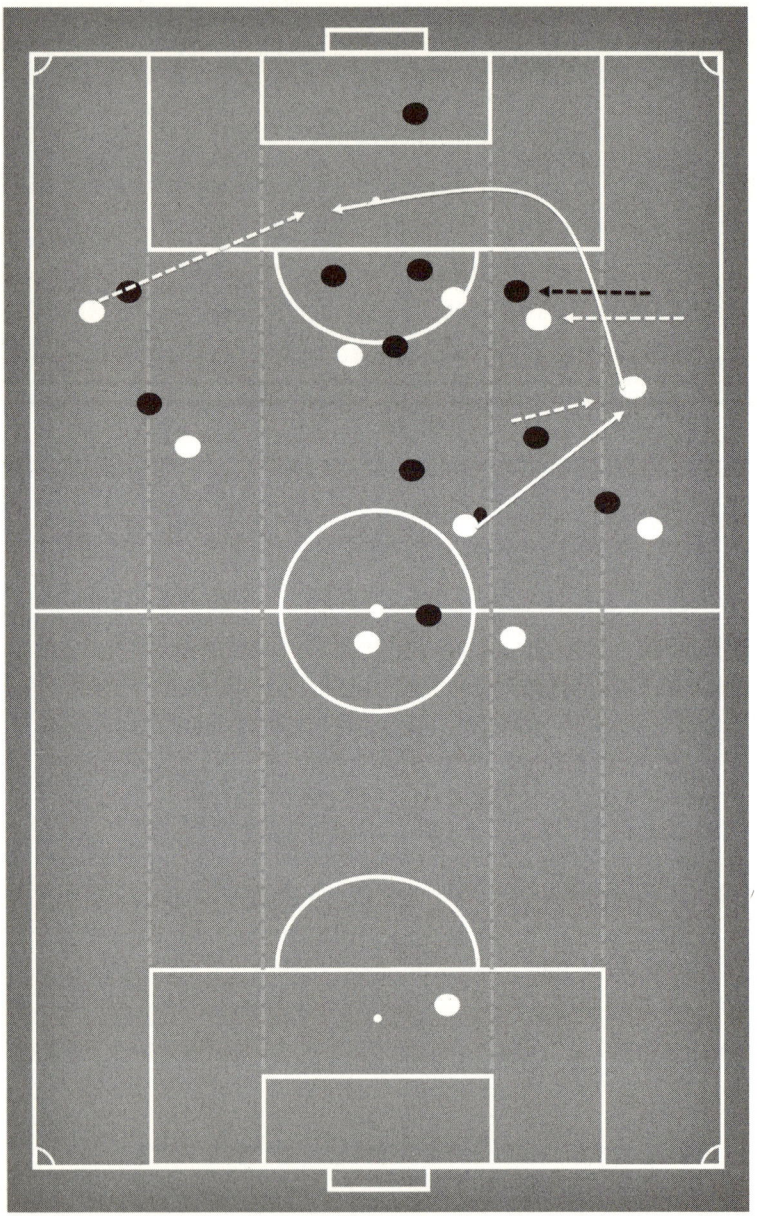

Figure 43

This ability to link play made the 8s extremely important in the final third and when they rotated into pockets of space they were invariably the option that was used in order to progress the play. This was especially true of Hernandez, who was one of the most active Leeds players in these areas of the pitch.

In *figure 43* we see an example of this.

The first thing to note is the rotation in the wide space. As Helder Costa, the right-winger, moves inside he drags his defender out of position. This creates the pocket of space in the wide area that Hernandez can then look to occupy. As the Spaniard rotates into this position the ball is then played wide to access this run. It is now that we see the importance of the 8s as the ball is received and then immediately played into the rear side of the penalty area where Jack Harrison is arriving having made a diagonal run.

Chapter 8
Ben White

When Leeds United announced the loan signing of 22-year-old Brighton & Hove Albion defender Ben White prior to the 2019/20 season, there was a feeling that the signing was about creating depth rather than adding to the quality of the first-team squad. Fast forward to the end of that season and White was being tipped to make the breakthrough with the senior England setup and was being linked with a permanent multi-million-pound move to Elland Road. In order to fully understand and appreciate the performance of this Leeds side over the course of the season, we have to acknowledge the impact that White had in the centre of their defence.

When White signed on 1 July 2019 there were two well established central defenders at the club in Liam Cooper and Pontus Jansson. They were firmly established as the first choice pair and despite some issues surrounding the relationship between Jansson and Marcelo Bielsa, it seemed unlikely that White would break them up. That was, however, until 8 July when Jansson was surprisingly sold to promotion rivals Brentford.

That sale led many fans of Leeds to question the effectiveness of the recruitment department at the club as they now seemed short in the centre-back position. From that point on though

White never looked back and by the end of the season he had played an incredible 4,471 minutes and established himself as the club's number one transfer target going into their return to the Premier League.

White had enjoyed something of a nomadic path to the limelight and he was initially a product of the Southampton youth system before being released by the south coast side at the age of 16. White, however, was not without a club for long and having been doing their due diligence on youth products in their area Brighton moved to sign the young defender almost immediately. Even at that point though there was no guarantee that White would make the breakthrough at first-team level and although he was excellent from a technical perspective there were still some who saw him as being undersized for his position.

At the start of 2017/18, White moved on loan to Newport County in the fourth tier of English football. It would be here that White would get his first real and extended exposure to first-team football and in a league where his physical capacity would be consistently tested. During the season White established himself as a key player for the League Two side and he impressed when Newport were drawn against Tottenham Hotspur in the FA Cup, which meant he had the job of marking the England international Harry Kane. By the end of the season White had been named as Newport's player of the year with the Welsh outfit's manager Michael Flynn calling him 'the best loan signing the club has ever made'.

When White moved back to Brighton after his loan spell they were trying to tie him down to a long-term contract amid interest from Tottenham, which was generated off the back of his performance against them in the FA Cup. In the end White signed a new deal but once again he found himself out on loan the following season when he moved to Peterborough in League One in January 2019. White again established himself early as a first-team regular in a strong Peterborough side and handled the step up in quality from League Two to League One comfortably.

It is interesting to note, when following White's progression through the leagues, that he has had significant exposure at each level of the football pyramid as he has moved through his loan spells. He showed that he could deal with the step up in quality from League Two to League One and then on to the Championship with Leeds. In retrospect, Leeds fans need not have been concerned as to whether White would be a capable replacement for the departing Jansson.

When White signed for Leeds he was a couple of months away from his 22nd birthday and as such he was already past the typical age range at which young players begin to fully establish themselves at their parent club. He is not tall for a central defender and is listed at 185cm, or 6ft 1in. This lack of height was a factor in the way that Bielsa used him as a central defender and invariably White was the free man in the back line as Liam Cooper took responsibility to mark the opposition forward.

While White did face some struggles in the defensive phase when it came to aerial duels, where he averaged 4.87 per 90 minutes with a success rate of 54.5 per cent, he made up for this with his positional sense and his ability when engaging and challenging the opposition ball carrier in ground duels. In these he averaged 9.2 per 90 with a 71.6 per cent success rate. For such a young player, White read the game exceptionally well and his positional sense and timing allowed him to defend in an extremely proactive style as he continuously seemed to be positioned in the right place at the right time to win the ball back for Leeds.

White is extremely versatile and he is comfortable in a wide range of defensive situations. He could defend in a deep block with the understanding of how and when to shift position to close passing angles and deny the opposition the opportunity to access the penalty area. He could defend in a high line and despite not possessing top-level pace he was rarely caught out of position because he read the game so well. He also turns his hips well and is fluid in his movements, which may seem like a small detail but it allows White to turn quickly in order to defend space behind the defensive line when the opposition look to play the ball over the top. More importantly, White is comfortable when forced to move out into the wide spaces to defend against quick strikers as the opposition are in transition. Again, his lack of real pace was rarely truly exposed in these situations.

In the build-up phase it did not take long for White to firmly establish himself as a key part of the way that Leeds would look to progress the ball through the thirds. He was a volume passer throughout the season as he averaged an impressive 48.67 passes per 90 with a success rate of 87.6 per cent. That number and success rate, however, does not come close to explaining how important White was to Leeds when they were in possession. The young Englishman quickly took to the preferred game model of Bielsa and understood the concept of verticality in possession very well.

He was not a central defender who would look to just do the safe thing with lateral passes across to the other central defender. Instead, White took risks and looked to connect progressive passes that broke through the lines of the opposition defensive structure. He averaged 7.51 progressive passes and 7.53 passes to the final third per 90. From a tactical perspective this gave Leeds an alternative to Kalvin Phillips, from the 6 position, or from Luke Ayling from right-back. White was able to fulfil the role of the player at the base of the wide diamond when Leeds were in possession of the ball and he had the passing range and vision to access all areas of the field when he was in possession of the ball. This made his passing especially interesting to Bielsa as White was able to collect possession of the ball and play the quick diagonal pass that accessed the wide player on the opposite side of the field who was isolated one v one against the opposition full-back. White was comfortable in possession and composed when under pressure – this was part of what made him such a perfect fit to this Bielsa system.

What was especially interesting about White in this system, however, was that he was equally comfortable when progressing the ball through vertical movements when he kept possession of the ball and drove through the opposition defensive structure. This became especially important for Leeds as the season progressed and teams began to drop more and more into a deep and compact block as a result of their potent attacking threat.

White averaged 0.79 dribbles and 1.21 progressive runs per 90 across the course of the season. These are impressive numbers for a central defender and it was not unusual for White to be the player who would step out of the defensive line in possession of the ball. Having a central defender behave in this manner forces the opposition defenders to step out of their defensive structure to engage the ball carrier. As soon as this happens, space is created within the defensive structure and Leeds were able to take advantage.

Now we will move on to some practical examples of White playing during 2019/20. All of the illustrations that follow are taken from matches played during that promotion campaign and will be used to further highlight the way that players worked within the tactical concepts that we have discussed through previous chapters.

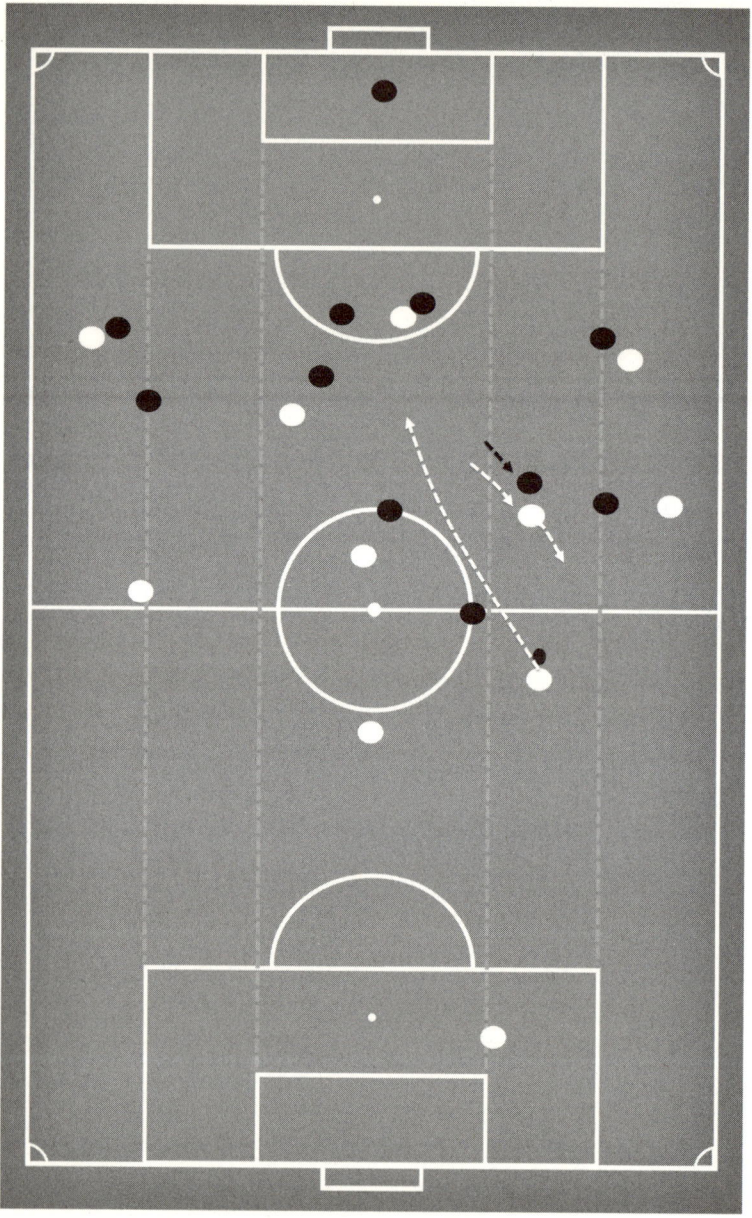

Figure 44

This first example of White in action comes from a match against Cardiff City and is displayed in *figure 44*.

This is a classic example of the rotational movements creating opportunities for team-mates to outplay the opposition. It also gives us an excellent example of just how good White was in possession and the problems that he would routinely cause the opposition defensive structure.

White is initially in possession just inside his own half and the opposition are not committing any players forward in order to provide immediate pressure on the ball. In many teams this kind of situation would lead to the central defender using the time and space on the ball to play a speculative pass that would often be played diagonally to try to access the far side of the pitch.

White, however, is far more nuanced than that. As the midfielder ahead of the ball rotates out into the half-space this opens up a large lane through the opposition defensive structure. White has the ability and confidence to drive in possession through this lane to take advantage of the opportunity presented. Having a central defender capable of driving forward in this manner causes chaos for the opposition as they have to move to engage the ball and therefore space is created elsewhere in their half of the field that Leeds can exploit.

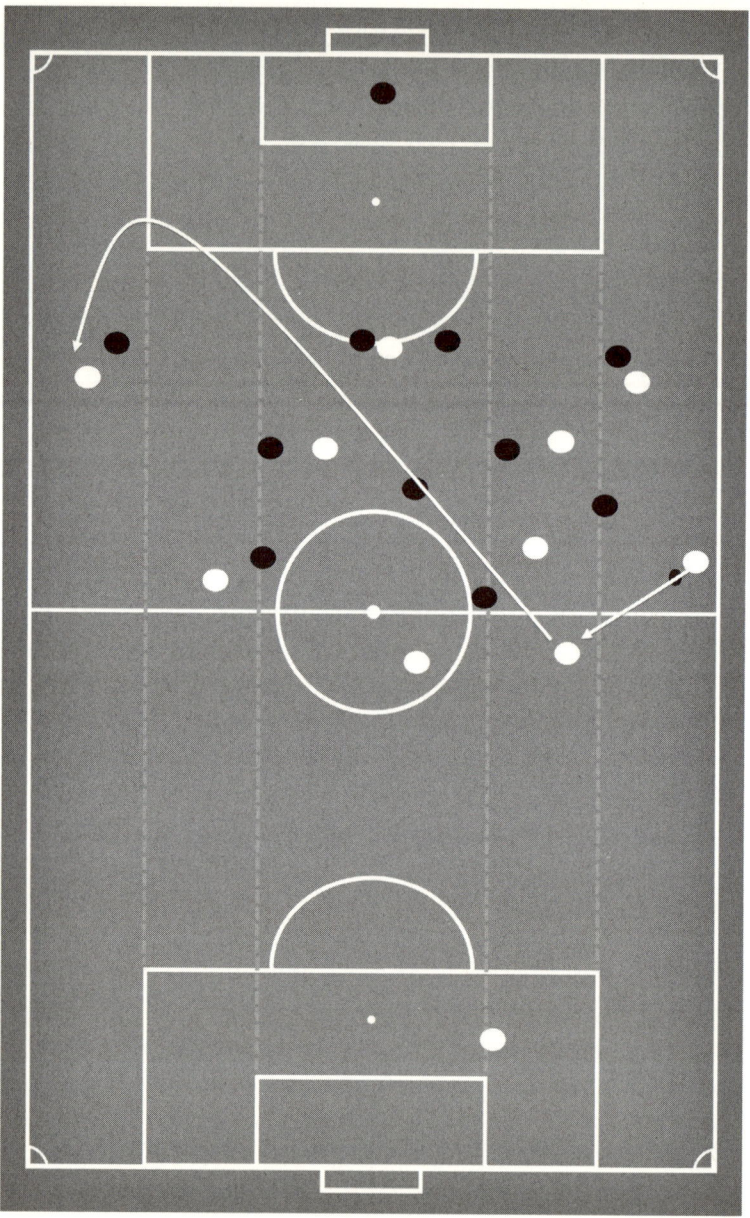

Figure 45

Of course, just because White can drive in possession in the manner that we have seen does not mean that this is always the correct choice to make. In *figure 45* we see another moment where White was in possession of the ball, this time against Bristol City.

White received the ball back after a throw-in from the right-back, Luke Ayling. The first thing to note is that we can see the overload beginning to form on the ball side of the pitch and there are options vertically for White to play into feet in order to progress the ball to a more advanced platform.

However, White appreciates that this is not the only option that he has open to him. Instead, he receives the ball and then opens up his body to play a long diagonal pass out to the opposite side of the field. This pass accesses the space where Jack Harrison, on the left of the attack, has isolated against the opposition full-back.

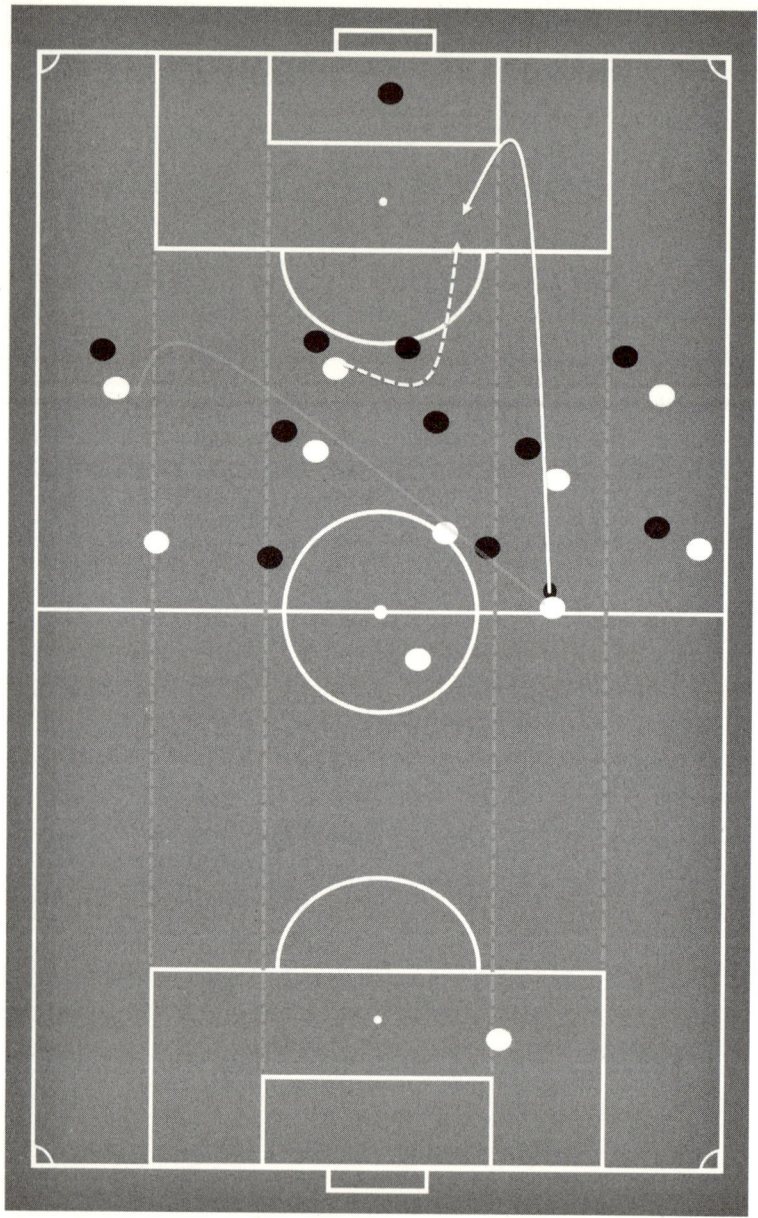

Figure 46

This threat and passing range that White possesses are a danger to the opposition and they were always aware that when the young English defender was in possession of the ball there was a threat of a diagonal switch of play.

Figure 46 shows an example of a time in which White used this to his advantage in order to fake a more vertical pass, again showing the concept of verticality in possession. This came from a match against Millwall.

White again initially has the ball, as is so often the case, in the half-space on his side of the field. There is a diagonal switch of play open for White to access that same pass to Harrison that we saw earlier. Indeed, White even opens up his body in order to make the opposition think that this would be the pass that was played.

In that moment, however, Patrick Bamford makes a run across the face of the defenders and then behind the defensive line. This movement allows White to play the pass that accesses the space behind the defensive line and creates a goalscoring opportunity for Bamford.

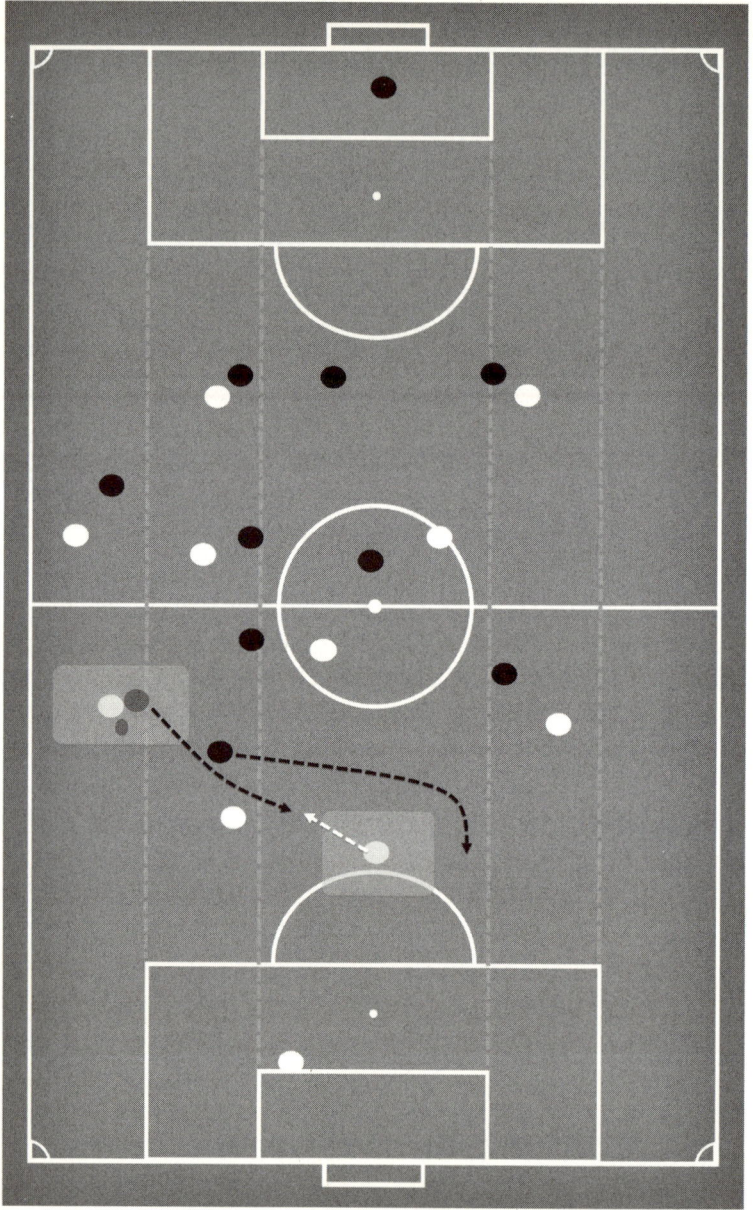

Figure 47

For all of White's huge threat in possession of the ball, we also have to acknowledge just how impressive he was in the defensive phase.

We have already talked about the fact that in the defensive phase or the defensive transition White was often left as the free man. This was, in part, because White was not that strong in terms of aerial duels but it was also because he was extremely effective with his positioning and his reading of the game.

Figure 47 is taken from a match against QPR and perfectly captures his defensive instincts. Left-back Stuart Dallas gets caught in possession and straight away QPR are able to attack two v two against Cooper and White. Cooper tries to challenge the ball carrier but loses his footing and therefore White is left in a two v one duel. He is intelligent enough to hold his central position and as the carrier takes a slightly heavy touch White jumps and challenges, winning the duel cleanly and carrying the ball away in transition.

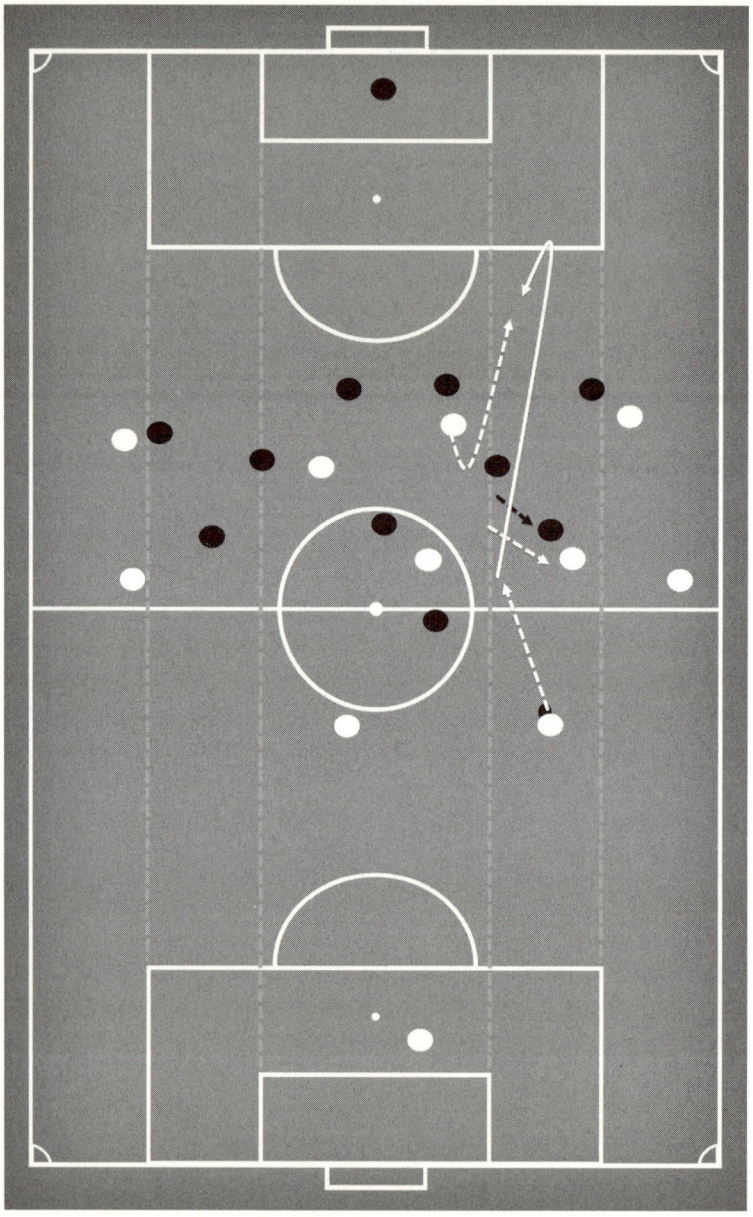

Figure 48

While the defensive side of the game from White was really important, especially in tight encounters, the reality is that Leeds enjoyed so much possession on most days that a key part of the young defender's performances was based around his ability in possession and especially with the clean progression of the ball.

In *figure 48* we again see an example of White in possession as rotations ahead create opportunities to play vertically, this time in a match against Sheffield Wednesday.

White is, again, in possession as we capture the moment. Once again the 8 directly ahead of the ball rotates out of his position. This creates an opportunity for White to drive forward into the gap and as he does so it forces the opposition to shift their defensive block in order to engage the ball carrier.

As White drives forward we again see Bamford making a movement back towards the ball before spinning and running in behind. This allows White to access the vertical pass through the defensive structure.

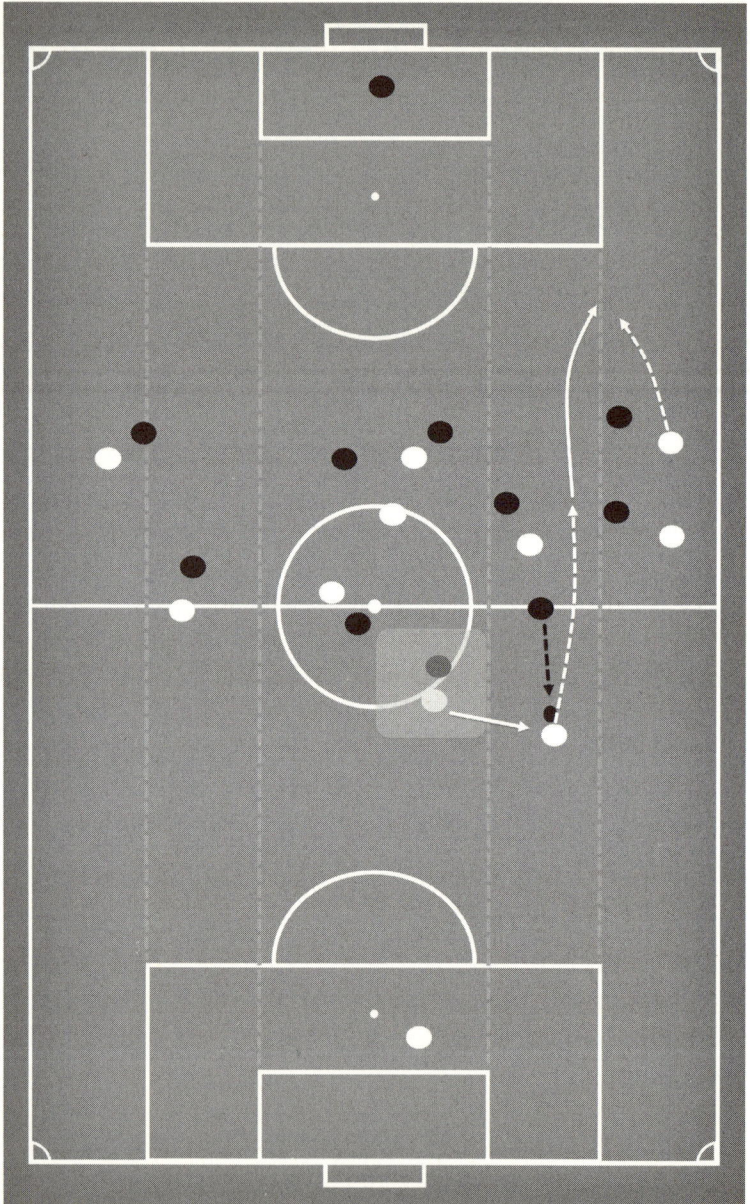

Figure 49

The composure that White displayed for Leeds was incredibly impressive, especially for such a young player. He never seemed flustered or rushed and always seemed to make the intelligent choice in possession.

In *figure 49* we see an example from a game against Preston North End which displays this perfectly.

The opposition had looked to attack quickly in transition via a long ball to the highest line. The aerial duel was won by Cooper and he knocked the ball down to White. At this point White has to take control of the ball and he has an opposition player moving quickly to press and close him down. There are many defenders who would become panicked in this position and look to hit the ball away.

Instead, White controls the ball and comfortably dribbles past the on-rushing defender. He then carries the ball further into the opposition half before calmly playing the ball through the defensive line for Helder Costa to run on to.

Chapter 9
Stuart Dallas

A large part of the mystique that surrounds Marcelo Bielsa as a coach lies in his ability to improve players, at almost any level. Indeed, When Bielsa first arrived at Elland Road there was considerable speculation in how the club would look to recruit players for the first-team squad with many in the media in particular of the impression that the club may look to target players who had worked with him in the past in order to provide their new coach with men who were familiar with his methods.

Instead, although there were some incomings, Bielsa displayed a willingness to work with the players already in place. This resulted in significant improvements in many of them but perhaps none more so than Stuart Dallas.

This improvement in Dallas, however, was not immediate. During Bielsa's first season in charge, 2018/19, we saw Dallas play a relatively significant role but as Leeds' form crashed towards the end of the season Dallas faded as a contributor. Indeed, had Dallas left at the end of that season there were few supporters who would have raised an objection.

Fast forward from that point to the end of 2019/20 and it was genuinely possible to make an argument that Dallas was deserving of the club's player of the year award, such was his impact. What was most interesting about his performances over the course of the promotion-winning season though was that he played in a wide array of positions, but more on that later.

Dallas was born on 19 April 1991 in Coagh, Northern Ireland. His career to date is interesting because he did not make the move to England at an early age, as so many other young Irish players do. Instead, he made his breakthrough at first-team level domestically as he played initially for his hometown club Coagh United and then for Crusaders. At this stage Dallas was an attacking winger who used his physicality and speed over the first ten yards to create separation from opposition defensive players. Over the course of the two seasons that Dallas spent with Crusaders he scored 26 goals across 85 appearances and got his first taste of European football when the Northern Irish side faced Fulham in Europa League qualification.

By this point Dallas was established as one of the strongest players in the Northern Irish leagues but he was still not on a professional contract and it was no surprise that he was being tracked by English sides keen on taking him away from his homeland and introducing him to the professional game. Ireland, both Northern and the Republic, still represents an interesting market for English, and even Scottish, clubs but in most cases talented young Irish players are spirited away from their homeland before they make any kind of significant impact at first-team level. In the end Dallas was already 21 when he made the move to England and joined Brentford, still in League One at the time, on a pre-contract agreement.

Initially Dallas found first-team minutes hard to come by and he left for a short-term loan to Northampton Town during his early stages at the London club. Gradually though, as tends to be the case with Dallas, he made himself an important player as his technical ability and direct attacking style helped him to stand out in matches when his side were struggling. Over the course of his time with Brentford we saw Dallas start to gain a reputation as a versatile player who was comfortable in filling a number of roles across the pitch. It was perhaps not that big a stretch therefore to start to see him as an attacking full-back who was dependable in all phases of the game. In the end, though, Dallas made it clear that he did not want to sign an extended contract and would be willing to allow his contract to run down and as a result Brentford were open to receiving offers for the player.

Brentford accepted a bid, reported to be around the £1m mark, from Leeds, and in August 2015 Dallas made the move north. This set the scene for his performance over the 2019/20 season where he emerged as one of the most versatile and important players at the club.

In the initial stages of the season the regular first-choice right-back Luke Ayling was injured and Dallas slotted in to that position. He played comfortably either at right-back (in the 4-1-4-1) or at right wing-back (in the 3-3-1-3) and was one of the key players in terms of his ball progression and ability to play the vertical passing game that Bielsa favoured so clearly.

Then, as Ayling regained fitness, there were injury issues in the centre of midfield and Dallas seamlessly slotted into the side as one of the two 8s alongside Mateusz Klich. Next, a relative lack of form from the two left-backs in the squad, Barry Douglas and Ezgjan Alioski, saw Bielsa shift the Northern Irishman across to the left. Once again Dallas never let his side down. Despite being naturally right-footed and therefore more likely to take a touch inside when receiving on the left he still suited the attacking game model that Bielsa favoured brilliantly and he started to develop a tendency to come inside to support the midfield in an inverted position when Leeds were in the attacking phase.

In possession, having converted back to deeper positions after spending most of his time as an attacking winger, Dallas was a key ball progressor for Leeds. He averaged 47.08 passes per 90 minutes and 19.22 of those were forward passes as he rarely looked to circulate the ball laterally or back towards his own goal. Indeed, Dallas averaged an impressive 7.68 passes to the final third per 90 and 9.66 progressive passes. These metrics were relatively balanced across all three roles that Dallas occupied across 2019/20 although when playing centrally as one of the 8s his responsibility was different with more of a focus on occupying central spaces on a high line and being positioned to receive the ball close to the opposition goal. When playing in either full-back position Dallas consistently impressed with his capacity to link the play in wide areas when Leeds were looking to overload the opposition. He was comfortable with the responsibility of playing at the base of the attacking structure in these overloads or rotating into one of the more advanced positions on the ball near side of the pitch.

Interestingly, as Dallas began to develop the tendency to drift inside into inverted positions on the pitch when the ball was on the far side, this played further into the concept of overload and isolation that Bielsa wanted. In these situations the movement of Dallas in towards the middle offered support in central areas to the 6 and allowed the two 8s to retain their higher positions safely. This movement also dragged an opposition player inside to cover the inverted run and, in turn, increased the opportunity that the wide player on that side of the pitch had to isolate himself against the opposition.

In the end Dallas played 4,232 minutes across the season, second only to Ben White, and he emerged as a player who could perform almost any function in this system. He is listed at 183cm or 6ft and has a powerful physique. This is a good size of player for a full-back and he uses his frame well in the defensive phase of the game. Even then, he only averaged 2.25 aerial duels per 90 with a success rate of 40.57 per cent although he was far more active in terms of defensive duels with 7.36 defensive duels and a success rate of 57.51 per cent.

As a former winger himself, Dallas understands the tendencies of a wide player and is capable of anticipating the movements of his direct opponent. He still has the pace that made him an active and capable winger but used this effectively to recover his defensive position when the opposition look to transition quickly into their attacking phase. He was an important part of the man-to-man defensive structure given his intelligence and capacity to read the flow of the game and adjust his position to deny the opposition space as they attacked. He is comfortable when isolated one v one against opposition players or when defending as part of a more established defensive block.

Now we will move on to examine some practical examples and visuals of Dallas in action during the 2019/20 season.

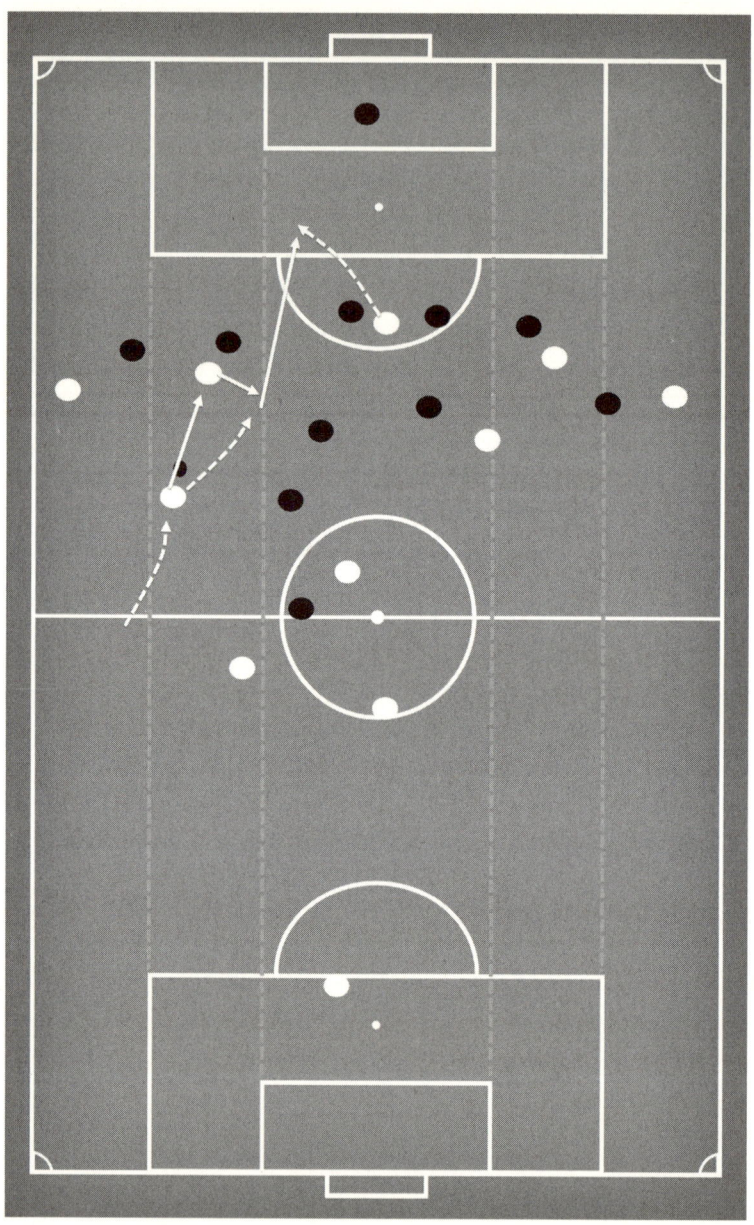

Figure 50

Dallas is an extremely intelligent player who has become central to the game plan used by Bielsa. He is very good at taking his position from the reference of not only the ball and the opposition but by the positioning of his own team-mates, especially the left-sided attacker. With Jack Harrison tending to stay wide when Leeds were in possession this tended to mean that Dallas would invert into the half-space where he could give an option centrally to aid the ball progression.

In *figure 50* we see an example from when Leeds faced Stoke City as Dallas affects the game from the half-space.

Dallas starts the movement in possession just inside his own half and with no immediate pressure on the ball he is able to drive into the half-space. As he advances forward he plays a pass to Mateusz Klich, who is ahead of the ball. Dallas continues his run and is then able to receive the ball back from Klich at a slightly more central angle. As he does so, he plays a vertical pass that breaks the defensive line and finds a diagonal movement from Patrick Bamford on the attacking line.

Straight away we see the concepts of isolation and verticality in action.

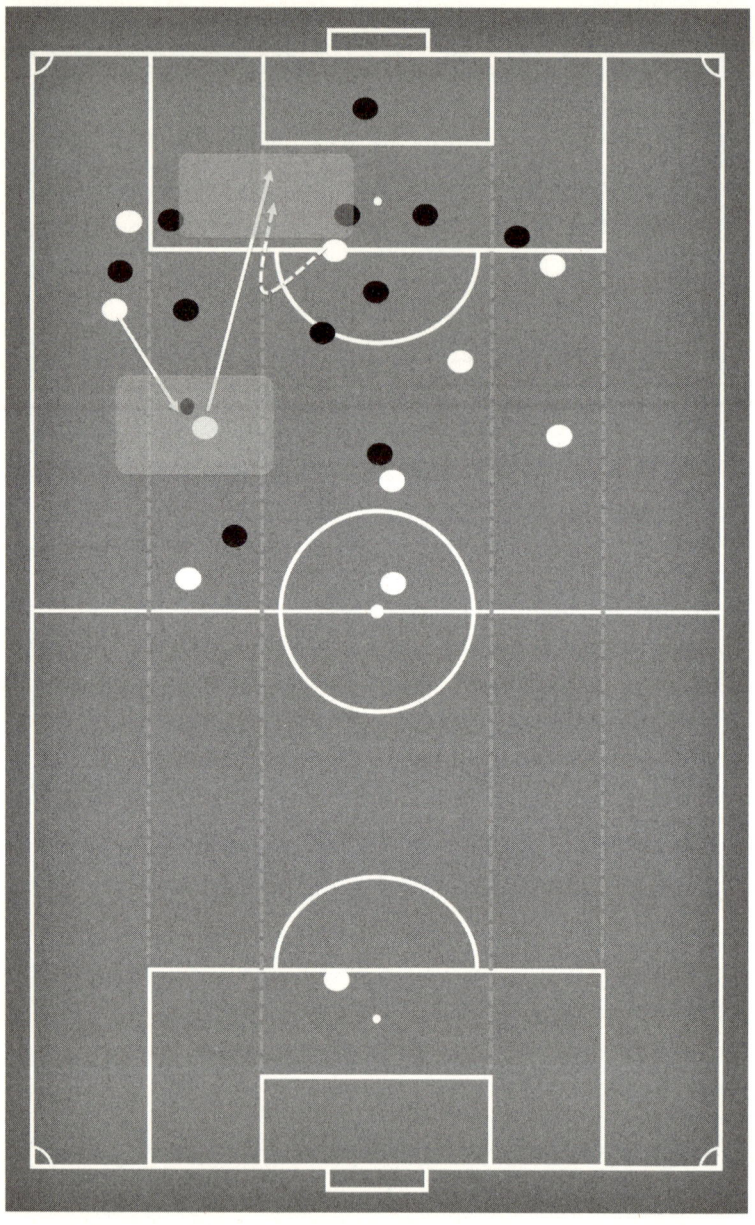

Figure 51

Next we again see an example of the way that Dallas was able to affect the game from his positioning in the half-space.

Figure 51 is taken from a match between Leeds and Luton Town.

This time Dallas is already positioned in the half-space as Leeds are firmly established in the attacking phase. The movement ahead of the ball from Klich as the 8 is key in this example as the Polish midfielder moves from the half-space out to the wide space, ahead even of Harrison. This rotational movement drags an opposition defender out of position.

Harrison takes possession of the ball and looks for the passing option in the half-space from Dallas. Because of the movement of Klich in the first instance, there is a vertical passing lane open from Dallas to Bamford. The English striker makes a movement back towards the ball before then spinning around and behind the defensive line. This movement allows Dallas to play vertically into this space.

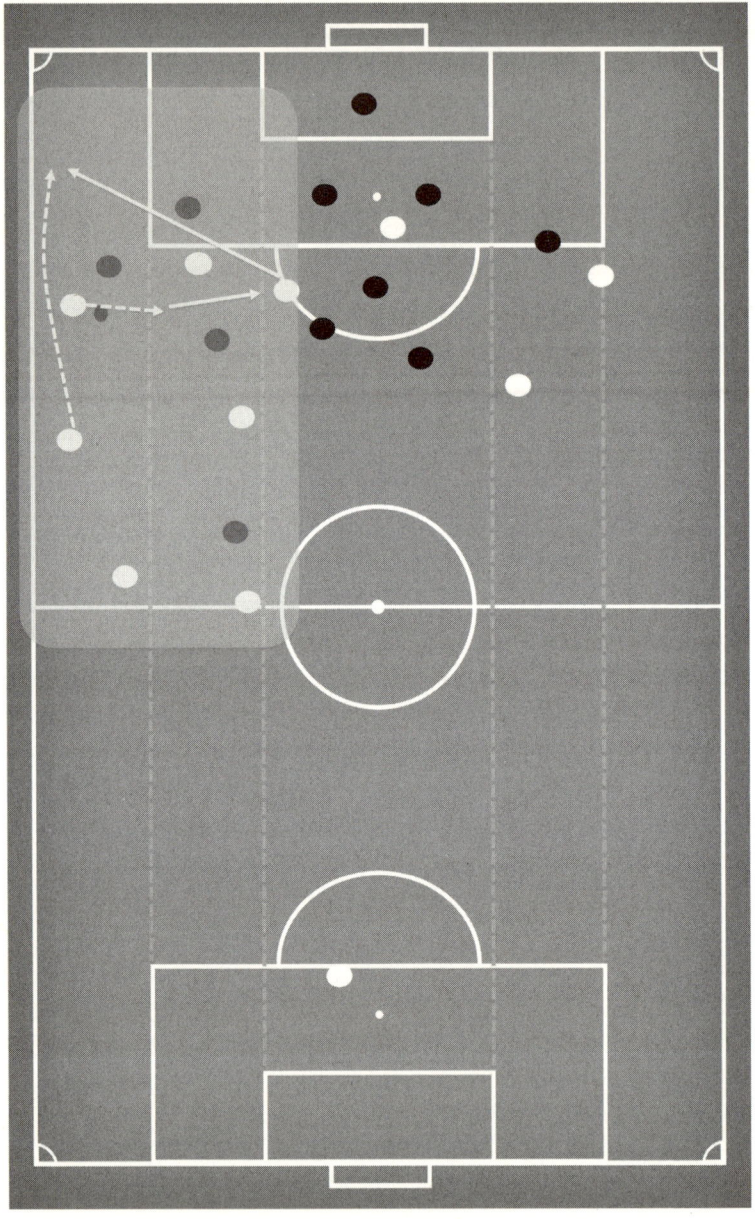

Figure 52

The intelligent movement from Dallas is one of the most important aspects of the Leeds build-up when the ball is on the left. We have already touched upon the fact that Leeds tended to attack down the right in previous chapters, but of course there were times when the ball was positioned out on the left.

We see an example of this in *figure 52* in a match between Leeds and Huddersfield Town.

This time the ball is positioned initially in the left channel with Harrison in possession. We see Dallas positioned behind the ball. The winger looks to drive inside in possession of the ball and as he does he rotates inside. This movement then triggers the opportunity for Dallas to move forward on to a higher line because Harrison has dragged a player inside with him. As Harrison moves inside he plays a combination pass with Pablo Hernandez and the Spaniard then makes an immediate pass out to the wide space where Dallas is moving vertically into space.

Once again the intelligence from Dallas to understand that his run should go outside and not inside is the key in this attacking movement.

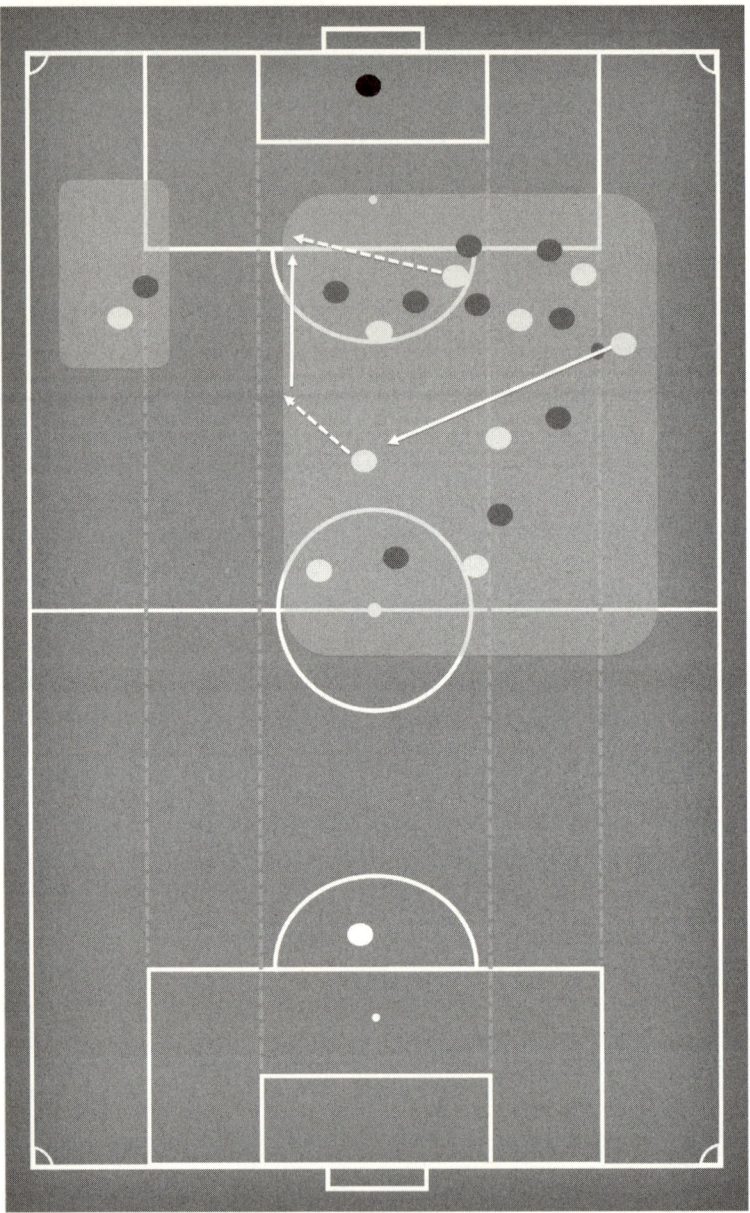

Figure 53

While this intelligence that Dallas displays on the pitch is interesting when the ball is on the left, it is also mirrored when Leeds are building their attacking play down the right.

We see this in action in *figure 53* in a match between Leeds and Bristol City.

Leeds are attacking on the right and we immediately see the concept of overloading one side and isolating a player on the other in action. Dallas is positioned in the central area at the left of the overloaded space and the man in possession uses the option of a pass to this space in order to quickly reset the ball.

Often in these circumstances you would expect to see Dallas then look to play to the isolated side of the field. Instead, he holds possession and drives towards the opposition area. This movement forces the opposition block to start to push forward and Bamford makes a mirrored movement as he moves laterally on the blind side of two defensive players. Dallas then has the quality to play the through pass into the path of Bamford in order to access the penalty area and create a goalscoring opportunity.

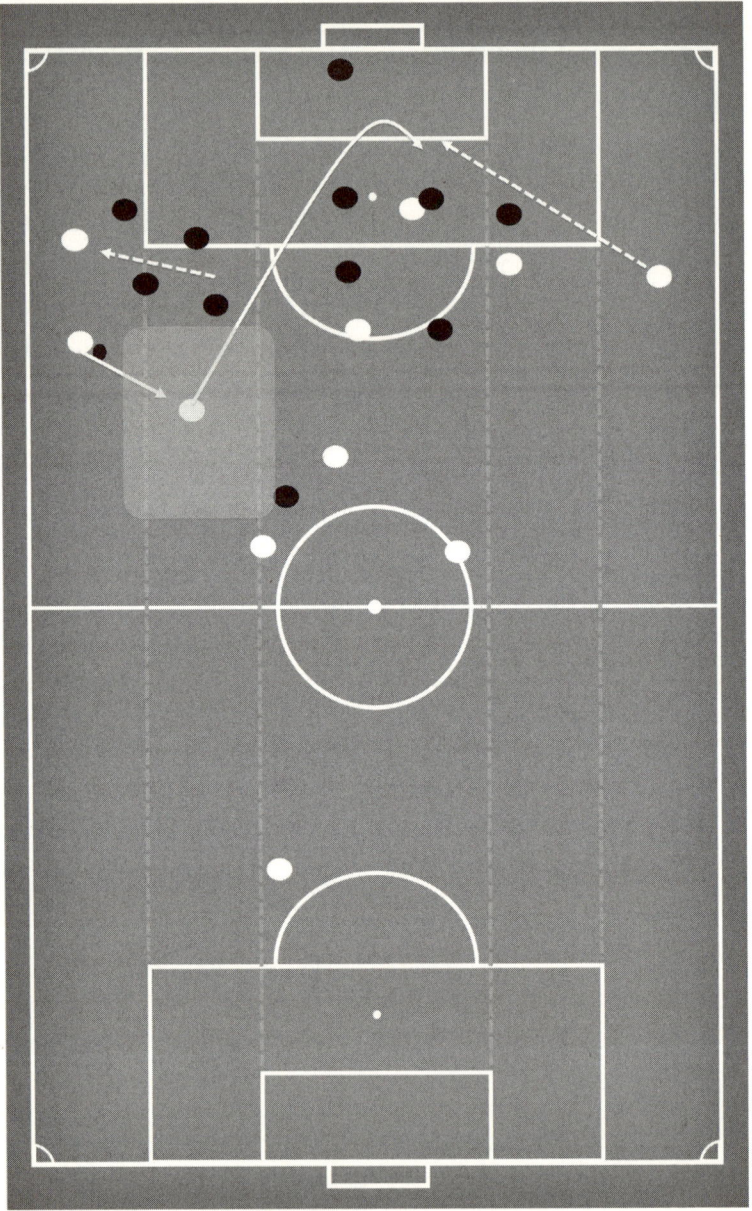

Figure 54

Now we are moving back to the kind of position and passing angles that we see from Dallas when he has possession of the ball in the half-space.

In *figure 54* we see an example of his passing range from this position in the match between Leeds and Brentford.

Once again Dallas is positioned in the half-space and ahead of him Klich has rotated out to the wide space. Harrison is in possession in this moment and he simply connects backwards towards Dallas who is able to accept the ball with no immediate pressure. There is an opportunity for Dallas to drive forward towards the penalty area but instead he pauses and as Luke Ayling makes a quick run from the opposite touchline we see Dallas play a perfectly weighted cross to find the run and create an immediate goalscoring opportunity.

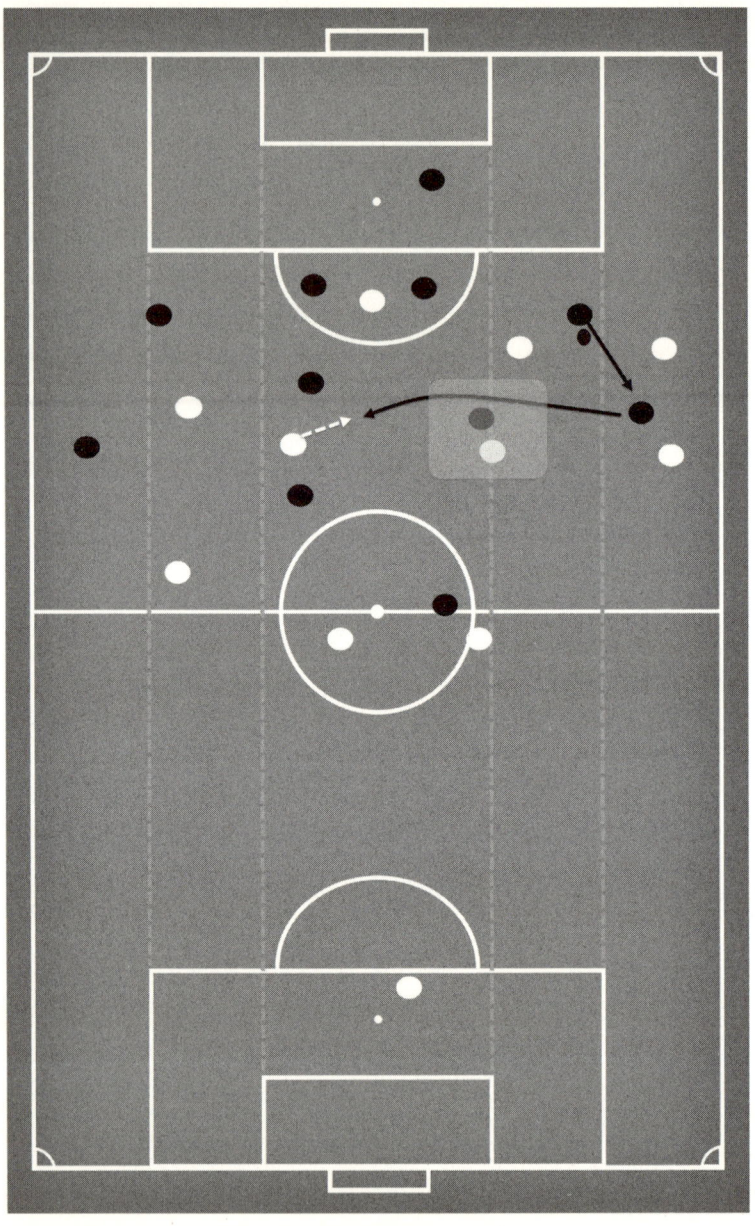

Figure 55

As well as being effective in possession of the ball, Dallas also thrives when being asked to recover possession in the opposition half of the field.

We see this in action in *figure 55* in a match between Leeds and Millwall. The opposition are looking to build their attack with a simple pass from the left-back to the left-sided midfielder. As that player takes possession though he plays a loose pass inside that misses the intended target. At this point Dallas is able to jump on the ball and win it back cleanly.

Chapter 10

Kalvin Phillips

For fans around the world, there is a holy grail in terms of the players they see represent their club every week. Every supporter wants to see a young homegrown player, who has been developed at the club's academy, make the breakthrough and become a first-team regular. For Leeds during the 2019/20 season that player was Kalvin Phillips.

Over the course of the season Phillips was firmly established as one of the best, if not the very best, 6s in the Championship with many starting to call for the young midfielder's inclusion in the senior England setup. International recognition did in fact come for Phillips but not until August, after Leeds had been promoted back to the Premier League. Before we break down the role that Phillips played in this Leeds team, however, we have to understand the route that he took as a young player and why playing as the 6 was never something that he had considered as he came through the ranks.

Not only is Phillips a product of the youth system at Leeds – he was also born in the city, on 2 December 1995. He has played his entire career at Leeds having joined the club as a 15-year-old in 2010 and has not even had so much as a short loan spell elsewhere. This is a player who is imbued with the same sense of passion about the game that flows through their passionate set of supporters. This is, in part, why the Leeds hierarchy were so calm when, after the 2018/19 season there were several big-money bids made for Phillips, with one confirmed suitor being the freshly promoted Premier League side Aston Villa. Despite speculation surrounding his future there was never any real risk of him making a move. Phillips was committed to the idea of helping his hometown side achieve promotion back to the Premier League and moreover he was committed to the challenge of working and learning under the guidance of Marcelo Bielsa.

As a young player, Phillips was naturally an 8 or a box-to-box midfielder with the ability to break into the opposition area and a reputation for possessing a fearsome shot at goal. It was in this position that Phillips impressed at youth level, and when he made the breakthrough at first-team level. Indeed, this was the role that he envisioned for himself when Bielsa arrived at Leeds. Those thoughts, however, were put to rest in the first meeting that Phillips had with his new coach when the players were surprised to find that Bielsa had already learnt not only their names but their strengths and weaknesses. There are few, if any, more detail-orientated coaches in world football than Bielsa and prior to signing the contract that saw him become the latest coach to try to take Leeds back to the Premier League the Argentinean had already carried out a full analysis of the squad.

In that first meeting as a group, Bielsa told Phillips that he saw the Englishman as a 6 or pivot as part of his tactical system. It speaks of the character of Phillips that he took this in his stride and accepted the challenge of learning the requirements of a new role. There are many young players who would have been less receptive to a new coach coming into a club and wanting to change not only their job but their specific position on the pitch. Phillips was immediately given specific training sessions designed to teach him the intricacies of the Bielsa game model. This was the point that the level of trust that Bielsa was placing in him really became evident. In all Bielsa's previous coaching jobs, the 6 was one of the key tactical positions both in possession and out of possession. It is fair to say that Phillips well and truly rose to the occasion.

In possession the 6 will always act as a single pivot and this is true whether the team structure is 4-1-4-1 or 3-3-1-3 with the 6 holding the centre of the pitch. Indeed, having pivots like the 6 and to a lesser extent the 9 is integral in the Leeds system because they act as constants with other players rotating in and out of space and moving high or low on to different lines in the attacking structure. Having the 6 always occupying a central space when Leeds are in possession ensures that the team always have a relatively fixed reference point around which they can build.

The 6 position is one of the most mentally intense in the Bielsa game model. It is not enough for the player in that position to understand his own role and the expectations of him; he has to understand how all of the other pieces of the tactical structure are supposed to work together. This allows him effectively to troubleshoot when the opposition transition from defence to attack. When you watch footage of Leeds in 2019/20 it really stands out that Phillips plays like someone who has far more experience than he actually does. He is often positioned in the right place at the right time to effectively prevent an attack before it becomes dangerous.

Indeed, when we apply data to the defensive discussion around Phillips his influence begins to become even more clear. In the league campaign Phillips accrued 3,489 minutes and in that time he averaged 9.05 defensive duels per 90 minutes with a success rate of 65.2 per cent. He also took part in an average of 3.51 aerial duels with 52.2 per cent proving successful. The aerial duel rates and the extent to which these were successful are especially interesting as this was an aspect of Phillips's game that Bielsa was especially keen that he worked on. It became a relatively common sight to see Phillips as the first line of defence as the opposition transitioned into the attack. He displayed excellent positional sense and reading of the play and tended to be positioned well in order to stop the attack in transition. He fits the role of a proactive midfield player almost perfectly and defends in an aggressive manner in that he would consistently step out to engage the ball carrier before they moved into a dangerous advanced position.

It is in the attacking phase, however, that we really see Phillips come into his own. First of all we have to acknowledge his intelligence in contributing to the build-up play. He excels in using the ball and the opposition structure as a reference point and ensuring that he is positioned in the right place to enable his team to build up from the first line. When the central defenders are being pressed Phillips shades back towards the ball but he also impressed with his adaptability when dropping back into the defensive line to form a chain of three with the two central defenders. What is especially notable is that he does not achieve this just by dropping on a vertical line to occupy the space between the central defenders, but by dropping into the position to the left of the two central defenders. This allowed the left-back to move to a higher line and enabled Leeds to progress the ball cleanly through the thirds and past the pressure.

In possession Phillips was a key ball progressor for Leeds. He averaged 48.13 passes per 90 minutes with a conversion rate of 84 per cent. As is often the case, however, passing rates on their own offer little by way of significance. Of those passes though we know that 13.96 of these were forward and that 7.53 per 90 were played into the final third. Now we are starting to build the picture of a midfield player who is important to the vertical style of play that Bielsa favours. All in all Phillips averaged 7.82 progressive passes per 90.

Now we will move on to looking at practical examples of the way that Phillips behaved in the Leeds structure in terms of the concepts and principles we have already covered.

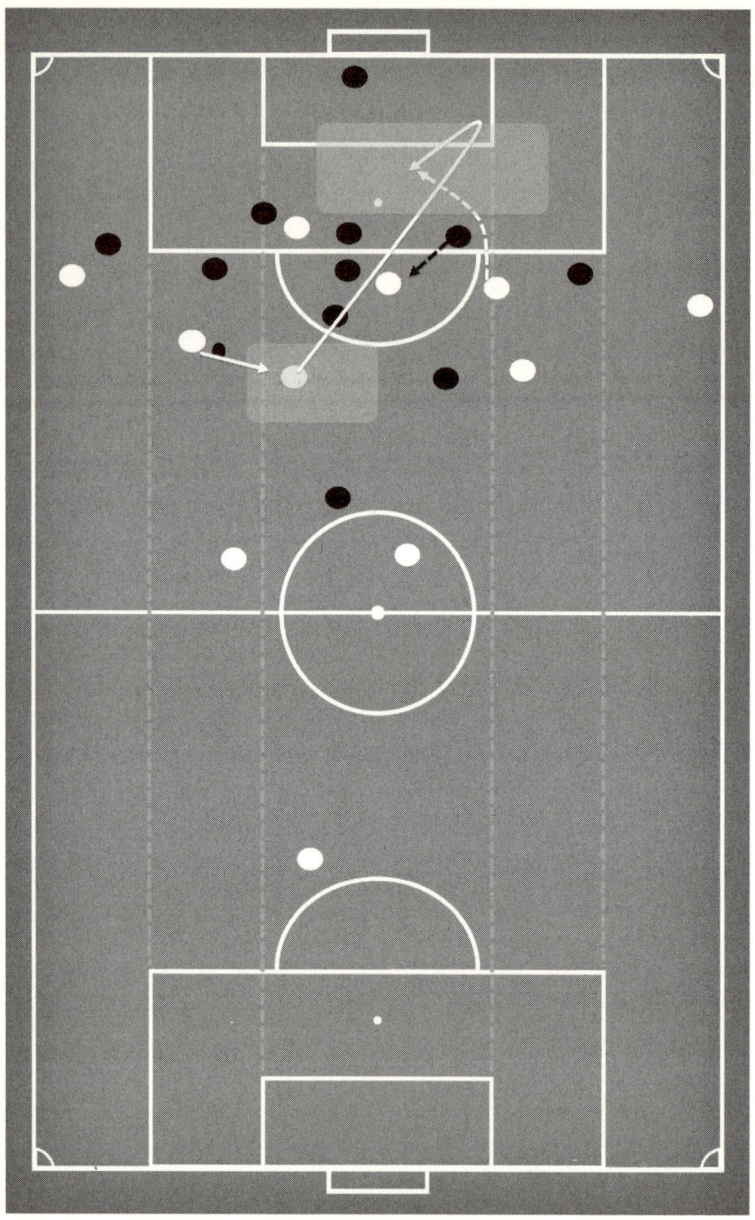

Figure 56

The first thing that we have to examine is the way that Phillips was able to control the game from the base of the attacking structure. From this position Phillips was a key ball progressor in terms of playing vertically and switching the angle of the attack. What is at times overlooked, however, is just how effective Phillips is when it comes to creating chances for his team-mates.

We see an example of this in *figure 56* from a match between Leeds and Cardiff City.

Leeds are in a period of continuous attack and as such they have forced the opposition defensive block back into a deep area. This means that Phillips, still operating as the 6 from a higher starting position, is able to collect possession in a much higher position.

As he gets the ball in space around 30 yards from goal there is an immediate reaction in the defensive line as the defender shown in the image moves to close down a ball near a Leeds player. This leaves the Leeds man at the back of the attacking structure free and as the opposition press and engage Phillips he shows the composure and vision to drop the ball over the defensive line into the penalty area for his free player to move on to.

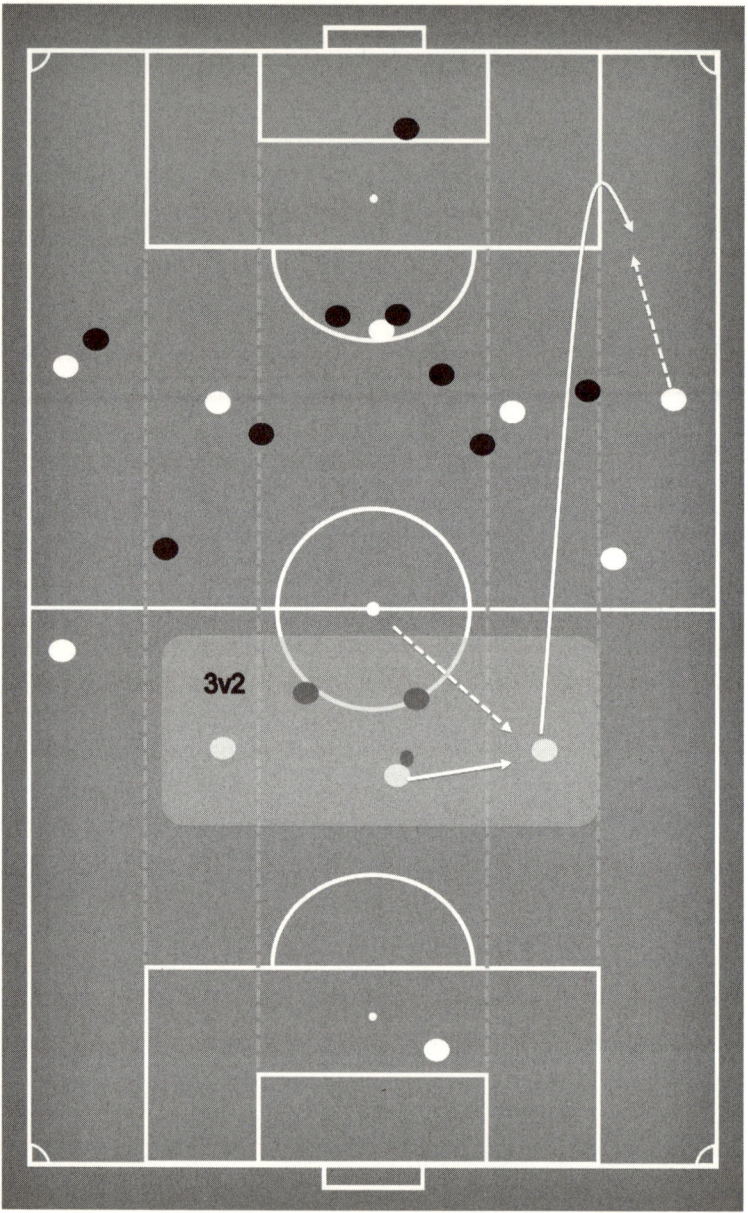

Figure 57

In an earlier chapter we talked about the way that Leeds under Bielsa would look to build from the back with a +1 principle of defenders compared to pressing opponents. When Leeds were in a 4-1-4-1 structure this meant that if two opposition players were pressing they needed to find a way to create numerical superiority. This was often achieved by Phillips dropping back into the defensive line to create a three.

We have an example of this in *figure 57* from a match against Sheffield Wednesday.

Here we see that Wednesday are pressing with two forwards against the two central defenders of Leeds. In order to facilitate the clean ball progression we see that Phillips drops back to the right-hand side and forms a back three with Ben White and Liam Cooper. This movement allows White to escape the press with a pass laterally to Phillips.

What is really impressive, though, is that when Phillips receives the ball here he still has the ability to play a vertical pass that releases the player behind the defensive line and into space.

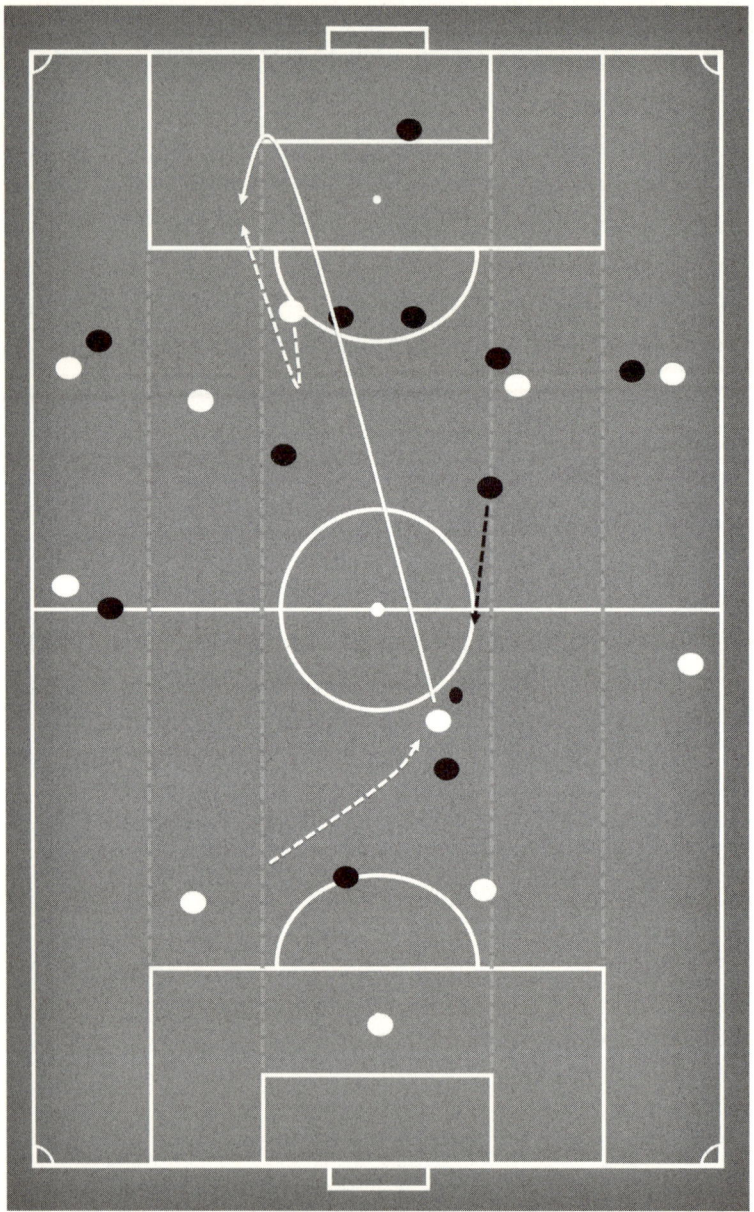

Figure 58

As well as being a great passer and progressor of the ball, with his passing range to access all areas of the field Phillips has the capacity to carry possession forward into advanced areas of the pitch when he has space to move into.

In *figure 58* we have shown an example of this from a match against Blackburn Rovers.

The play was stretched and Phillips picked up the ball close to his own penalty area. He has space to move in as the opposition midfield block is already deep and dropping deeper to cover the threat of the Leeds 8s who are still positioned high. Phillips is able to drive almost to the halfway line before an opposition midfielder moves to press and engage the ball. As the opposition player closes him down, however, we again see that Phillips has the composure and the ability to still pick out an accurate vertical pass that accesses space behind the defensive line.

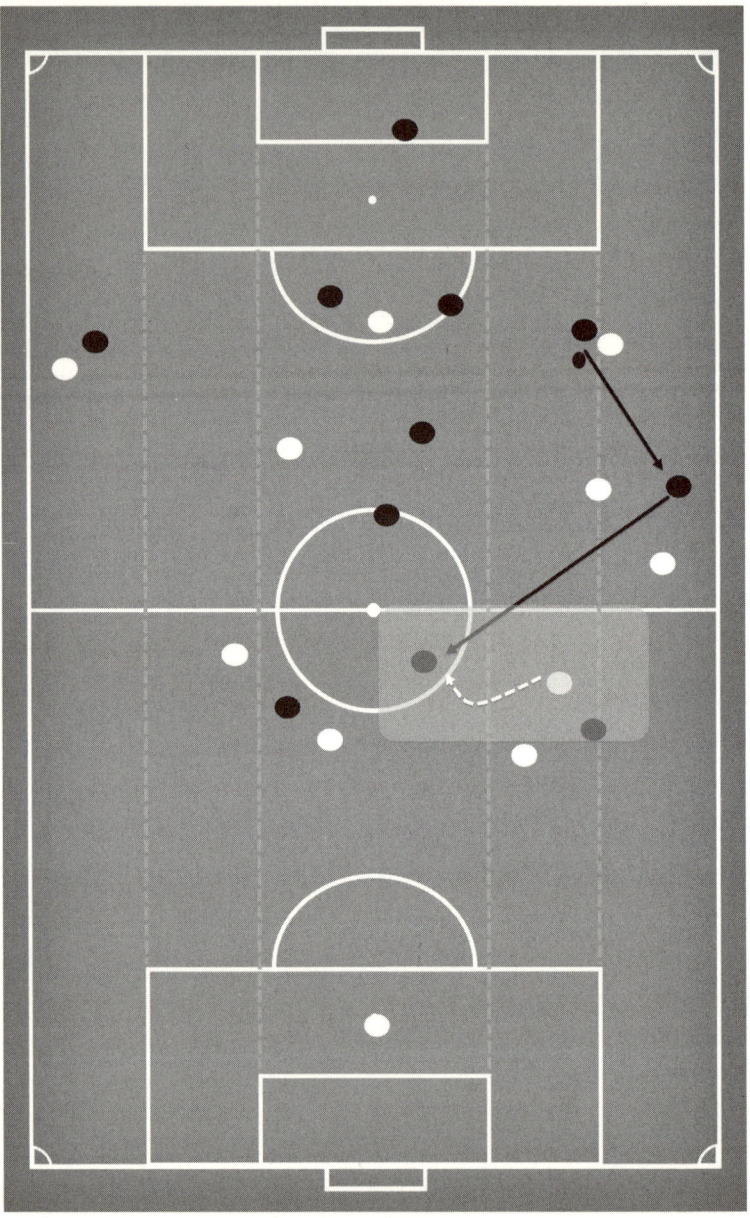

Figure 59

As well as being a key player in terms of the way that Leeds would look to build the attack and progress the ball, it is fair to say that Phillips was also important with his ability to engage the opposition attack with aggression and timing to win possession back.

In *figure 59* we see an example of the way that Phillips read the game and moved across to win the ball as quickly as possible as the opposition were looking to attack into the final third. This example was taken from a match against Swansea City.

The opposition, in the first instance, win the ball back close to their own area but they then combine quickly through a series of vertical passes. These passes eventually find a free player in the central area of the pitch and here Phillips is forced to adjust his defensive position to engage the ball. He does not reach the receiving player before the ball but he is still able to engage and win the ball back for his team.

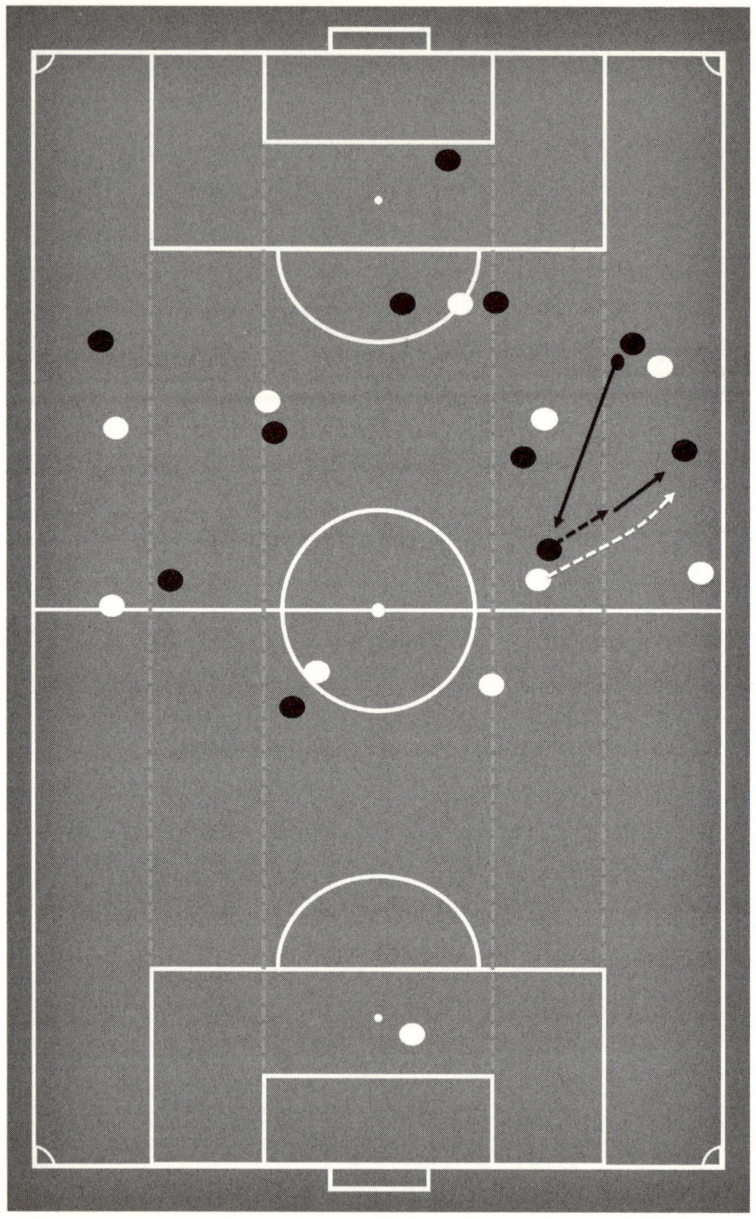

Figure 60

Phillips was also extremely effective when defending from behind the ball in moments where the opposition would be looking to probe in order to find an opening behind the Leeds defensive line. Often it would be Phillips who would be the player who drove the opposition back as he moved to engage and press the play from behind. This was key as when the opposition looked to attack quickly with direct passes there was always the chance that the high press from Leeds would be outplayed.

We have an example of this in *figure 60* from a match against Luton Town.

Luton play a pass forward to the player being covered by Phillips, who engages and presses quickly and the man who has received possession is forced to move back towards his own goal. He then tries to play the ball off to escape the press but Phillips simply continues his movement and quickly presses the new ball carrier. This effort and aggression pays off as Phillips is able to win the ball back and start an attacking transition for his team.

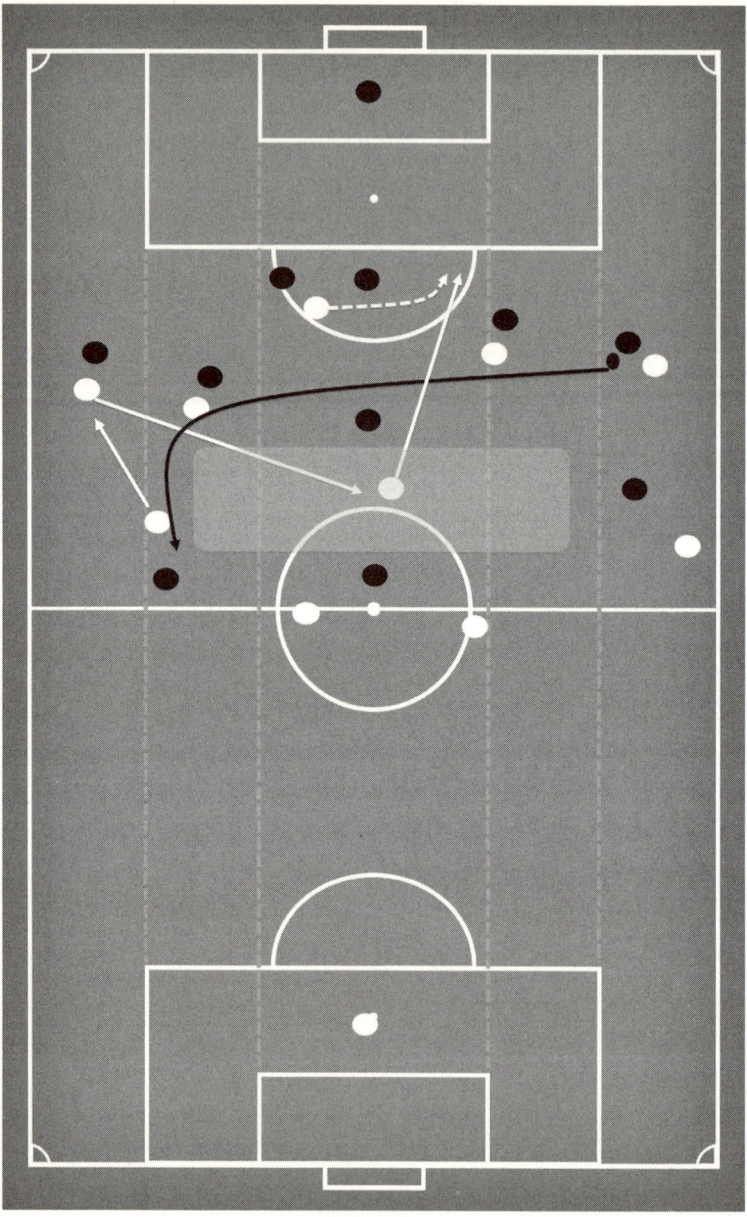

Figure 61

To finish our examination of the way that Phillips fits into the structure we will circle back to just how strong he is when taking possession and controlling the game in the centre of the pitch.

We see in *figure 61* in a match against QPR that the opposition initially have possession of the ball in their own half. The man with the ball looks to play a long and direct vertical pass to the far side of the pitch. This is poorly hit and Stuart Dallas is able to win the ball in an aerial duel before finding Jack Harrison on the left wing. From here the ball is then moved back inside to Phillips, who is holding a controlling position as the reference point in the central position.

Phillips immediately accepts possession of the ball and then calmly opens his body. He looks as though he is going to play the diagonal pass to the far side but this is a feint and instead he plays a perfectly weighted pass through the defensive line to find the run of the striker into the penalty area.

Chapter 11

Mateusz Klich

When you watched Leeds play on their way to promotion in 2019/20, one of the things that will have struck you the most is that the players on the pitch seem to perfectly match the style of play favoured by Marcelo Bielsa. It ran from the first-choice centre-back pairing of Ben White and Liam Cooper, who were composed in possession and resolute when defending, to the full-backs of Luke Ayling and Stuart Dallas who contributed effectively in every phase. This extended into the midfield where Kalvin Phillips, the 6, looked every bit the young star and Pablo Hernandez oozed class and experience as the attacks flowed through him.

There are, however, perhaps no players in that Leeds squad who quite encapsulate the playing philosophy of Bielsa quite as well as Mateusz Klich. Klich is the very definition of a modern multi-functional midfielder. If Phillips and Hernandez represent the brains of the team then Klich is their lungs.

In any moment of a game we can see Klich around the ball and in the defensive phase he will be either pressing and engaging the ball carrier or shutting down potential passing lanes. In the attacking phase he occupies space intelligently and often favours the half-spaces and even wide areas where he can lose his immediate marker before crashing back towards the ball in order to receive a pass. He offers technical ability and steel in equal measure and will often act as the player to commit the 'professional' foul at the right time in order to slow the opposition transition and allow his side to regroup in their defensive shape.

There is no doubt that Klich firmly established himself as a key player but when Bielsa arrived to take charge this outcome was by no means a foregone conclusion. Indeed, Klich had up to the point of Bielsa's appointment struggled to establish himself as a part of the first-team squad let alone as an automatic first choice. This should perhaps not come as a surprise, however, as Klich is something of a late bloomer in a football sense.

The early part of the career of the Polish midfielder was anything but straightforward as he impressed enough to earn a series of moves but never seemed to convince his coaches that he was deserving of a regular place in the team. He made his breakthrough at Cracovia in his homeland having impressed as a youth prospect. He then impressed in Polish football with his energetic style and in 2011 he made the move to Germany to sign for VfL Wolfsburg for a fee reported to be in the region of £1.5m. This represented the largest sale in Cracovia history and appeared to suggest that the German side regarded him as an important player for the future.

Instead, however, Klich was never given a chance to put together a run of matches in the first team and he found himself moving again, this time on loan to the Dutch side PEC Zwolle. At this level Klich began to come into his own and the Dutch side made the move permanent. It was at this point that Klich really started to settle into his game as he began to acclimatise to a higher level of competition than he had experienced while playing in Poland. Klich was an important part of the squad that qualified for the Europa League and also beat Ajax to win the Dutch Cup

Final. In a twist to the story, however, Wolfsburg had inserted a buy-back clause in the deal and they activated it in 2014 to bring Klich back to Germany.

In hindsight this decision seemed ill-conceived as Wolfsburg boasted a midfield unit that already had the mercurial Kevin De Bruyne as its focal point. Once again Klich found himself on the outside looking in and the successes of his time in Holland faded quickly. Again Klich found himself on the move although this time within Germany as he dropped down to the second tier to sign with Kaiserslautern. This, again, saw Klich start to at least play first-team football but in keeping with the nomadic nature of his career he was transferred, after just one full season. Once again Klich found himself going back across the border to Holland as this time he signed with FC Twente. At the Dutch club Klich managed 14 goal contributions (goals and assists) over the course of his only year there as he displayed again that he had the ability to be a force at this level.

These performances attracted the interest of Leeds and after just one season at FC Twente, Klich was transferred to the English club. You would be forgiven for believing that at this point our section in this chapter charting the nomadic journey of Klich had come to an end. You would, however, be wrong.

Klich only stayed in England for six months in the first instance as he struggled to impose himself on the first-team squad. Leeds' then-coach, Thomas Christiansen, appeared to have little trust in the Polish midfielder and at that point the club accepted a loan offer as Klich again moved to Holland and this time to FC Utrecht. Klich had been adamant when talking to the Leeds head of recruitment, Victor Orta, that he would be back and that this was not the end of his Leeds career.

He was correct in this statement and when, after six months, he returned to Leeds he encountered a new coach in the shape of Marcelo Bielsa.

Bielsa was, by all accounts, initially unsure of Klich. He appreciated his technical work and his physical profile but Bielsa was not sure which position suited his skillset the most. Indeed, there are reports that at one stage Bielsa considered using Klich as a central defender and while his aggressive nature and passing ability mean that he could have played in this role, we know with hindsight that something would have been lost in the midfield. So instead Klich became one of the two free 8s in the system and over the course of the 2019/20 season he was one of the most impressive performers across the English leagues.

From a physical point of view, Klich is listed at 183cm or 6ft and he has a powerful build. He uses his size well, especially when dropping back towards the ball in order to receive the vertical passes that are played into central spaces. He covers ground well and angles his runs intelligently to either access pockets of space in the attacking phase or cut off potential passing lanes for the opposition in the defensive phase.

Klich was a force of nature in this Leeds team. In the attacking phase he effectively contributed in almost every facet of the game. Across the league season he played 4,035 minutes and averaged 48.07 passes per 90 minutes with a completion rate of 81.4 per cent. Again these passing numbers and completion ratios are relatively unhelpful in isolation. When we consider that Klich was not typically used as a part of the ball progression phase and that he would tend to receive the ball in space around the final third, these numbers become more interesting. Klich also produced several other interesting metrics during the promotion-winning season, averaging 1.65 shots, 2.7 crosses and 1.45 dribbles each game. Klich was a player who seemed capable of doing anything as he drove his team forward.

In the defensive phase Klich was equally as important as he averaged 7.16 defensive duels and 5.78 ball recoveries in the opposition half. Klich was one of the most positionally aware players in the team and although his first role was to drop into a more compact defensive position and pick up his man in the man-marking system, he was also often the player who would react in the first instance when a pressing trigger was activated. Klich would move to press the ball while also keeping his man in his cover shadow. This meant that while Klich was engaging as an important part of the press he was also still ensuring that the opposition could not escape the press by accessing the pass to his man.

Now we will move on to view some in-game examples of the way that Klich played for Leeds across 2019/20.

Mural of Marcelo Bielsa painted on the side of a building near Hyde Park in Leeds.

Leeds players and Bielsa celebrate with the Championship trophy at Elland Road on 22 July 2020.

A typical pose from Marcelo Bielsa as he analyses the match between Leeds and Swansea City on 12 July 2020.

Bielsa watches the match between Leeds and Bristol City while sitting on his now infamous bucket. 15 February 2020.

Patrick Bamford finds space to strike at goal in the match between Leeds and Barnsley, Elland Road, 16 July 2020.

Jack Harrison and Luke Ayling celebrate with Mateusz Klich after the Polish midfielder scores. Blackburn Rovers vs Leeds, Ewood Park, 4 July 2020

Leeds players celebrate the opening goal in a match against Leeds and Huddersfield Town, Elland Road, 7 March 2020.

Jack Harrison attacking with intent in the match between Hull City and Leeds at the KCOM Stadium. 29 February 2020

Bielsa gives his team instructions in their match against Middlesbrough at the Riverside Stadium. 26 February 2020

Helder Costa keeping possession of the ball in tight spaces. From the match between Nottingham Forest and Leeds at the City Ground, 8 February 2020

Marcelo Bielsa and his coaching staff surveying the action in the match between QPR and Leeds at the Kiyan Prince Foundation Stadium. 18 January 2020.

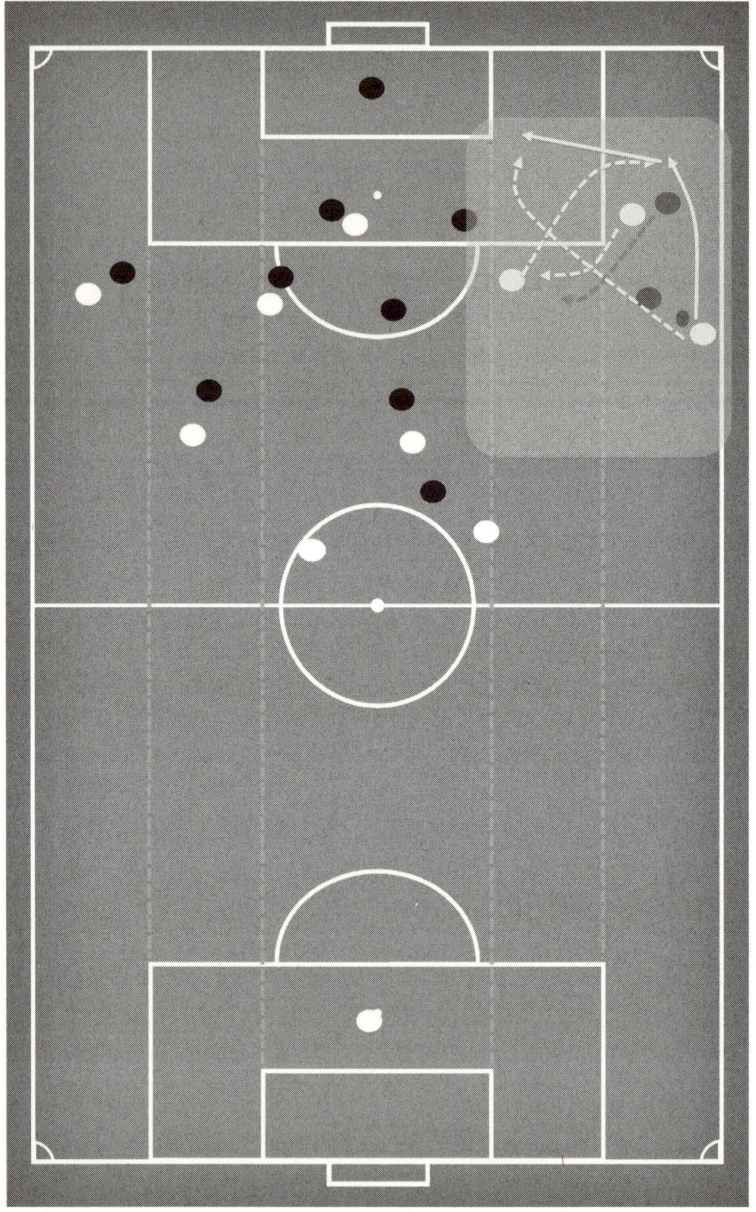

Figure 62

The first thing that really stood out as we saw Klich in this promotion season was the intelligence of his movement and how hard he worked to find space in the attacking phase. Klich was often a player in constant motion as he rotated in and out of space in order to move opposition players out of position or create opportunities for his team to play into an advanced platform from where they could attack.

The first example in this chapter can be seen in *figure 62* and is taken from a match against Barnsley.

The play is concentrated out in the wide-right areas where Leeds are trying to find their way past a difficult defensive block from Barnsley. Luke Ayling is in possession of the ball and the first rotation sees Helder Costa move inside from the advanced position that he was initially occupying. This creates a pocket of space that Klich immediately looks to move into and occupy. This movement from the Polish midfielder is the key to unlocking the defence and Ayling finds the pass to access this space.

The movement also sees Klich receive and shield the ball and allow Ayling to make an inverted run into the space that Klich had left. Klich then finds the angle to feed Ayling as he moves into the area.

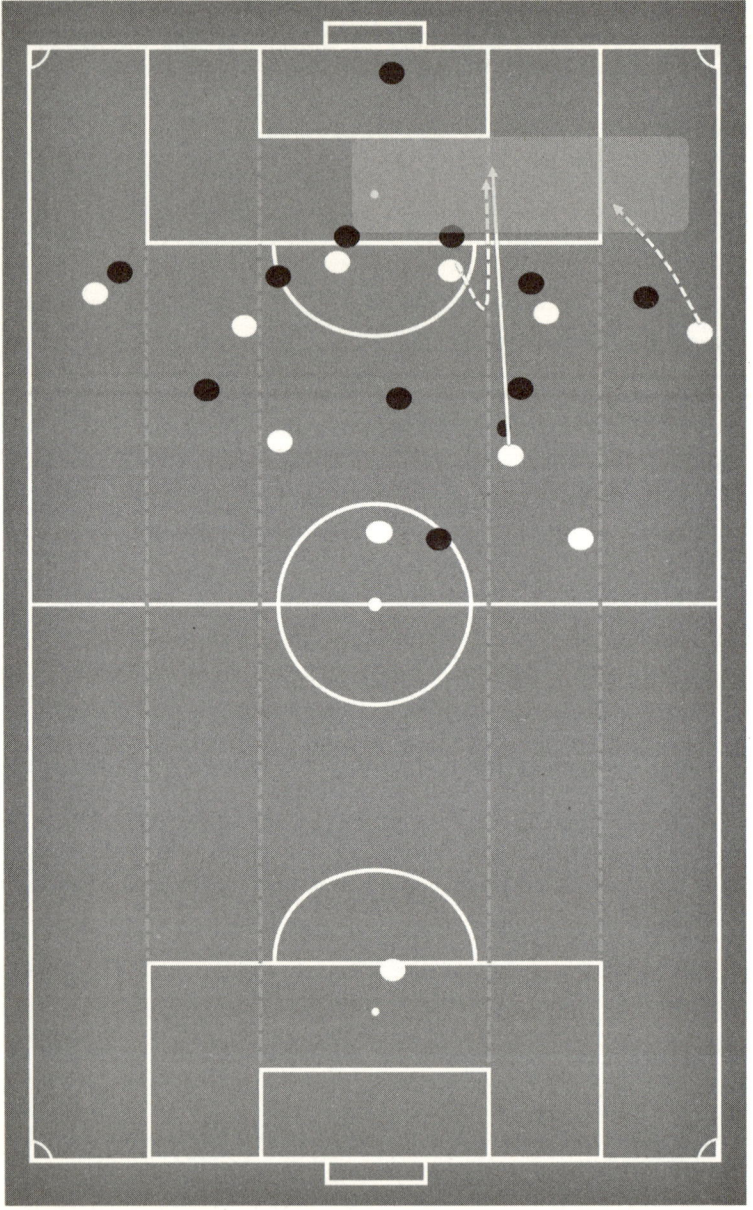

Figure 63

Klich has a clear tendency to move into high positions on the field as early as possible and from these he can receive vertical passes and link in with attacking team-mates to break down defensive blocks. He can also, however, rotate backwards in order to aid the ball progression as once again this speaks to his work rate and constant motion to find space in which he can receive the pass from a team-mate.

In *figure 63* we see an example of this movement from that same match against Barnsley. Again, Barnsley are aggressive defensively and they work hard in order to prevent Leeds from finding an easy route through to goal.

Klich has dropped to the base of the midfield to get possession of the ball. Costa makes a run from the wide right position and Klich initially shapes to play this pass to the winger. Instead, he shifts his weight and plays a driven ball through the vertical passing option into the penalty area.

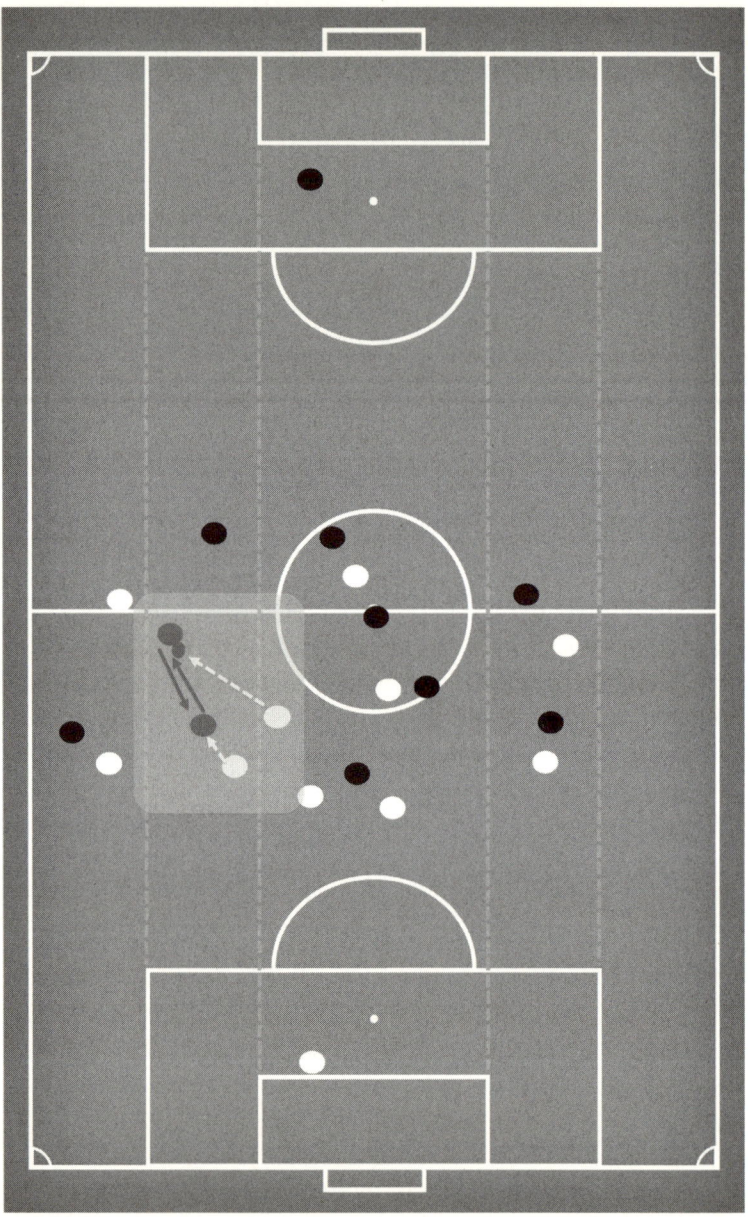

Figure 64

The work rate from Klich also, naturally, extends to the defensive phase as he works hard across the width of the midfield to deny the opposition the chance to play through. He perfectly understood the expectations that Bielsa had on his defending players and executed what the coach wanted almost perfectly.

In *figure 64* we see an example of this defensive work from a match against Cardiff City as the opposition tried to break through in the Leeds half of the pitch.

The man initially in possession for the opposition looks to play a pass forward to link with a slightly more advanced team-mate but that player is pressed from behind aggressively by Kalvin Phillips as he prevents the man receiving the ball from turning. This pressure forces the ball back to the initial Cardiff player in our example. It is at this point that Klich then moves aggressively forward to press the ball played back towards the Cardiff goal. Klich quickly covers the gap and engages the ball before winning it and starting an attacking transition for his team.

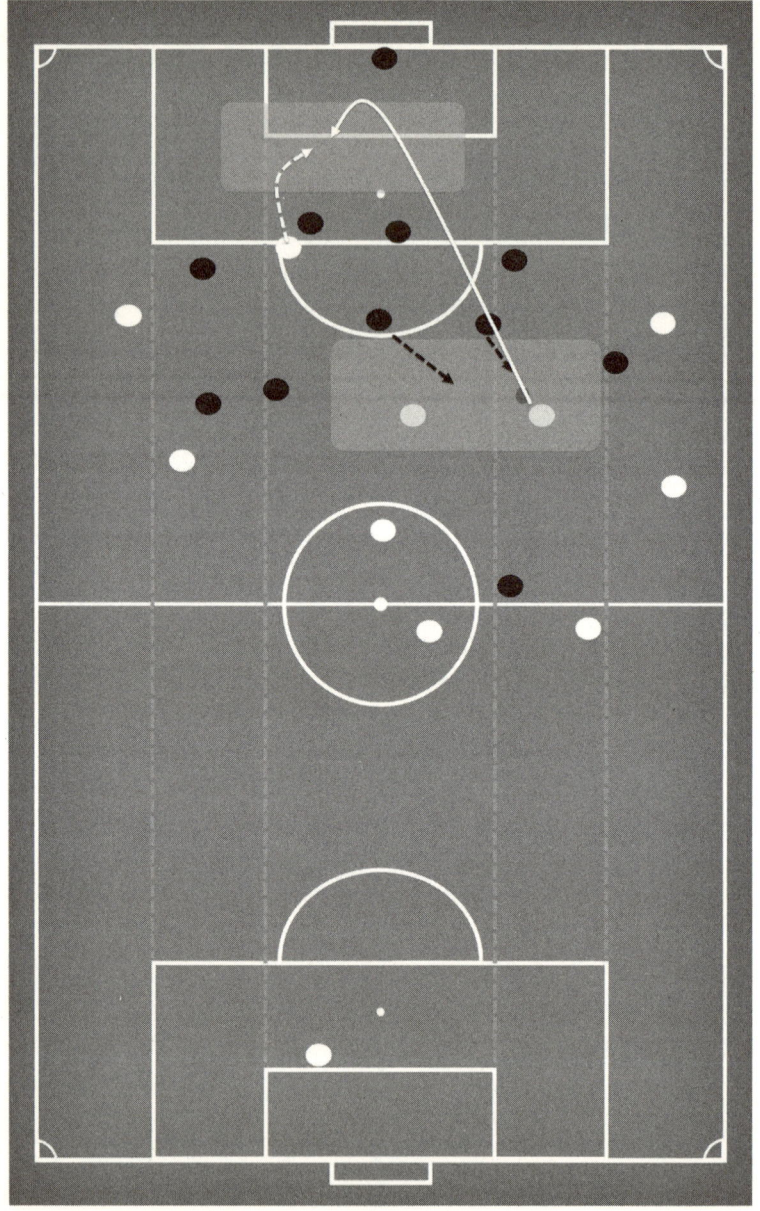

Figure 65

A big part of why Klich was so important for Bielsa was that he was incredibly press-resistant. He was a safe option for team-mates to access wherever he was on the pitch and he tended to use his technical ability to control the ball and his physical strength to shield possession and prevent the opposition from easily winning the ball back.

This press-resistance extends to Klich remaining calm as he is facing an opponent moving to press the ball. His decision-making was consistently strong.

In *figure 65* we see this press-resistance and decision-making in action in a match against Hull City.

Klich ended up taking possession of the ball in the right half-space and he had the defensive block ahead of him with no obvious vertical passing option. As soon as Klich received the ball the opposition started to move to engage and press him in an attempt to either win possession back or force Leeds to go backwards.

Klich, however, was able to remain calm before clipping a perfect pass to the back of the penalty area. This accessed a run made on the blind side of the defender by Patrick Bamford and the striker ended up scoring in this situation with a flying header as he directed the ball back across the goalkeeper.

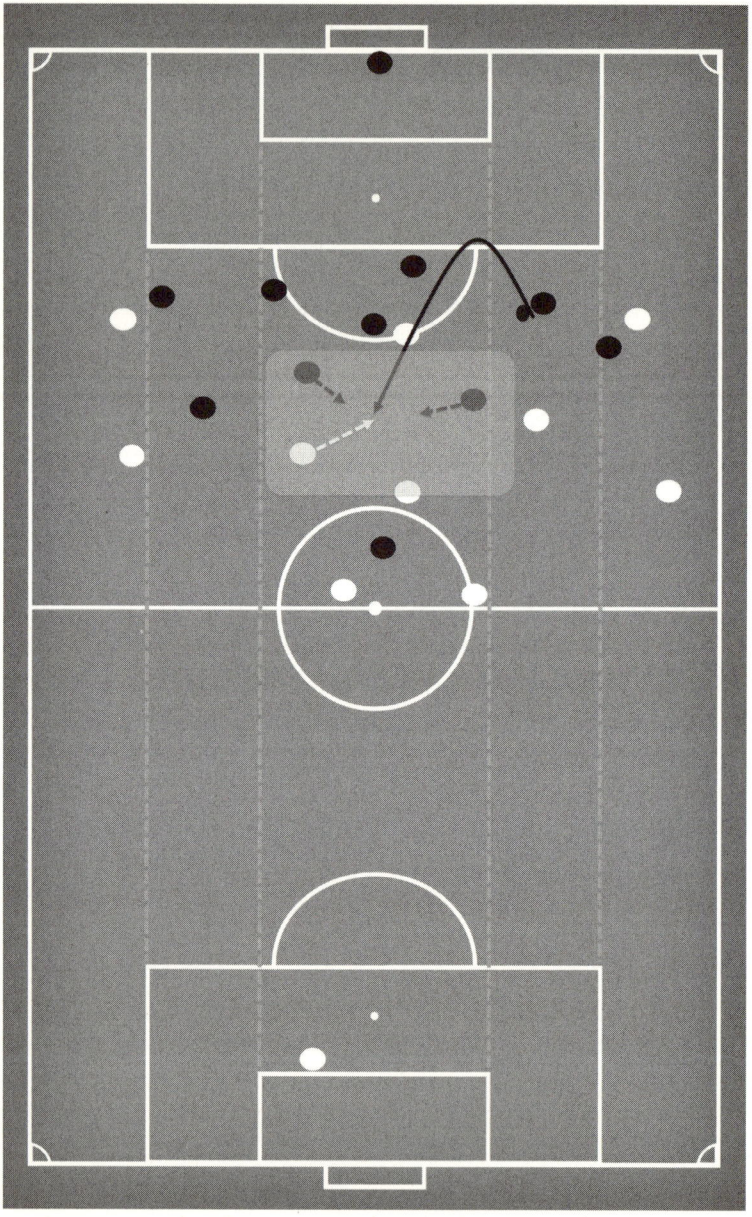

Figure 66

Now we will circle back to the aggressive way that Klich was able to consistently win the ball back from the opposition before then driving forward to create opportunities for his team-mates.

This example can be shown in *figure 66* in a match against Reading. Initially the ball was played long and high by Leeds but the pass was inaccurate and a Reading player was able to head the ball way comfortably. This clearing header landed in a central position and two Reading players moved to pick up possession. However, Klich was also close to the ball and despite being outnumbered two v one he was still able to win the duel and regain possession.

From this position Klich then drove forward with the ball before managing to shoot at goal from the edge of the penalty area.

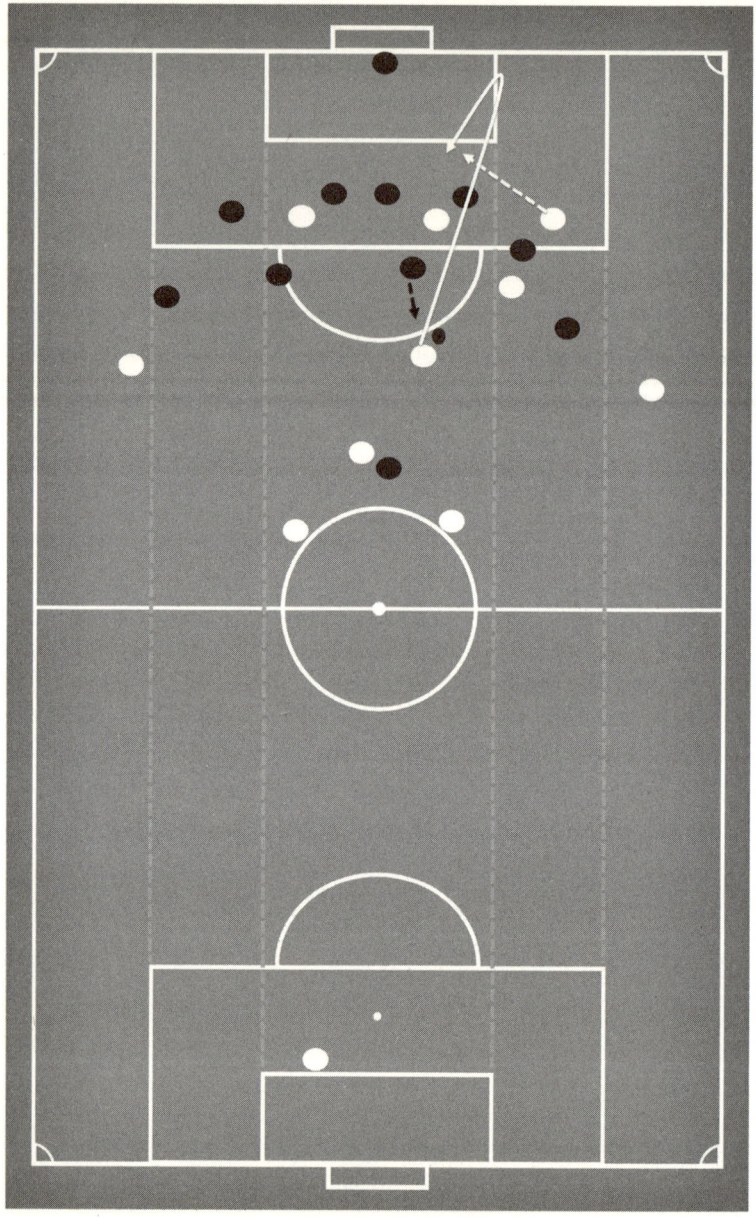

Figure 67

We will finish this chapter again looking at the way that Klich was able to maintain his composure and create goalscoring opportunities for team-mates in the face of pressure from the opposition, this time in a match against Nottingham Forest.

We see this final example in *figure 67.*

Leeds are again in a well-established attacking position and they have therefore pushed the Forest defence back into a deeper block. Again, we see that Klich has rotated around to a position at the edge of the penalty box and he is free to receive possession in this area. When he does accept the ball here, however, the opposition again look to push out to engage and press him.

This time Klich waits for Helder Costa, from the right of the penalty area, to make an intelligent run behind the defensive line. He is able to time the pass perfectly to play the Portuguese winger in on goal.

Chapter 12
Pablo Hernandez

For all of the emphasis that Marcelo Bielsa places on a highly systemised approach to building his tactical system, he also finds space for creative players who add an extra dimension to their side in the attacking phase. Indeed, while there are specific instructions in the initial build-up phase in terms of occupation of space and rotations and in the defensive phase with the man-to-man-marking system and -1 pressing concept, the same is not true when the ball travels into the final third.

When Leeds are able to occupy these advanced areas Bielsa is happy to allow his team to become more creative in their attempts to then progress the ball forward. There are still some specific concepts which are adhered to, such as rotations and overloads in the wide spaces, but players are encouraged to get creative in terms of their passing angles and movements around the edge of the penalty area.

It is in these positions that their most experienced player really comes to life as Pablo Hernandez provides the creative spark and ingenuity that helps Leeds to break down even the most stubborn of defensive blocks. The career trajectory of Hernandez is exceptionally interesting, as is the way that the midfielder has altered his role and the way that he plays on the pitch in order to adapt as advancing age has affected his physical abilities. When Bielsa first arrived at Elland Road prior to the 2018/19 season the Spaniard was earmarked for the right-midfield slot. This was, after all, a position that Hernandez had occupied throughout his career.

As the campaign wore on, however, Hernandez began to drift inside into the half-spaces and central areas more often. By the time that 2019/20 came around, Hernandez was still playing on the right but only in name. Eventually Bielsa moved Hernandez inside to occupy the 8 position alongside Mateusz Klich and he never looked back. For an experienced player who had been capped at senior level by the Spanish national team to be willing to adapt his game to meet the needs of his coach and team speaks volumes about the character of Hernandez.

Hernandez is a product of the prolific Valencia academy and broke into their first team in 2005/06, but his profile was as a fast right-footed winger with good feet. At this point in football's history it was still normal practice for wide players to be played on the same side of the field as their dominant foot. If Hernandez was to come through today the chances are that he would develop as a left-winger with a tendency to invert in possession and attack into the half-spaces. Instead, he was seen as a more creative player with the speed to create separation from defenders and then access the penalty area through crosses or dribbles from the wide spaces. Although Hernandez was highly rated at the club he was initially included in a deal that saw another player move from Getafe to Valencia. After just one season with Getafe, however, Hernandez returned to Valencia, who exercised a buy-back option and then signed him to a long-term deal.

Hernandez ended up staying at Valencia until the start of the 2012/13 season when he made a surprising move to join Swansea City in the English Premier League. Hernandez was a big hit with the Welsh side and fitted well with their ball-playing philosophy. In the end Hernandez only played 57 matches for the Swans over his time at the club but it was during this spell that he made a connection that would eventually lead him to Elland Road and to Bielsa.

We will speak more of this connection and its importance later on in this chapter.

When Hernandez decided to leave Swansea there was a general sense that he was starting to decline. A player who had relied so heavily on his ability to use his pace in order to beat defenders was now struggling to have a significant impact in the attacking phase. He was still technically excellent but many onlookers at the time felt that the Spaniard's lack of physicality was starting to become an issue.

At this time the growth market in terms of ageing international players who were looking to ease off before starting to think about retiring was not in China or the US but in the Middle East. In 2014, Hernandez agreed to a move to the Qatari league to join Al-Arabi. At this point in his career it would have been easy for him to start to slow down and collect what was undoubtedly a significant wage. But he would not be finished with the English game.

Hernandez was 31 years old when he received a text message from his fellow Spaniard and former Swansea coach Pep Clotet. The text was not part of a recruitment mission but rather an expression of excitement from one football obsessive to another. Clotet had just agreed a deal to join the coaching staff of Gary Monk at Leeds and he was excited at the prospect of joining a club with such a storied history in the game. Clotet was surprised, then, when Hernandez responded that were he needed he would be happy to come back to England. The deal from that point was concluded relatively early and Leeds had secured the signing of a truly mercurial talent.

By this point Hernandez had adapted and learnt to play through his head and not his legs. His positioning was always intelligent and he excelled at finding pockets of space in the opposition defensive structure in which he could receive the ball. When he did get possession he showed soft feet and the ability to retain possession under all kinds of pressure. In short he showed signs of being a player who would be key for Bielsa and his specific tactical identity. Indeed, Bielsa has been quoted as saying that Hernandez was responsible for 'making the game fluid' and not the tactical system itself. This is testament to the ability of the Spaniard to control and dictate the tempo of the Leeds attacking play as they moved the ball into the final third.

Over the course of 2019/20 we saw Hernandez play 2,685 minutes but his ability in those was absolutely key in Leeds winning the title and gaining promotion to the Premier League. Over the course of the whole season he managed 20 goal contributions with nine goals and 11 assists. He averaged 62.01 passes per 90 minutes with a 76.7 per cent success rate. Of these passes, though, 22.26 were played forward and 11.2 were into the final third. When playing as one of the 8s Hernandez developed more of a tendency to be the player who dropped back into the midfield block to receive the vertical passes from the 6 or from the central defender. He was often the man who would receive centrally before then looking to play the next vertical, or progressive pass. By the end of the season Hernandez was averaging 13.88 progressive passes per match.

Hernandez was also a force in and around the penalty box, which shows when we break down his individual metrics in this area. He ended the season averaging 2.45 shots and 3.52 dribbles but he also helped his team to access the penalty area. Here he was making 2.75 crosses and 5.8 passes to the box with 1.11 key passes. In the attacking phase the contribution from Hernandez was nothing less than superb.

There is no better word to describe the Spaniard other than mercurial. Now, though, we will turn our attention to looking at some practical examples of the performance of Hernandez throughout 2019/20.

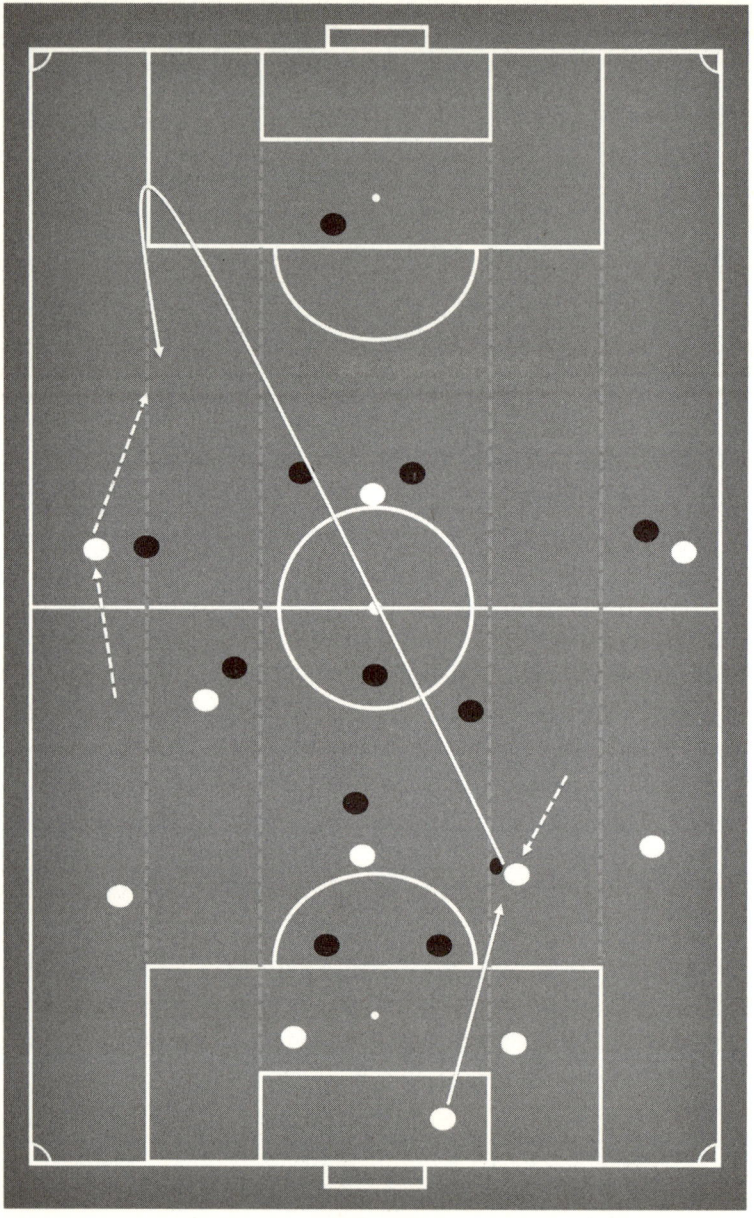

Figure 68

We will start with an example of the vision and urgency that Hernandez brings to this Leeds side. This is shown in *figure 68* and is taken from a match between Leeds and Derby County.

Neither team has set their structure yet as Leeds are about to take a goal kick. There are several players who are slowly moving into their positions ready for the ball to restart. Hernandez, though, is not resting back. Instead he makes a movement quickly back towards the penalty area and demands the ball from the goalkeeper. Wisely the goalkeeper uses this option and fires a vertical pass to the Spaniard.

This is where we truly see the vision of Hernandez as he receives the ball and immediately touches it out of his feet and plays a direct pass diagonally over the top of the opposition defensive line. This pass finds Jack Harrison running into space and immediately, thanks to Hernandez, Leeds have moved from their own half to create a goalscoring opportunity.

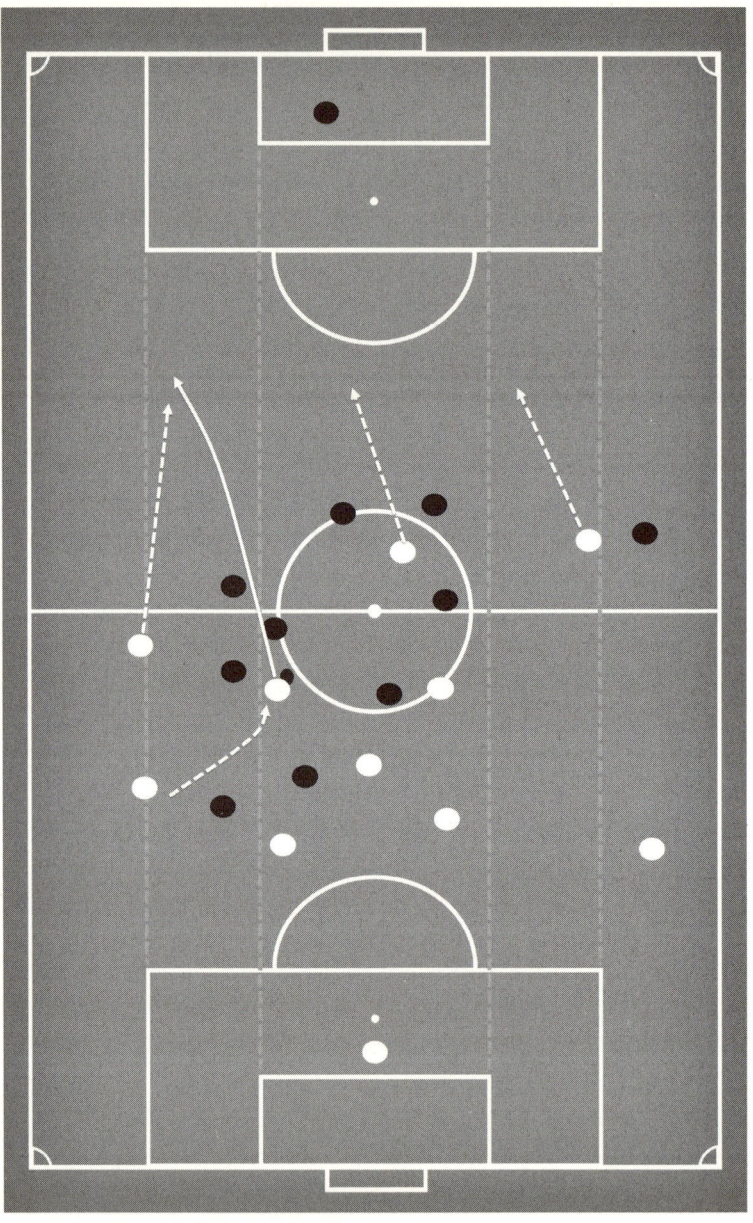

Figure 69

Our next example is taken from the same match and again shows Hernandez taking possession of the ball in a deep area and then progressing the play for his team.

We see this example in *figure 69.*

This time Hernandez has dropped back on the left-hand side of the pitch and collected possession deep inside his own half. He immediately looks to drive his side forward as Bielsa would want him to. He rides a challenge from an opponent and looks as though he is going to go to ground but keeps his balance. From this point on his body is open towards the right side and there are two runners looking to access space behind the defensive line. The easy pass would be to try to play one of these two players into space.

Instead, Hernandez fakes that pass and forces the defenders to shade that way before reversing the ball back to the left where there is a third runner moving from a deeper position.

This is verticality in action from Hernandez.

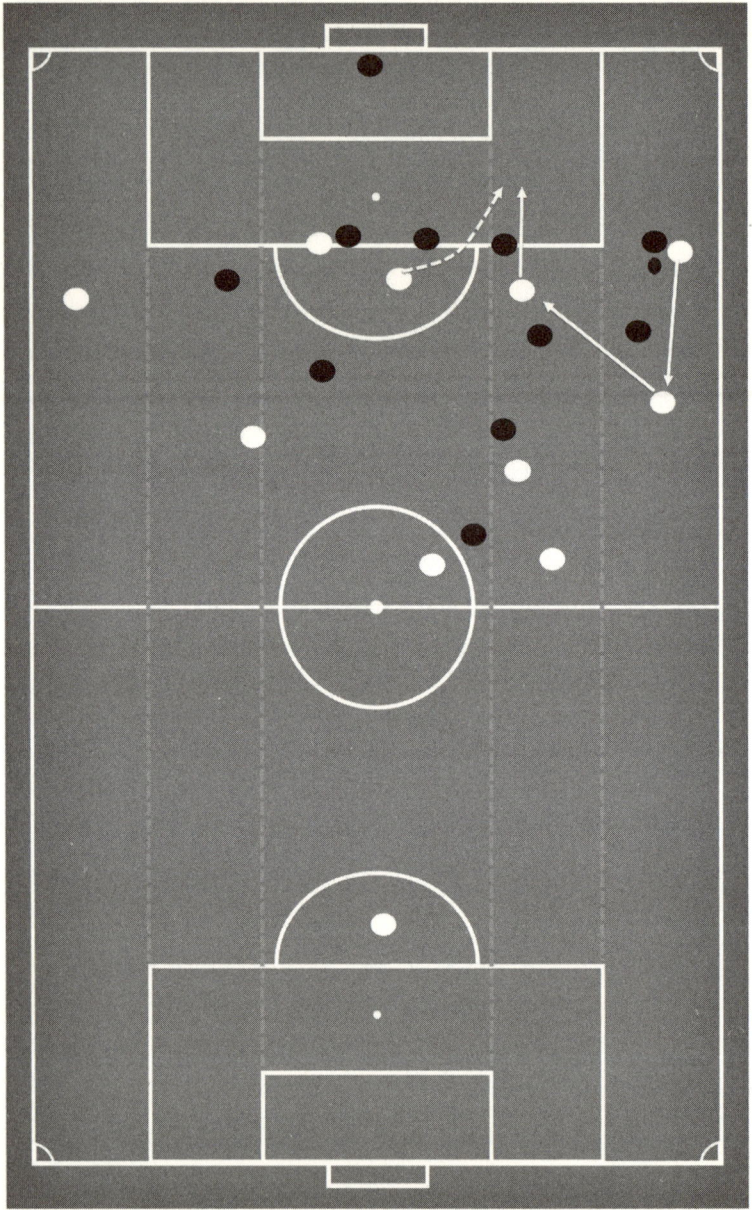

Figure 70

Hernandez is an extremely intelligent footballer who seems to have an ability to always be in space when receiving the ball. This, when combined with soft feet and excellent technical skills, make him an extremely difficult opponent to face. This is especially true in the final third and around the penalty area where his ability to bring others into play and navigate tight spaces is fantastic.

We see an example of this in *figure 70* from the match against Hull City.

Here we see Hernandez positioned in the half-space just on the edge of the penalty area. The ball is set back from Helder Costa to Luke Ayling before a diagonal through ball accesses the feet of Hernandez on the edge of the area. As the Spaniard takes possession of the ball he is quickly pressured but Mateusz Klich, the second 8, is making a run to overload that section of the pitch and connect with his colleague.

The key to this next moment is in the disguise in the pass from Hernandez who shows no sign of even seeing Klich before he plays the pass through and accesses the run on the defender's blind side.

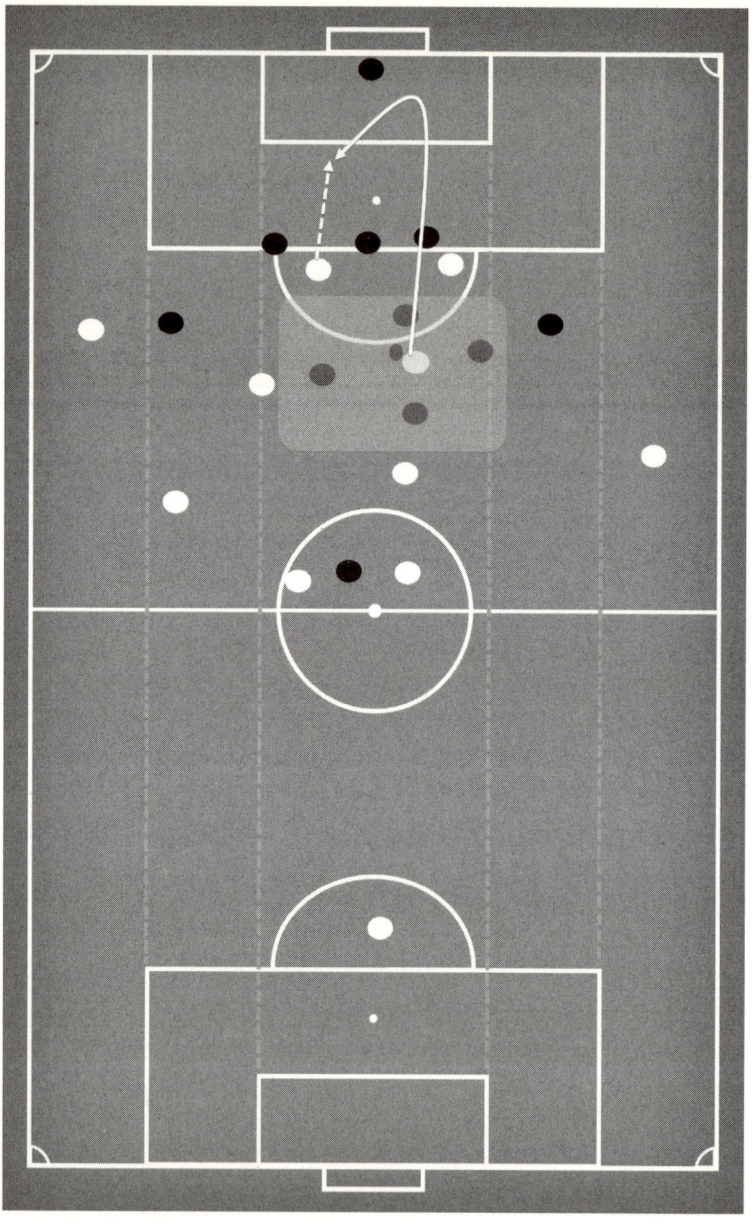

Figure 71

Regularly throughout the course of the season we would see Hernandez seem to have time as he collected possession of the ball, even when surrounded by opposition players and put under pressure. He rarely seemed rushed and had the ability to slow the game down before making the right choice almost every time.

This ability, to almost pause in possession, was such an interesting contrast to the all-action, high-tempo style of many of the other Leeds players.

We see an example in *figure 71* of a moment in the match between Leeds and Blackburn Rovers.

You can see that as Hernandez takes possession centrally, he is in a pocket of space but surrounded by four defensive players. It is this ability to create separation in these moments that really makes Hernandez stand out. He is able to wait now, despite pressure closing in, for the run of the more advanced player to happen. As this takes place Hernandez simply lifts the pass perfectly over into space to create a goalscoring opportunity for his team.

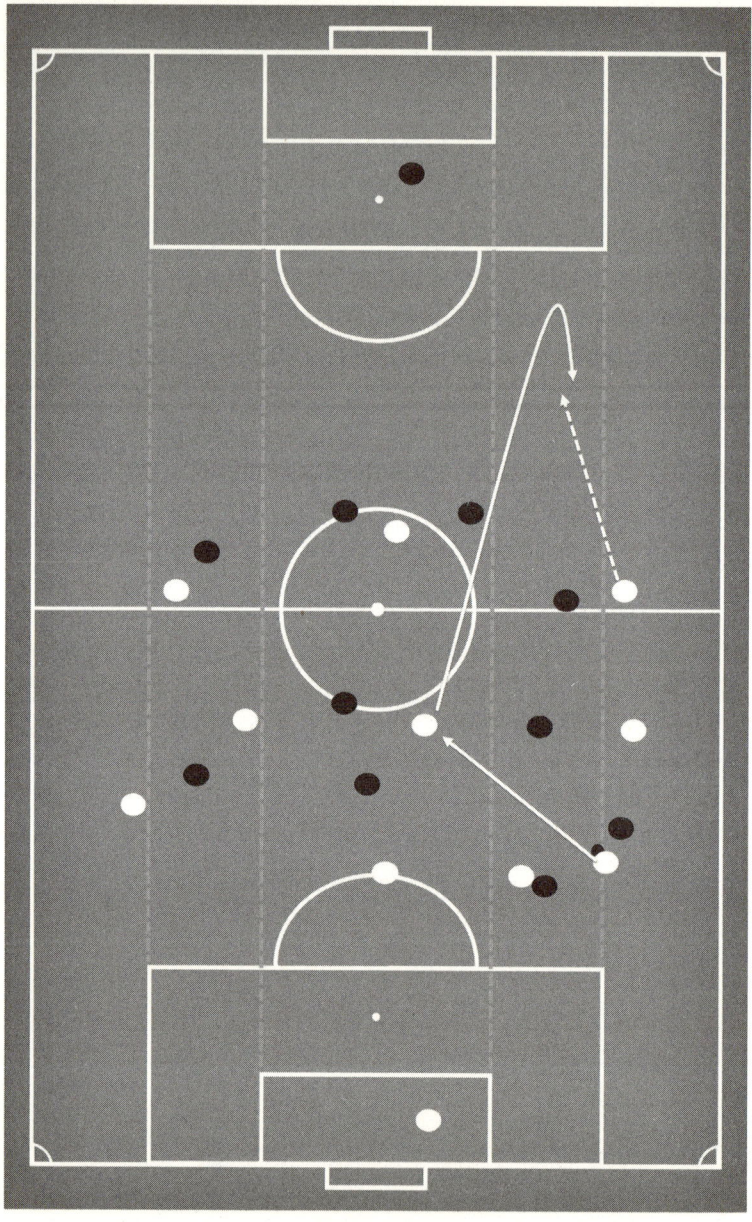

Figure 72

One of my own favourite things about watching Hernandez play is that at any moment he has the ability to either slow the game down or speed it up. He lulls the opposition into slowing down and then quickly ups the tempo again to take advantage of space in the opposition defensive structure.

In *figure 72* we see this in action in the match between Leeds and Fulham.

Again Hernandez is dropping back in to provide an option to progress the ball from the defensive third into the middle third of the pitch. Ayling has just won the ball back for Leeds and he quickly plays the diagonal pass into the feet of the Spaniard. Here we could either see Hernandez slow things down or increase the speed and this uncertainty makes it difficult for the opposition to deal with the threat.

This time Hernandez has dropped back towards the ball and demanded possession because he understands that there is a vertical passing option that will outplay the defensive line of the opposition. He does not even take a touch and instead immediately plays the ball over the top and outside for the wide forward to gather and run through on goal. Once again this shows the value of verticality.

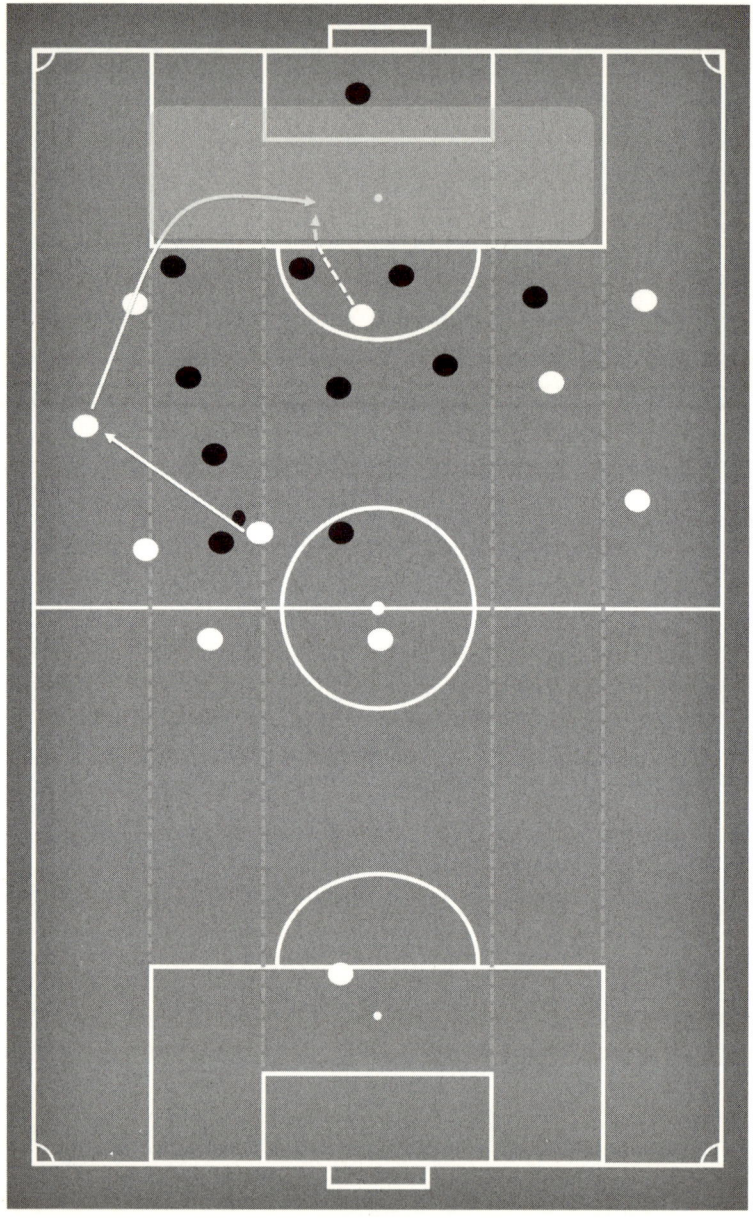

Figure 73

Our last example of Hernandez in action comes from the same match.

This illustration, shown in *figure 73*, shows how versatile the Spaniard is from a positional point of view and again shows how the rotational movements for attacking players, in the established attacking phase, worked for Leeds under Bielsa.

This time Hernandez eventually picks up possession on the left-hand corner of the penalty area. As the ball is built up from Phillips to Harrison we see that Hernandez has made a movement out to the left-hand side ahead of the ball. The pass is played into him as, yet again, he has created separation from the defensive players.

Once more the key in his pass is the disguise that he shows on the ball. He is shaping to play a deep ball across to the right but instead curls it across in the last moment to access the run of the attacking player moving into the penalty area.

Chapter 13
Jack Harrison

Over the course of the 2019/20 season and as Leeds faced more opponents who were intent on sitting in deep and compact defensive blocks, it became increasingly clear that having an outlet retaining a wide position was key, especially on the left. It was evident that with the preference of Leeds to attack down the right, where Pablo Hernandez, Helder Costa and Luke Ayling formed a capable and exciting triangle, there was a need for balance and width on the opposite side.

This width was invariably created by a player who Leeds do not even own in Jack Harrison, on loan from Manchester City. The promotion-winning season was actually Harrison's second year on loan at Elland Road and with Marcelo Bielsa's team back in the Premier League he would then join again for a third spell.

The case of Harrison is especially interesting because it is the only clear example that we have of the relationship of Bielsa and his Manchester City counterpart Pep Guardiola. The two coaches share a deep respect for one another and before Guardiola took up his first role he flew to Argentina to spend time with and learn from Bielsa. It is clear that there is a large degree of trust from the powers that be at Manchester City that Harrison will be well coached by Bielsa and will be developed in a tactical system that has some similarities to that used at the Etihad.

In his first season, Harrison perhaps flattered to deceive to an extent. He looked good in isolated patches but too often he was passive in possession and was not looking to attack and engage the opposition defensive block often enough. Instead he would often slow the play down with a lateral or backwards pass or look to attack the full-back before being easily dispossessed. Indeed, if you asked many Leeds fans during the 2018/19 season who they preferred on the left then the answer would most likely have been Jack Clarke as the youngster developed a reputation for coming off of the bench and changing the game in a positive manner. This lack of consistency in the final ball is not something that is especially unusual for a young attacking player but it was an area of his game that Harrison would have to develop if he were to get to the next level.

After agreeing to again join for 2019/20, it became clear very quickly that Harrison had indeed been working on his game. He spent time during pre-season in the gym working on his ability to act with explosive movements that would allow him to better gain an advantage over his direct opponent. More than this, though, he has also talked openly about spending time watching footage of himself with a view to understanding where his strengths and weaknesses lay.

When the new season started we saw a much sharper version of Harrison take to the field. He no longer had the same hesitancy in possession and although he was still raw in terms of the quality of his final delivery, when he had the ball in wide areas it was now possible to watch Harrison and see a wide player who would fit the tactical system of Bielsa and of course Guardiola.

That Harrison has the drive to improve himself should come as no surprise to those who know and understand the route that he has taken to get to this stage of his career. Indeed, while there are several players within this Leeds team that have been down nomadic or indirect routes, there are few who have travelled the same path as Harrison.

As a young player he was part of the youth system at Manchester United and although the coaches there liked him and rated his abilities he never really stood out from the middle of the crowd. It was at this point that Harrison's career took a decisive turn and he owes that to his mother. In a lot of cases, when parents get involved it can be for the wrong reasons. In this case, however, Harrison's mother was sharp enough to realise that although her son showed promise there was no indication that the coaching staff were prepared to push him in order to maximise his potential.

Instead, the family started to research alternative options and they came across a private school in Massachusetts, USA. Harrison made the move abroad and immediately benefited from the exposure that is afforded to high-school athletes in the United States. He won individual awards and was announced as the youngest player eligible for the 2016 MLS Superdraft. He was drafted as the number-one pick by the Chicago Fire but, due to the nature of American sports, he was almost immediately traded to New York City. This saw Harrison added to the City Football Group, a multi-club ownership group with Manchester City as the cornerstone. This move therefore put him into the development system of Manchester City.

Harrison almost immediately, and despite his young age, earned a place as a first-team regular at New York City. He spent nearly two years at the club and impressed hugely with his direct, attacking style of play. There were many clubs who were starting to show an interest in bringing him back over the Atlantic from New York and as such it came as no surprise that Manchester City exercised an option to take Harrison to the Etihad. It was a circuitous route for a player to go through only to end up in not just the same country but the same city as he had previously left.

Although Harrison had impressed with his performances in the MLS there was still a need for him to get used to the pace and the expectations of professional football in England. As such he was sent out on loan almost immediately to Middlesbrough in the Championship. In the end, over the course of half a season, Harrison only made four first-team appearances.

The following season Harrison made the first of his loan moves to Leeds and he started to show genuine signs that he would be able to adapt to Premier League football. And in 2019/20 he really made a genuine step in his development as a regular first-team player at the Championship level.

Over the course of that season Harrison played 4,050 minutes of first-team football as he firmly established himself as the first-choice player on the left. He had 6.04 dribbles, although only with a 55.5 per cent success rate, and 4.04 touches in the opposition penalty area per match. This starts to show the profile of a player who had a tendency to be isolated on the far side of the field away from where the attacks were generally built up. He finished the season with 14 goal contributions in the league (six goals and eight assists) but it was his positional sense and willingness to be tactically disciplined that convinced Bielsa of his importance to the project.

His crossing was still relatively inaccurate as he attempted 4.6 crosses per 90 with a 27.5 per cent success rate, but this tends to be on par with all but the very best crossers of the ball in world football. He also averaged 4.78 passes to the penalty area, in keeping with the fact that Leeds looked to combine in tight spaces in and around the penalty area.

Now, once again, we will move on to consider the practical examples of the way that Harrison contributed to this game model.

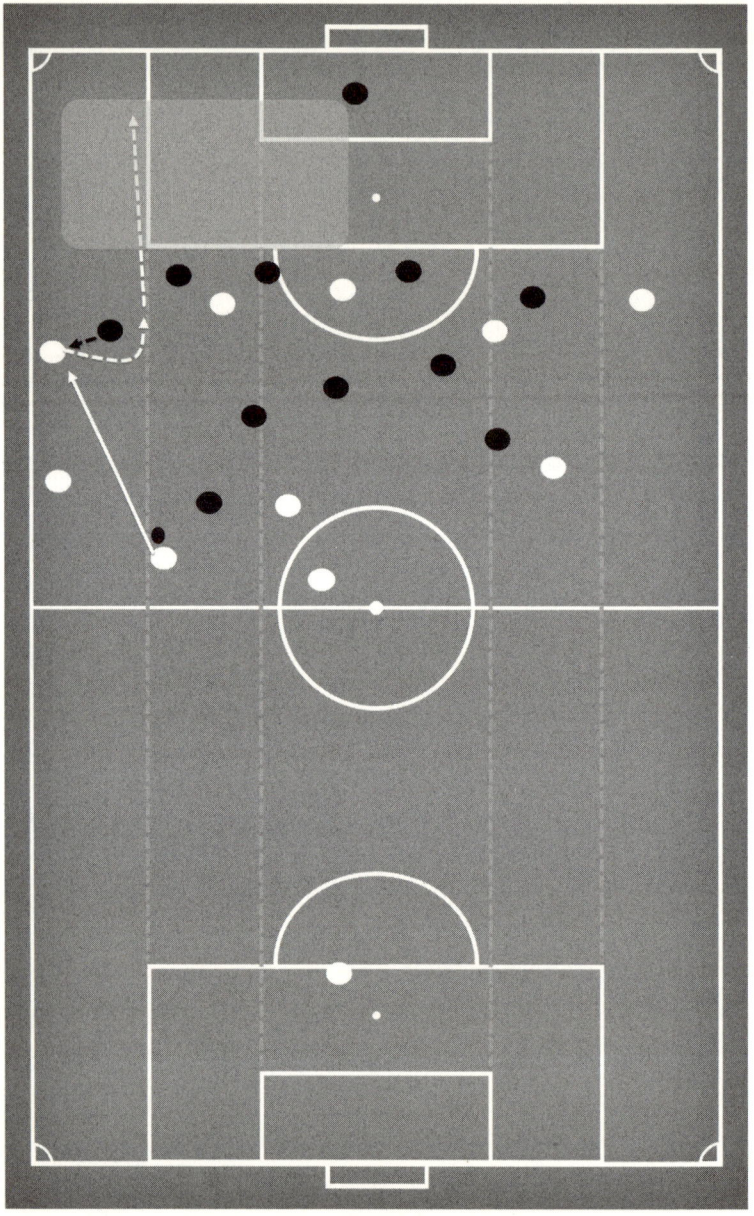

Figure 74

There can be no doubt that one of Harrison's biggest strengths is his ability and willingness to carry the ball at the opposition. While he has the technical capacity to play in combination with team-mates when he has close connections to them, he is more regularly isolated wide with defensive players.

Harrison has a direct style and whenever he takes possession, whether wide or in the half-space, his first instinct is to engage the first defender and move the ball towards goal.

In *figure 74* we see an example of this in action in the match between Leeds and Barnsley.

Liam Cooper is initially in possession in the left-sided centre-back position and although there is an option to play safely to the left-back he instead uses the vertical passing option in to the feet of Harrison, who has dropped into a deeper position in order to receive the ball. As Harrison takes possession in this area of the pitch he is quickly closed down and engaged by a defensive player.

Harrison is press-resistant and understands how to accept pressure and allow the defensive player to make contact before rolling past them. In this instance he quickly outplays the defender and his first instinct from this position is to quickly drive at the penalty area. He moves into a dangerous area before looking to connect a cross into the central area where team-mates are attacking the box.

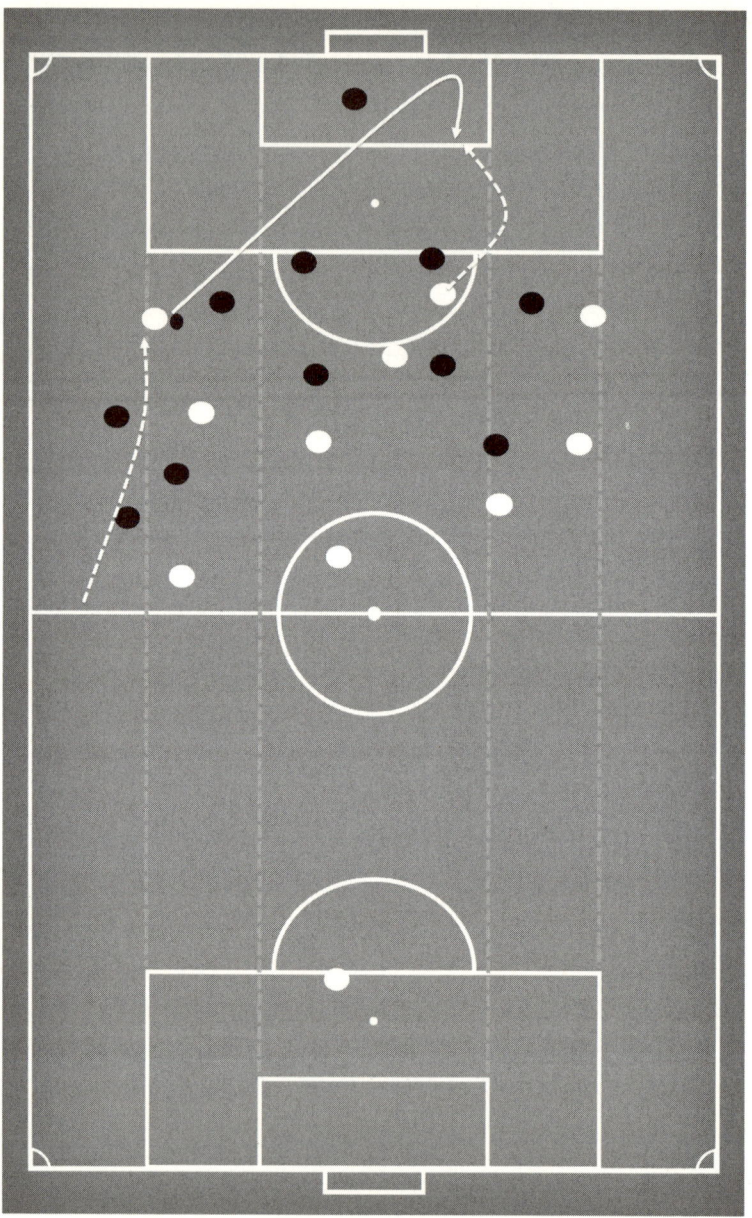

Figure 75

Harrison is not only capable of receiving and playing in advanced positions. He also impresses when collecting the ball in moments of transition in deep positions before driving forward and engaging the opposition defensive block.

In *figure 75* we see an example of this from the match between Leeds and Luton Town.

Harrison initially picks up possession deep inside the opposition half before looking to move forward to affect the opposition defensive block. His movements are quick and decisive, a term that tends to describe his playing style almost perfectly, as he goes past defensive players who are trying to engage him.

When he reaches the edge of the opposition penalty area we see Harrison look to play a deep cross over to the far post. Patrick Bamford has made the move from the 9 position to attack the far post but as the cross comes in the striker fails to make contact with the ball.

This is part of the reason that cross completion statistics can be misleading. Harrison has played the ball into the perfect area but the striker has failed to make contact. It is the player playing the cross that is effectively 'penalised' in this scenario where actually there should have been a completed cross.

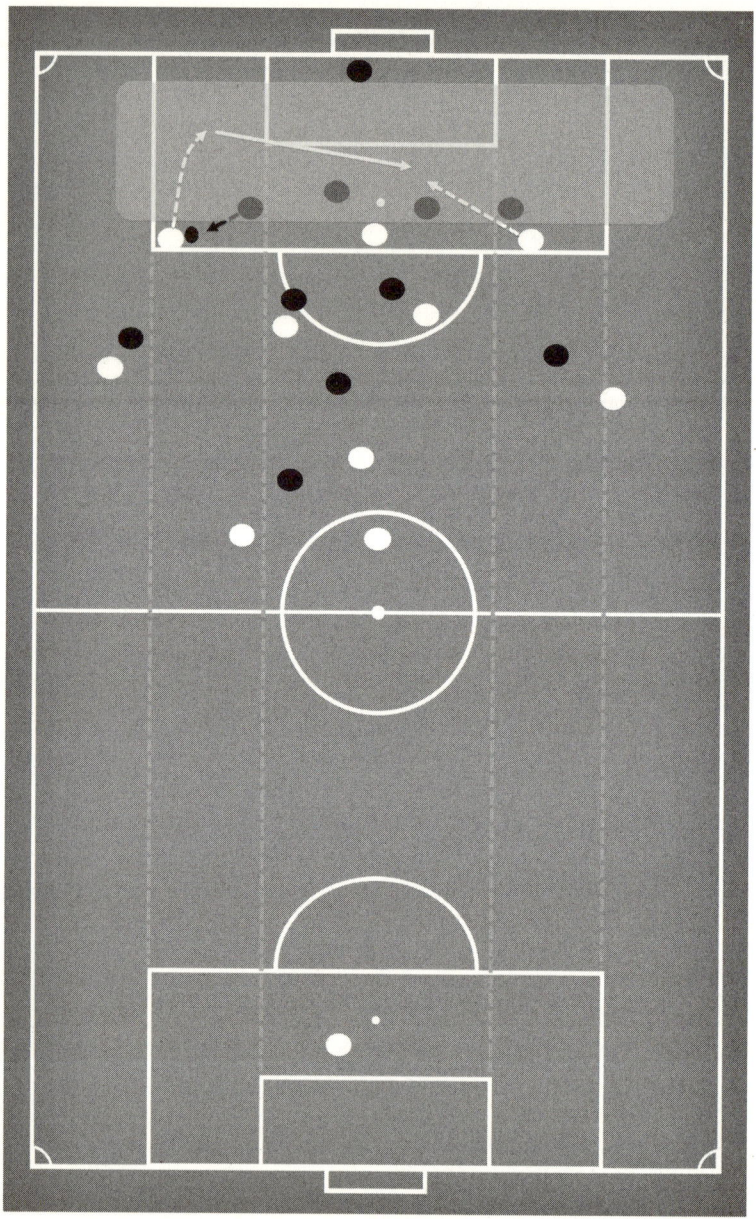

Figure 76

Harrison has the physical capacity to carry the ball at speed and for some distance but he can also receive it in tight areas high up the field comfortably. There are some wide players who are noticeably better at one aspect of receiving than the other, whereas Harrison was versatile in that he was comfortable in either situation.

In *figure 76* we see an example of the match between Leeds and Reading when Harrison received the ball just inside the opposition area without much time or space to react.

The key here is in the spacing from Leeds. The opposition defensive line is narrow but there is space in the wide areas of the penalty area and there is support behind the ball from the 8s moving high in order to occupy space in the final third.

When Harrison receives the ball he is immediately engaged by the opposition defender who moves to close down. It is in these tight spaces that wide players have to have the technical capacity to operate. Harrison slows the game down and is able to pause while the defender moves to engage and then he quickens the play as the defender approaches and beats the defender on the outside. He then has the composure to pick the correct ball with a cross played back across goal for the opposite side winger to attack.

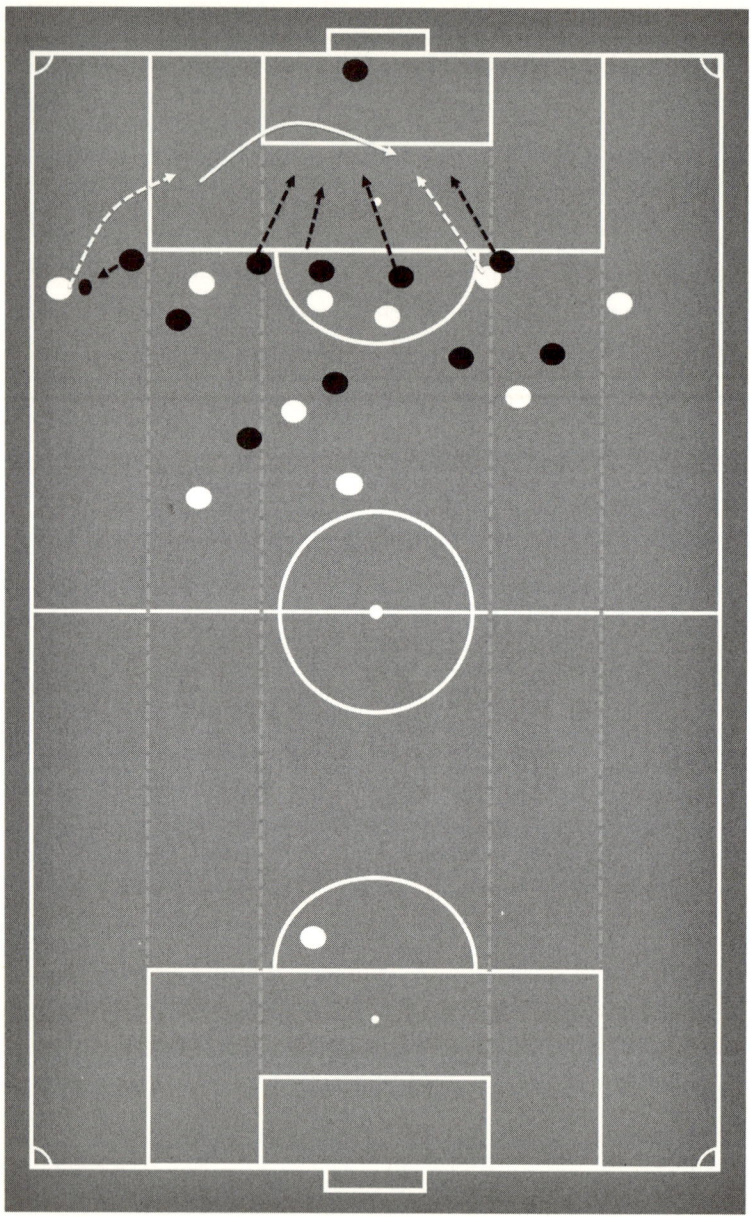

Figure 77

This ability that Harrison has to attack the opposition defenders quickly and decisively makes him so important to Leeds when they move into the final third. He will always look to attack and engage the opposition as quickly as possible and this tends to prevent the other team from being able to move covering players across quickly enough to deal with the threat.

In *figure 77* we again see a situation where Harrison has received possession isolated against a defender on the left, against Wigan Athletic. Again the attacking movement ends in a dangerous ball across into the area.

In this example Leeds are in a more established attacking position and as such the defenders for Wigan are compact and in a deep structure already. As Harrison receives the ball he is in the wide area and again the opposition defender on that side of the pitch is forced to move across to engage the ball to try to stop the winger producing a dangerous delivery into the area.

Harrison, again, pauses and slows the game down as he waits for the defender to engage and then quickly changes tempo to move past the man. This leaves the defender off balance and unable to get back to attempt a second challenge.

As Harrison moves into the area the defensive line of the opposition has started to crash back and there is no immediate option for the wide player to get a shot at goal. It is here that we see his composure as he remains in control and is able to play a perfectly weighted ball to access the only attacking player moving into the area.

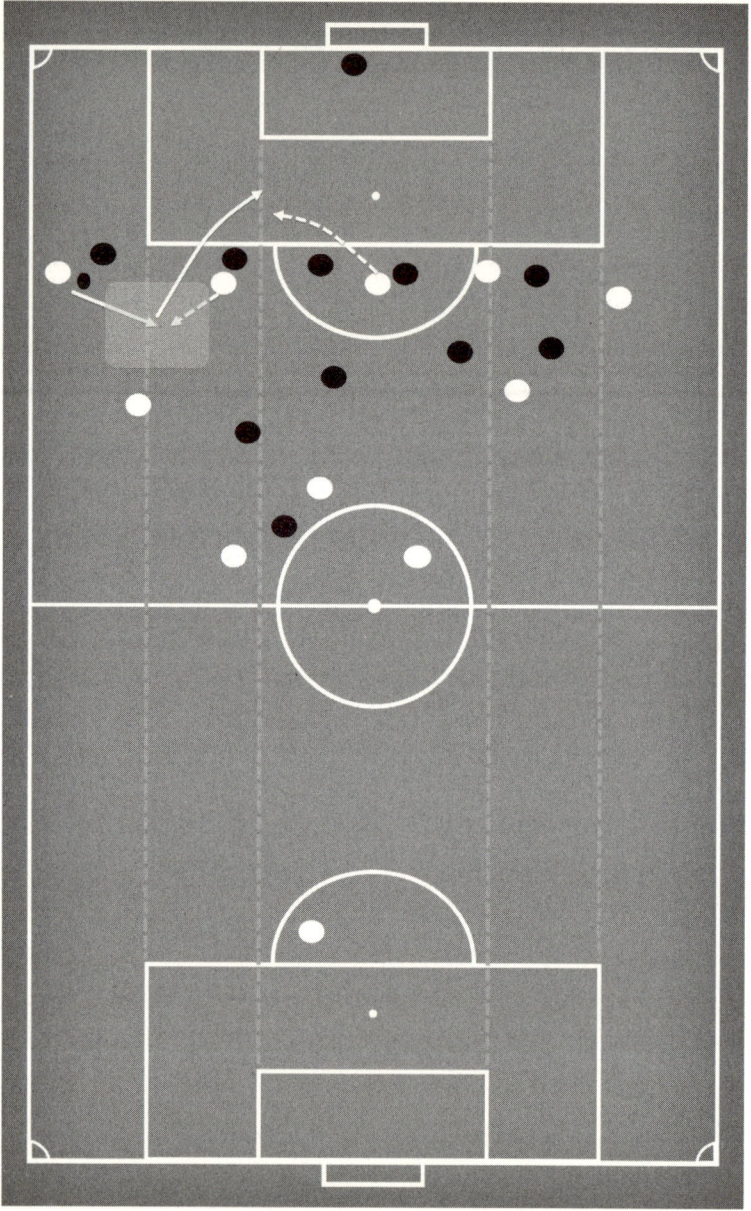

Figure 78

Harrison's technical ability allows him to receive the ball in the final third and then connect with team-mates when the opportunity presents itself.

In *figure 78* we see a clear example of this as Harrison receives the ball in the half-space with a team-mate on the outside of him. This is an example from the match between Leeds and Fulham.

Mateusz Klich has rotated into the wide space and Harrison has moved inside. This is a typical movement that we tended to see on the right of the Leeds attack and not on the left but we have to bear in mind that football is extremely fluid and as concepts and ideals provide the framework there is still versatility allowed in the system by Biesla.

As Klich receives the ball we see that Harrison is initially closely covered by a defensive player. He moves into the half-space and away from the defender and is able to create enough separation to collect possession. This allows the ball to be shifted inside for Harrison to take possession.

This small movement by Harrison not only allows him to collect the ball in a pocket of space but created the opportunity for Bamford to move across on the defender's blind side into the penalty area. Once again we see the technical ability of Harrison to collect the ball in a tight area and then his vision to find the pass through the defensive line to find this run.

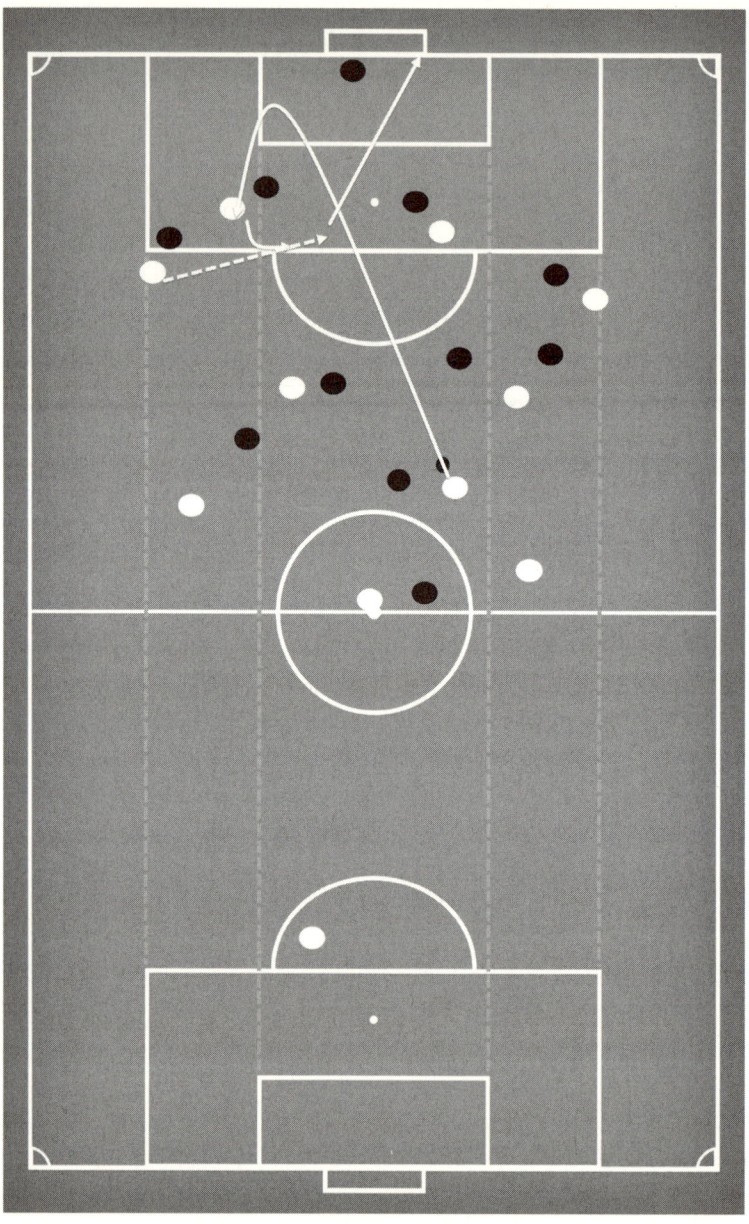

Figure 79

While the role of the wide players in this system used by Bielsa during 2019/20 was to provide and maintain width there were also times in which they had to move inside to support in the penalty area.

We see an example of this in *figure 79* as Harrison not only connects and receives the ball inside but scores an important goal for Leeds against Blackburn Rovers.

This time the ball is initially at the base of the attack with Kalvin Phillips. He looks to play a quick pass into the penalty area where Bamford has taken up position on the far side against a defensive player. As Bamford receives the ball he wins the aerial duel and knocks the ball back.

It is at this moment that Harrison has started to make a movement across from the left-hand side of the area in order to support underneath the striker. This movement means that he can receive the pass back. As defenders move to engage and press Harrison the wide player simply continues his path across the area and then fires a shot low into the far corner of the goal.

Chapter 14

Patrick Bamford

In football today, transfer speculation is one of the staples of the media. Whether the transfer window is open or not there are dozens of stories every day written about players who may be available or which positions clubs will be looking to recruit. This is certainly the case for a club like Leeds United whose significant fan base will generate interest in transfer windows.

In the time that Marcelo Bielsa has been at the club, one position has generated more speculation than any other, perhaps understandably given its importance: the 9. For the majority of 2018/19 and 2019/20 that position has been occupied by Patrick Bamford, much to the annoyance of a large number of supporters. At this point we probably have to look quickly behind the curtain and accept that this book is being written as Leeds are already playing in the Premier League in 2020/21. We therefore know that Bamford has taken to the higher level extremely well and is now converting chances at a much better rate than we perhaps saw over the course of the previous two seasons in the Championship.

At this point I should reference that this is something actually predicted by the excellent Josh Hobbs, who writes for the equally excellent Leeds blog All Stats Aren't We. In an article Josh argued that the Premier League would actually suit the style of play of Bamford better than the Championship. In the Championship, Leeds faced defences that were deep and compact with a lot of penalty box entries coming from wide areas. In the Premier League the feeling was that Leeds would play in more open games against teams who were more likely to look to attack them. This would result in more chances falling to the 9 in areas where there were fewer concentrated defensive blocks, therefore the conversion rate should be higher.

Indeed, the crux of the issue the fans initially had with Bamford centred around the issue of goal conversion. Leeds were so dominant in matches that they would regularly create goalscoring opportunities. The fact that so many chances were missed showed Bamford in a poor light. As we will see later on in this chapter, however, the overall performance of Bamford was still good enough to justify his place in the starting line-up under Bielsa.

Bamford is listed at 185cm or 6ft 1in and has a strong build. He is also left-footed and has a tendency to prefer to play over to the right where he can interlink with team-mates and help with the overloading of the opposition on that side of the pitch.

What is interesting about Bamford is that his career progression has been anything but that of a player who was destined to reach the top level. He made his professional debut with Nottingham Forest in the 2011/12 season, having come through the youth setup at the club. In the end though he would only play in two matches before being sold for a reported £1.5m to Chelsea.

From this point on the career trajectory of Bamford is one of a typical player in the Chelsea youth setup where he played in under-23 games and impressed enough to earn a series of loan moves without actually ever getting close to becoming a first-team regular there. In the end he would spend five seasons at the Premier League club without making a single appearance. With that said, however, over the first few loan spells away from his parent club Bamford at least displayed a clear ability to score goals.

Initially he moved on loan to MK Dons for the 2012/13 season and ended the campaign with 18 goals from 37 appearances. Next, he took a step up in quality in terms of team-mates and the opposition and signed on loan for the second half of the following season for Derby County in the Championship. Once again Bamford impressed although he did not set the league alight with eight goals from 21 appearances.

The next season was the last loan for Bamford in which he impressed as he joined Middlesbrough for an initial six-month loan, although it was eventually extended until the end of the season. Over the course of this spell at the north-east club Bamford scored a very respectable 17 goals in 38 appearances.

At this point in his career Bamford still represented significant value for his parent club as a young English striker who was displaying the ability to score goals. What happened next, however, greatly affected his reputation. Loan spells at Crystal Palace, Norwich City and Burnley saw Bamford accrue just 19 appearances over the course of three seasons with no goals scored. He suffered from injury issues over the course of this time but the performances were still a significant concern for Chelsea and it was at this point that they decided to cut their losses.

Luckily, at least one of those loan clubs had fond memories of the striker and in January 2017 Bamford signed for Middlesbrough for a fee reported to be in the region of £5.5m. Bamford played for the majority of the season and although he split time playing as a 9 and as a wide forward his performances greatly improved and the goals started to flow again.

With that said, however, it was still something of a surprise that after only a year and a half at the club Bamford was on the move again as he signed a four-year contract with Leeds prior to the 2018/19 season. It has been widely discussed that this transfer was largely a result of the fact that Victor Orta had moved to Leeds as the head of recruitment. He had held that position at Middlesbrough and still had an extremely high opinion of Bamford.

Fast forward to 2019/20 and it was evident that Leeds were still not 100 per cent sold on Bamford as the first-choice 9. This was despite the fact that Bielsa liked the player and appreciated his work rate off the ball. That season saw Leeds win a fierce battle to take the highly rated young striker Eddie Nketiah on loan from Arsenal. Many onlookers felt that this move would see Bamford moved to a back-up role as Nketiah was expected to start as part of the deal. Instead, Bielsa displayed his trademark loyalty and retained faith with Bamford as the 9.

Over the course of the 2019/20 season we saw Bamford play 3,675 minutes in the Championship. He ended the league campaign with a perfectly respectable 16 goals, although his xG across the course of the season was 24.28 so this was an underperformance of 8.28. Single-season xG differentials can be difficult to use for any significant analysis but they do provide a snapshot that requires further investigation. Bamford averaged 3.21 shots per 90 minutes and 5.14 touches in the penalty area. He was an extremely active part of the attacking play for his side although this was not purely something that we could measure via data.

Bamford displayed excellent work rate in terms of pressing the opposition and closing down passing lanes and was also an important part of the build-up play with his willingness to drop deep to receive the ball at his feet with pressure in behind him.

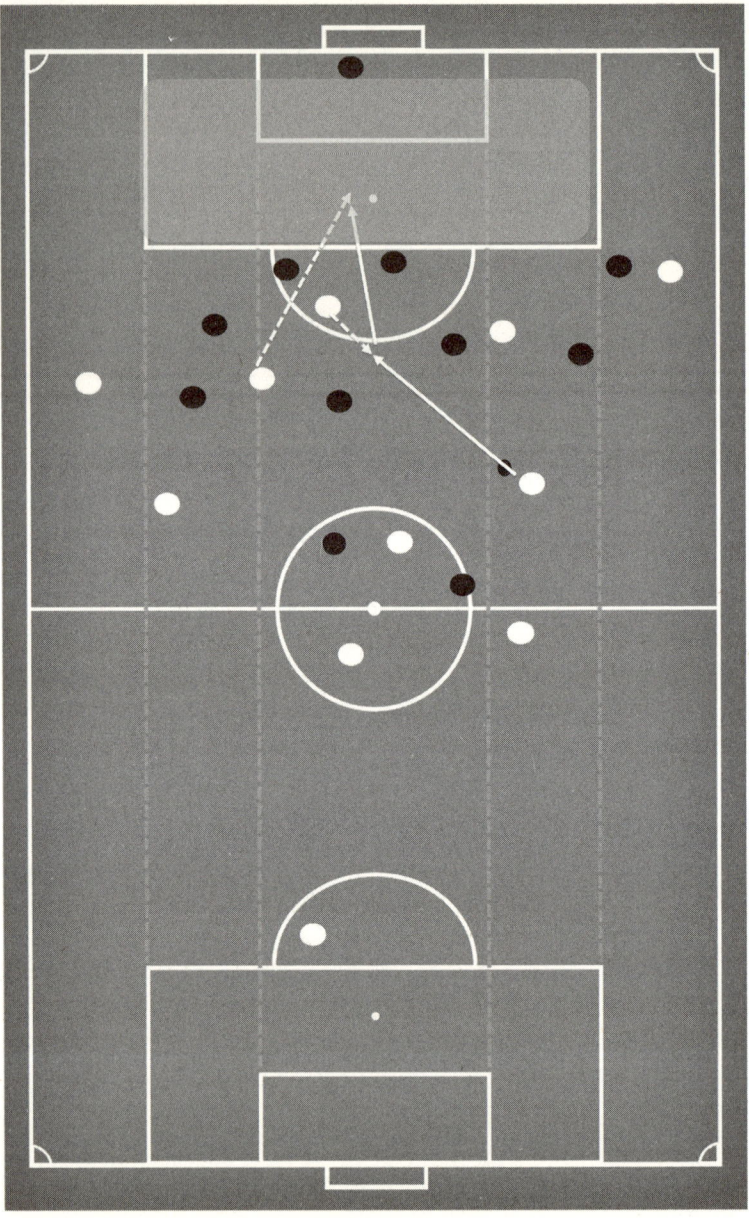

Figure 80

For as much as Bamford is the primary goalscorer in this system, he also works extremely hard in terms of showing backwards towards the ball in order to provide connections as possession is progressed forward.

This work rate and ability to create relationships with players in deeper positions was one of the key reasons that Bamford was able to see off the challenge from Nketiah in the battle to be the first-choice 9 in this side. We have an example of this in *figure 80* in the match between Leeds and Millwall.

Luke Ayling has possession of the ball in the right half-space having made an inverted movement into that area. As he is looking to progress the ball towards the penalty area it is Bamford who makes the movement back to allow the vertical pass to be played into this zone.

As Bamford moves back towards Ayling, he rotates away from the highest line and creates space that can be occupied. As Bamford takes possession we see Mateusz Klich make a move beyond the ball to attack the space that Bamford has created. Bamford is able to connect the pass through the defensive line to find Klich moving into the penalty area.

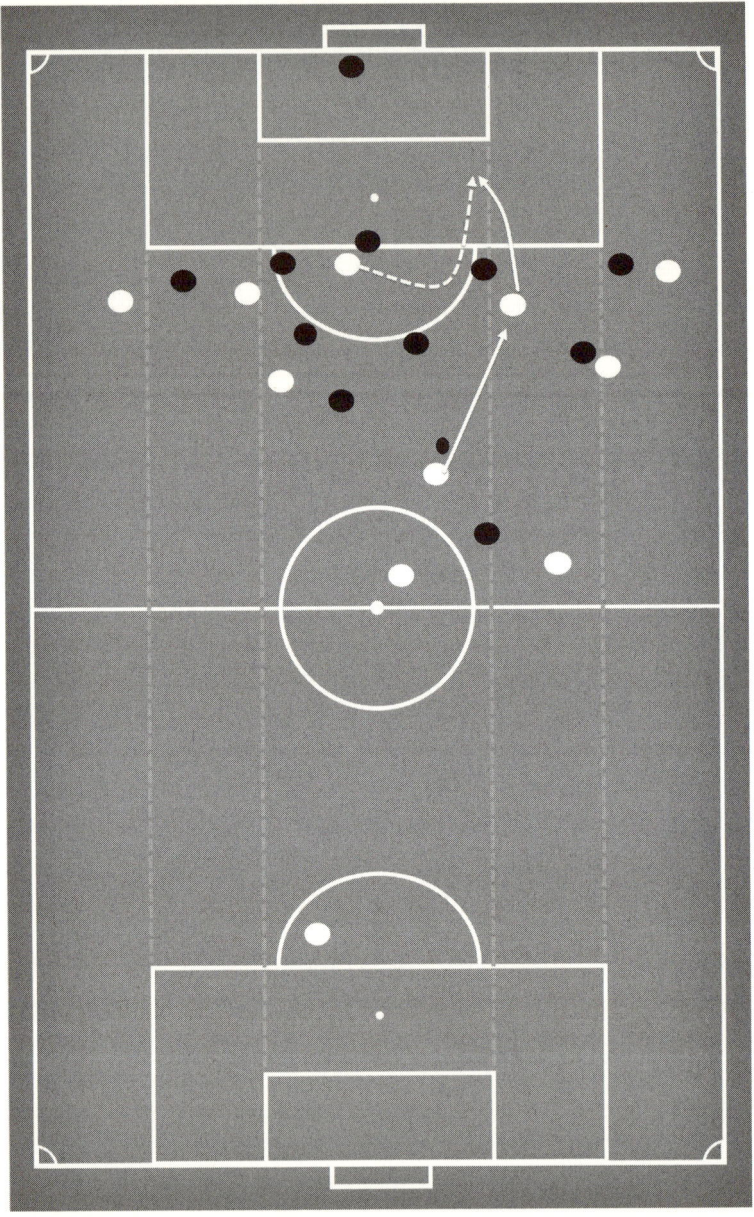

Figure 81

Bamford is an extremely intelligent forward player. He displays a tendency to position himself on the shoulder of the defender and likes to drift on to their blind side away from the position of the ball. This means that as the defender shifts concentration towards the ball Bamford is able to make quick movements to lose the marker and move into space to receive possession.

In *figure 81* we can see an example of how this movement works in a match between Leeds and Queens Park Rangers.

The ball is initially positioned, once again, with Kalvin Phillips at the base of the attacking structure and he looks to play the vertical pass into the final third. His pass finds Pablo Hernandez, who is positioned in the half-space on the right-hand side of the pitch. This pass forces a defensive player to move to engage Hernandez and drags that player out of the defensive line. This creates an opportunity for Bamford to rotate across in order to access the space that this defensive player has emptied.

The key lies in the timing of the run from Bamford and as his defender turns his concentration towards Hernandez on the ball we see Bamford make a quick movement across the face of the defender. He angles his run to ensure that he stays onside and this run allows Hernandez to find the pass past the defender to access this run and create an opportunity for Bamford to shoot on goal.

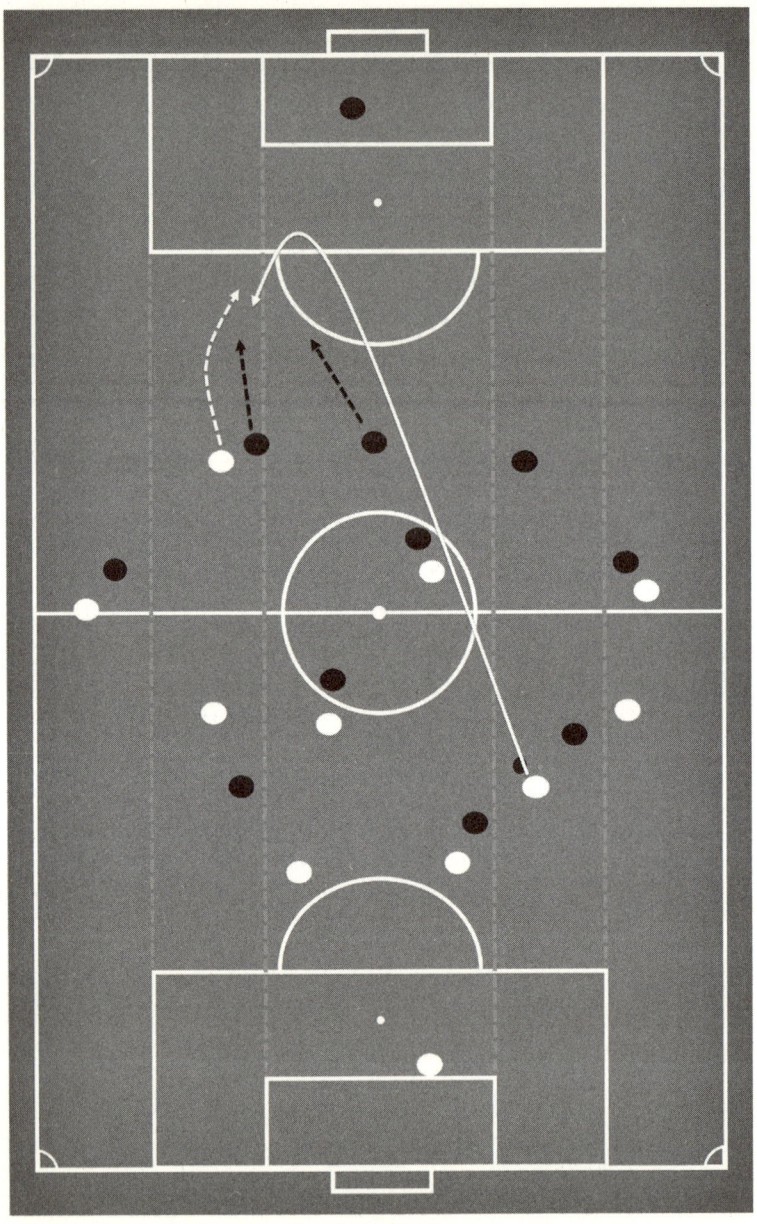

Figure 82

In moments of quick transition, when Leeds look to play vertically to hit space behind the defensive line, we again see the movement of Bamford to drift from defenders and attack space as the key to enable this kind of passing from back to front.

In *figure 82* we have an example of this from a match between Leeds and Stoke when Bamford is able to create separation before taking possession of the ball and scoring in transition.

The ball is initially in the possession of Hernandez as the Spaniard has dropped back into the half-space in order to enable the progression of the ball. As soon as Hernandez picks up possession he turns and looks to play vertically, as they are coached to do by Bielsa, and we see Bamford recognise this as a visual cue to create separation and make a run behind the defensive line.

Bamford initially is covered by a defensive player but as Hernandez plays the ball over he is intelligent enough to angle his run away from the defensive player. This prevents the defender from being able to make contact or disrupt the motion of the run from Bamford. This means that Bamford is able to collect possession before moving in on goal ahead of the defender and finishing the chance.

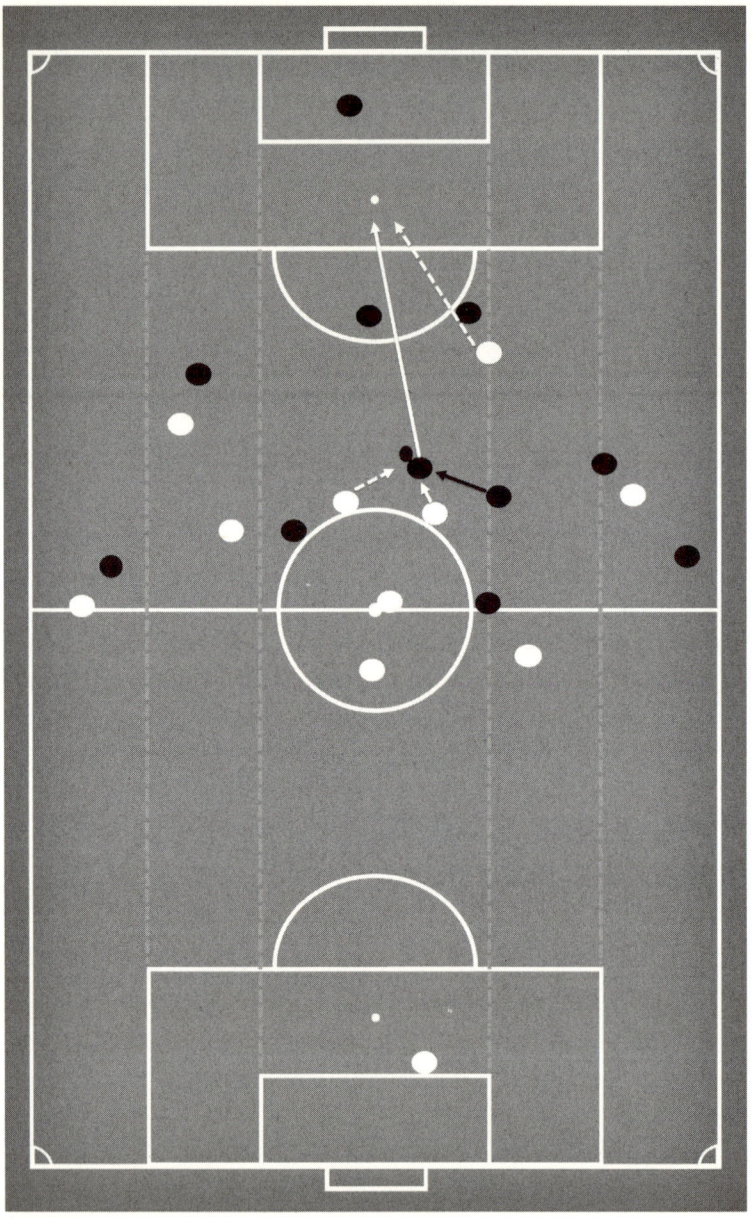

Figure 83

Bamford is a player who consistently looks to take up pockets of space and positions, even when the opposition have the ball, to make sure that as soon as Leeds are able to win the ball back he is ready to make quick movements in order to present passing options to outplay the defensive line.

In *figure 84* we see an example of this as Bamford eventually scores against Blackburn Rovers.

The opposition have won the ball in their own half and are looking to build and escape pressure. Bamford is initially positioned on the edge of the half-space and the central area and he is closely watching the situation and the position of the ball. The press engages and the ball is won back almost immediately. At this point Bamford immediately makes a run to attack the space between the defenders. The player who has won the ball back is able to play it quickly through to Bamford and the striker collects possession and finishes the chance.

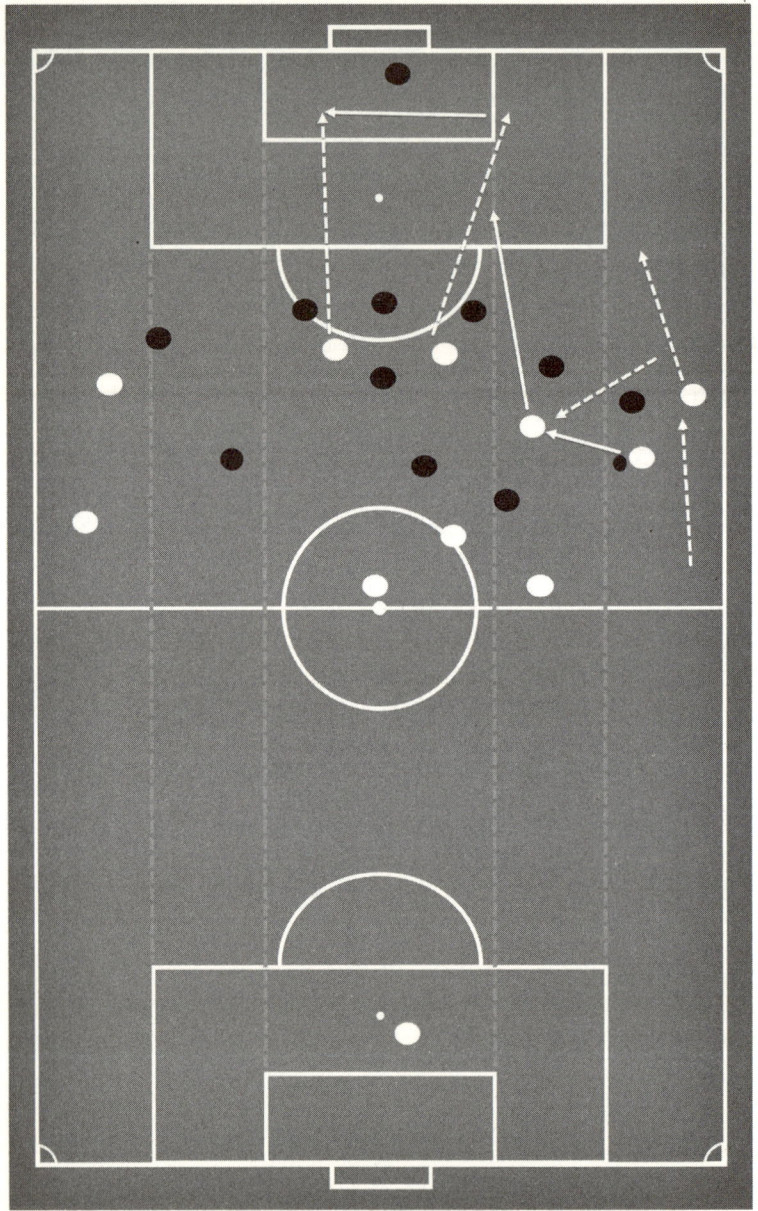

Figure 84

Bamford's attacking instincts actually fit very well with the attacking concepts that Bielsa uses with Leeds. He quite often is the player on the periphery of the attacking movement as possession is progressed vertically and rotated through the thirds but when the opportunity presents itself he tends to be the player who is in position to attack the ball as it moves into the penalty area. We see an example of this in *figure 84* as Leeds use rotations and verticality to break through into the penalty area before the ball is played across for Bamford to finish at the back post.

Pablo Hernandez initially has possession on the right and Helder Costa makes an inverted movement to rotate past the ball. This creates the space for Luke Ayling to rotate forward in the wide lane. This rotational movement creates chaos for the defenders as they are looking to pick up players moving in and out of spaces.

The ball then moves to Costa, who is able to play a vertical pass that releases Klich into the area. The Polish midfielder is then able to play the ball across the face of goal and Bamford is ready to finish at the far side.

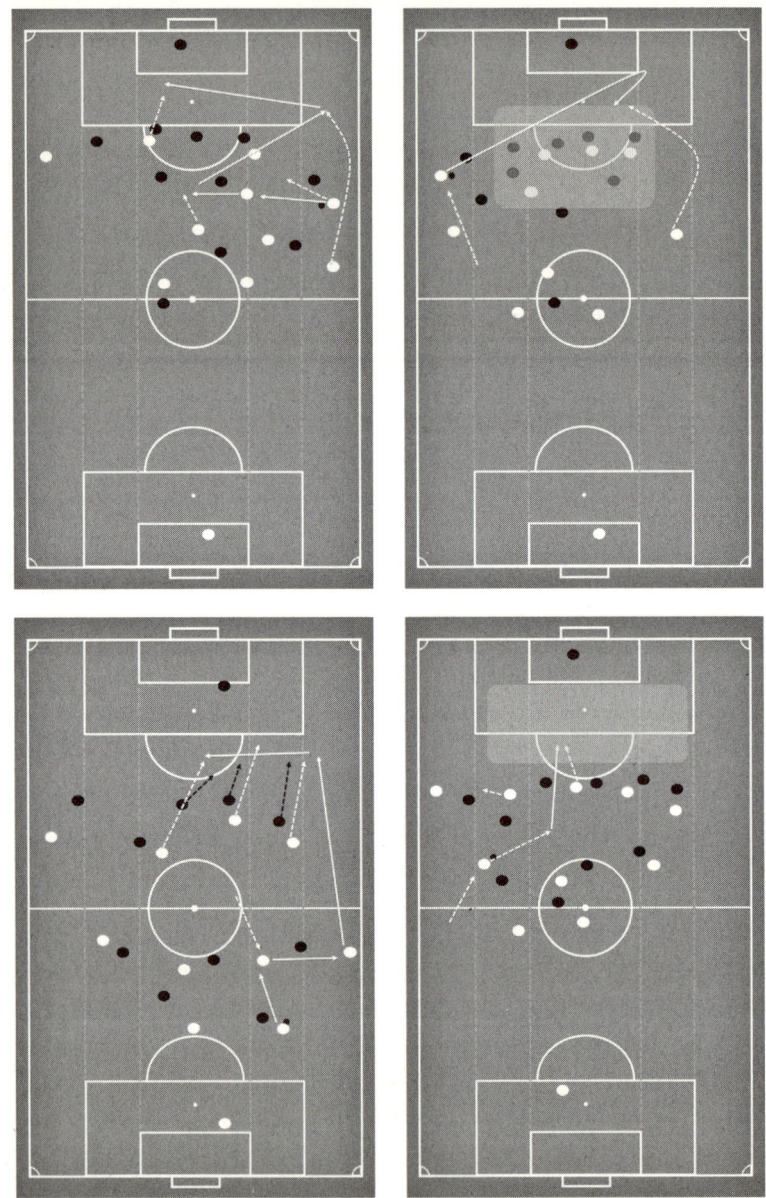

Chapter 15

Anatomy of a goal

As we come to the end of this book we have examined the tactical concepts used by Marcelo Bielsa at Leeds United over the course of the 2019/20 season which saw the club promoted back to their rightful place in the Premier League. We have discussed and displayed the importance of such central ideas as verticality and rotations and shown how Bielsa coached his team to perform and act when out of possession. We have also taken the time to examine the back stories of some of the key players within this team before showing how they acted and interacted within these central concepts that dictate the overall game model.

All that remains now is for us to look at some of my own favourite goals scored by Leeds during the season in order to further show the concepts in action.

Before we start it is worth pointing out that these goals do not necessarily represent the 'best' and they are not ranked in order. Instead they are intended to further enforce the concepts that you have, hopefully, learnt about during this book.

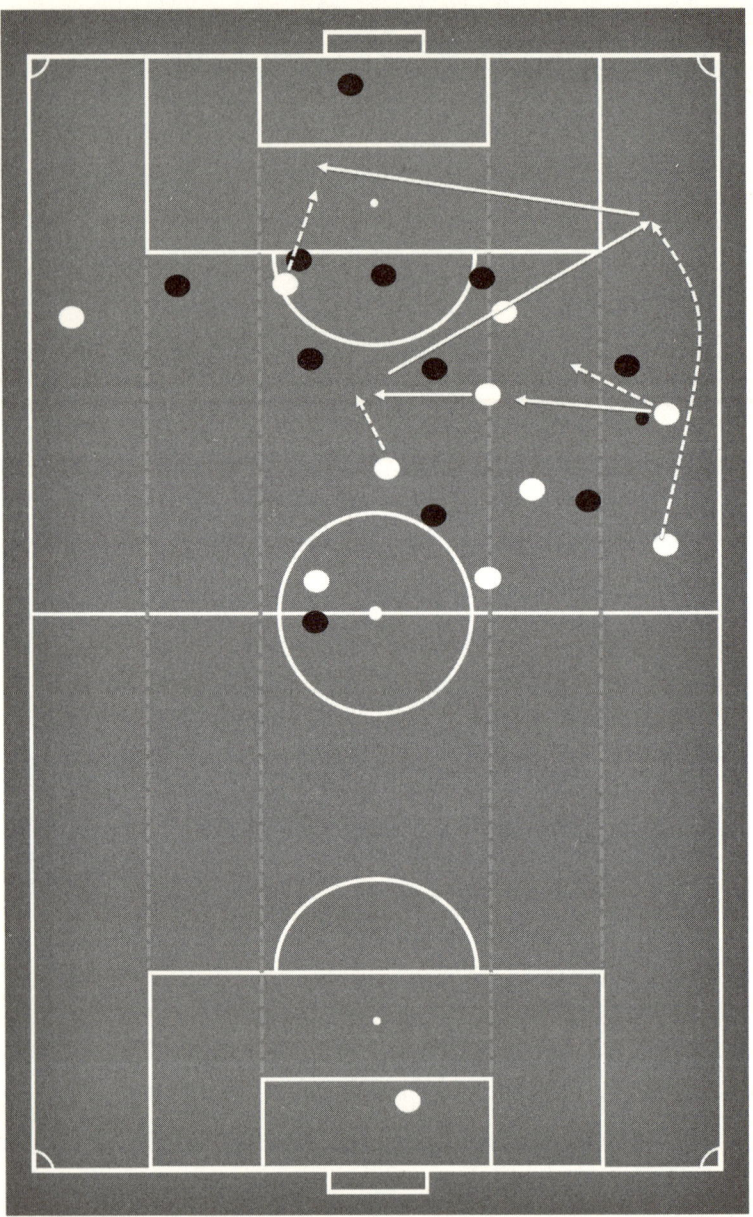

Figure 85

1) Patrick Bamford vs Millwall, 28 January 2020

Our first goal shows the concepts of overloads and rotations in the final third with the 9, Patrick Bamford, being the player to benefit from some excellent attacking interchanges in the build-up to the chance being created. We show this in *figure 85*.

Initially, the ball is positioned on the right-hand side of the pitch with Helder Costa with a defensive block from what looks a well-set opposition. The Portuguese winger connects inside with a simple pass to Pablo Hernandez who is positioned just about in the half-space. As Costa plays this pass he angles a run into the half-space himself and empties the wide area as he takes the defender with him.

The play has not yet fully developed and Hernandez plays a second lateral pass to the second 8 in Mateusz Klich, who has stepped forward. Now there has been a run off the ball by the right-back who is attacking the empty wide space. Klich plays a simple ball out to this side and Luke Ayling is released towards goal.

As Ayling collects the ball we see Bamford, positioned at the far side of the penalty area, make a run off of the defender towards the back post. The cross is received and finished.

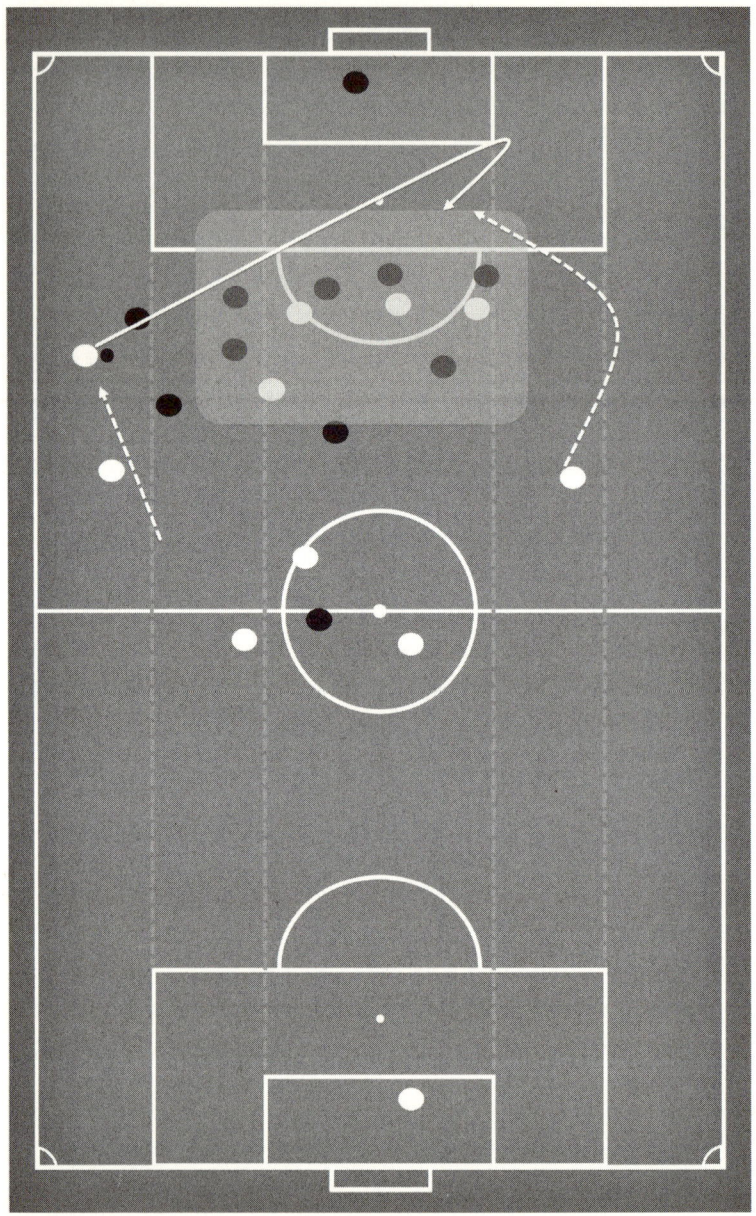

Figure 86

2) Luke Ayling vs Huddersfield Town, 7 March 2020

Next we have a goal from an unlikely source in the shape of right-back Ayling. This goal again highlights overloads and rotations as well as the way the pitch is spaced in the attacking phase to ensure that there is always width to stretch the opposition out. We have shown this in *figure 86.*

This time the ball is positioned in the left half-space with Hernandez, who drives in possession towards the wide area where there is space. We can see that the central areas around the penalty box are compact and overloaded as Leeds look to flood these spaces with attacking players. This central occupation creates the opportunity with space open around the back post which can then be attacked.

Ayling, initially in a deep position, makes an unchecked run around the back of the penalty area in order to access this space and receive the cross when it comes in from Hernandez.

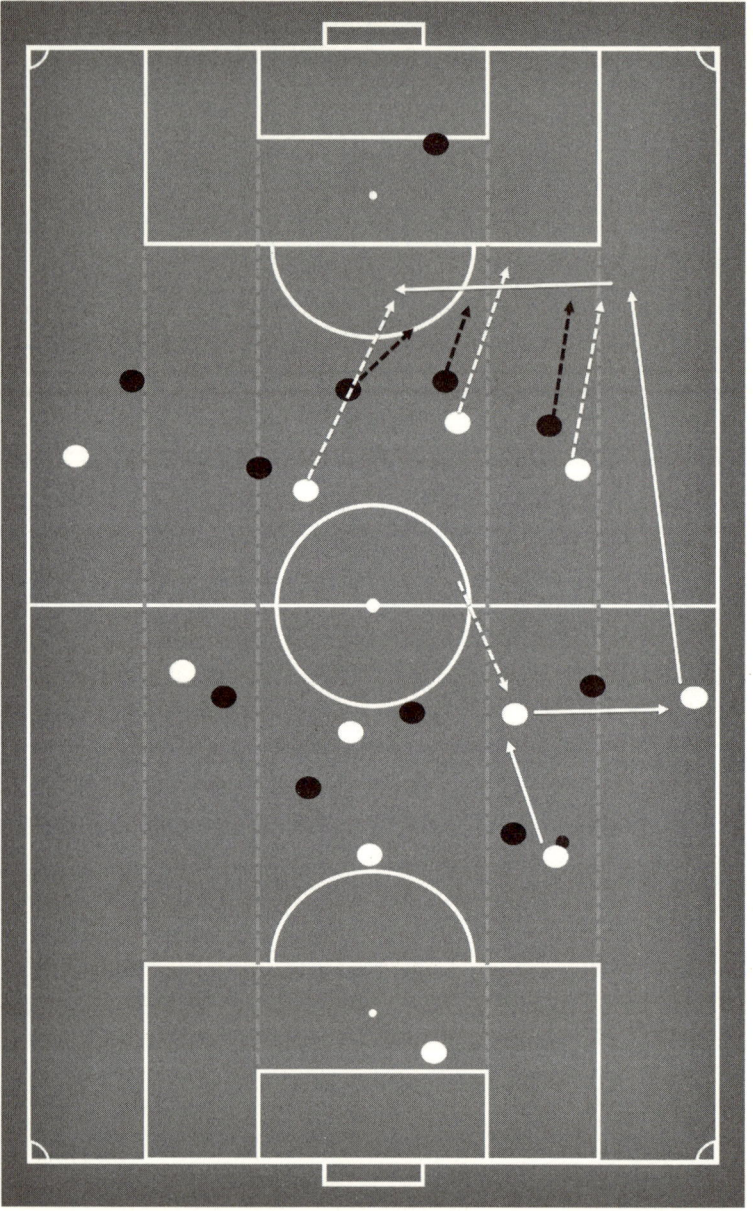

Figure 87

3) Pablo Hernandez vs Stoke City, 9 July 2020

Now we will see the first of two goals from the same match as Hernandez scored by arriving at the edge of the penalty area to get on the end of a great flowing move. The main concept that we see in action here is verticality as the ball is played through the opposition defensive block quickly.

The ball is initially with Ben White in the defensive line and Mateusz Klich drops back into a deeper position to offer a passing option vertically. As he collects the ball and a defensive player moves to engage he plays the pass immediately out to Ayling in the right-back slot. The ball is then again played vertically to access the run of Helder Costa in the wide position moving beyond the defensive line.

At this point the attack and defence are all trying to occupy the best positions around the penalty area. The ball is pulled back and Patrick Bamford steps over it to confuse the opposition. That allows Hernandez to control the ball and strike it cleanly into the opposition goal.

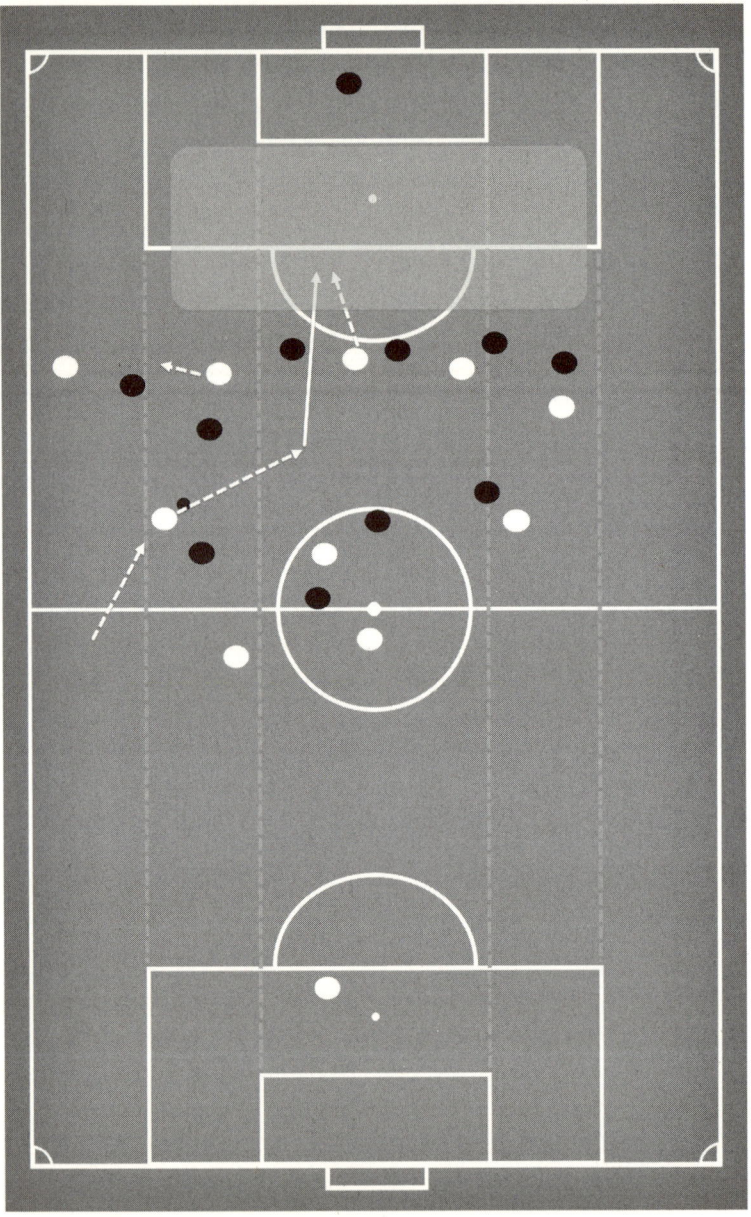

Figure 88

4) Helder Costa vs Stoke City, 9 July 2020

The key concepts this time are rotation and verticality as Costa breaks beyond the defensive line to finish an opportunity. This is shown in *figure 88*.

This time the key creator is Stuart Dallas, who takes the initiative to drive inside when in possession. The Northern Irishman initially takes the ball in the left-back slot and he carries it in an inverted movement towards the half-space. The key to the creation of this space for the run is that Hernandez makes a movement from inside to out and pulls away an opposition defender. This gives Dallas the opportunity to carry the ball and then ahead of the run we see that Costa has moved into a central position.

The Portuguese winger makes a well-timed movement off of the ball to run behind the defensive line and the pass is played through from Dallas to access this space between the defensive line and the goalkeeper.

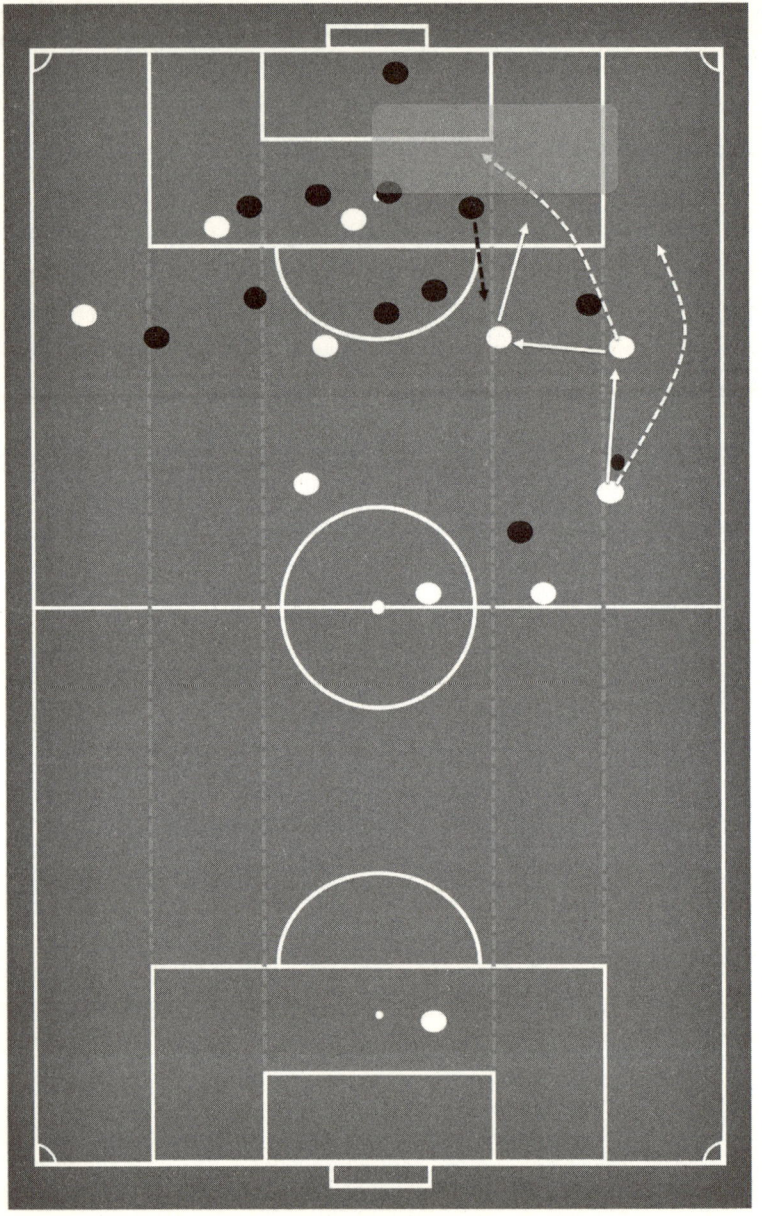

Figure 89

5) Stuart Dallas vs Charlton Athletic, 22 July 2020

Once again the key concepts that we see are overloads and rotations. This goal is shown in *figure 89*.

The play is being progressed down the right and it is here that the interplay from Leeds forces a breakthrough and creates the goalscoring opportunity. The ball is initially positioned in the wide area with Ayling and he plays the forward pass in to Stuart Dallas, who immediately shifts possession inside to Hernandez in the half-space. The key here is that Ayling has made an overlapping movement through the outside space and this distracts the defensive players. Dallas then makes a similar movement to run into the penalty area at an angle.

Hernandez not only plays the through ball but he plays the pass through the defender's legs to find the run of Dallas for the Northern Irishman to score.

Conclusion

By gaining promotion to the Premier League in the 2019/20 season there is no doubt that Marcelo Bielsa has gained his place in Leeds United folklore. You can make the argument, however, that even without the promotion this would have been the case anyway. Sometimes there are coaches who join a club and fit so perfectly, not just in football terms but with the character of a city, that they become legends almost immediately. Jurgen Klopp at Liverpool is one example and the theory also applies to Bielsa and Leeds.

Bielsa came to Leeds and gave the fan base the only thing that they truly wanted. He gave them a team that played in the image of the city – all-action, attacking and relentless. Suddenly Leeds were playing the kind of football that their fans had yearned for and gradually the rest of the world started to pay attention. Media coverage and interest grew and with that came the hype. None of this mattered though, as Leeds fans had already accepted and adopted the eccentric Argentinean coach as one of their own and the support that they had for him was total.

Witness the scenes from around the city during the course of 2019/20. Leeds fans posting selfies on social media with the coach as they discover him wandering the city, in the supermarket, in a coffee shop, or in a park. If Leeds is a city that is down to earth and without pretension then it fits Bielsa like a glove, in the same way that Bilbao did when he first moved to Europe.

The concepts we have covered here provide the technical and tactical framework for Leeds as a team. They instruct the behaviours of the players in and out of possession and provide a reference point so that the players understand the expectations that Bielsa has of them. It is noteworthy from a coaching point of view that over the course of the season the players began to fully embody these concepts. They rotated and overloaded, they attacked and defended with full commitment, and this led to them becoming so successful, as opponents were often blown away when faced with their attacking force.

For me, a large part of the beauty of football is that it is so subjective. You and I could watch the same match sitting side by side and come away with very different takes on the game. A 0-0 draw could be boring to some but for others the tactical battle that led to both teams being shut out could be intriguing and interesting. It will come as little surprise to you after reading this book that I come down on the side of the latter.

Football tactics, however, need not be an overly complicated subject. My sincere hope is that the concepts we have discussed as you have worked your way through this book have been described and explained in such a way that is accessible and enjoyable for you.

Thank you for taking the time to read a book that I have poured so much of myself into.